Staging Gertrude Stein

Staging Gertrude Stein

Absence, Culture, and the Landscape of American Alternative Theatre

Leslie Atkins Durham

palgrave
macmillan

STAGING GERTRUDE STEIN
© Leslie Atkins Durham, 2005.

First published in 2005 by
PALGRAVE MACMILLAN™
175 Fifth Avenue, New York, N.Y. 10010 and
Houndmills, Basingstoke, Hampshire, England RG21 6XS
Companies and representatives throughout the world.

PALGRAVE MACMILLAN is the global academic imprint of the Palgrave Macmillan division of St. Martin's Press, LLC and of Palgrave Macmillan Ltd. Macmillan® is a registered trademark in the United States, United Kingdom and other countries. Palgrave is a registered trademark in the European Union and other countries.

ISBN 1–4039–6934–5

Library of Congress Cataloging-in-Publication Data

Durham, Leslie Atkins.
    Staging Gertrude Stein : absence, culture, and the landscape of American alternative theatre / by Leslie Atkins Durham.
        p. cm.
    Includes bibliographical references (p.) and index.
    ISBN 1–4039–6934–5 (alk. paper)
    1. Stein, Gertrude, 1874–1946—Dramatic works. 2. Experimental drama, American—History and criticism. 3. Avant-garde (Aesthetics)—United States—History—20th century. 4. Stein, Gertrude, 1874–1946—Stage history—United States. 5. Stein, Gertrude, 1874–1946—Dramatic production. I. Title.

PS3537.T323Z5883 2005
812'.52—dc22   2005051028

A catalogue record for this book is available from the British Library.

Design by Newgen Imaging Systems (P) Ltd., Chennai, India.

First edition: October 2005
10 9 8 7 6 5 4 3 2 1

Printed in the United States of America.

Contents ⤴

Acknowledgments ᕽ

This book is the memento of a long journey; needless to say the debts I incurred along the way are as great as they are many.

The project began at the University of Kansas, first as a seminar paper and then later it became my dissertation. I'd like to thank Ron Willis for the class that inspired me to begin this work. I owe much gratitude to my dissertation committee: John Gronbeck-Tedesco, Jack Wright, Iris Smith, John Pultz, and most especially to Mary Karen Dahl, who pushed me farther than I thought I could go and who endured many, many drafts of each chapter as I struggled to find my historical and theoretical way.

The dissertation became a book while I was at Boise State University. Without the support of a faculty writing group, that very likely would not have happened. Our membership was somewhat fluid, but the core group included Marcy Newman, Michelle Payne, Tara Penry, and Jacqueline O'Connor. The paths of writing and revision are arduous. Their insights and friendship kept me going. Special thanks are owed to Jacqueline O'Connor who read chapter after chapter, but perhaps even more importantly, who believed in me and the project when I didn't. She propels me toward all things worthy. I am incapable of thanking her enough. A Faculty Research Associates Program grant at Boise State provided me with course release time so I could steer the manuscript toward completion. My thanks also go to the chair of the Theatre Arts Department, Richard Klautsch, for his assistance and encouragement during this last phase of the project.

Pieces of various chapters appeared in the following journals. I am grateful for the advice of the editors of these journals for their assistance in refining my work. Portions of chapter 2 appeared in "Reinscribing Primitivism: Frank Galati's *Gertrude Stein*," *Text and Presentation* 23 (2002): 33–44 and in "Performing Gertrude Stein: Faith Ringgold's Signification on Primitivism in *The French Collection*" in *Florida Atlantic Comparative Studies* 8 (2006). Portions of chapter 4 appeared in "A Pop Parade of American Fantasy: Staging National Identity in *The Mother of Us All*" *The Journal of Dramatic Theory and Criticism* 16.2 (Spring 2002): 33–46. Portions of the epilogue appeared in "Hashirigaki" *Theatre Journal* 55.3 (October 2003): 516–8. I'd also like to thank Palgrave's anonymous reviewers for their invaluable questions and comments on the way to the book's final form. The book would be a far less valuable document without the photographs that help bring the history of Gertrude Stein's work in production to life. In collecting the photographs, the following people helped me in numerous ways: Michael Willis of the Glimmerglass Opera, Chris Kam of the Foundry Theatre, Leigh Golden of the Beinecke Library, Clay Hapaz of the Wooster Group, Cindy Layman of the Santa Fe Opera, Cindy Bandle of the Goodman Theatre, Klaus Grünberg, Celene Reno, and Bea and Victor Shifreen. To all of these people I am truly grateful. My final set of thanks goes to my family. They've helped me in every way imaginable: financially, intellectually, and emotionally. My sincerest thanks go to Christopher and Sharon Atkins, Douglas and Rebecca Atkins, Jean and Albert Dimmitt, Ann and Gene Durham, to my beloved husband Craig, and most recently to my daughter Kate. Special thanks are owed to my father. He is my mentor and my model. I trust he recognizes a tribute in the first line of the acknowledgments and in every long sentence that follows. My final thanks goes to the true, dear friend I lost right before the project was completed. For six years Maggie sat with me while I worked; she offered the unflagging encouragement I craved. Would that I had worked faster so she could celebrate with me at the journey's end.

Introduction ∽

After all anybody is as their land and air is.
Anybody is as the sky is low or high,
The air heavy or clear
And anybody is as there is wind or no wind there.
It is that which makes them and the arts they make.[1]

Gertrude Stein wrote none of her plays on American soil. In 1903, when she was twenty-nine years old, she sailed to France, determined to forge the kind of artistic and personal identity she felt prohibited from creating in what she considered the provincial and conservative United States of the early twentieth century. Before she died in 1946, Stein returned to America only once—for a lecture tour from October 1934 through May 1935, timed to coincide with the grand successes of *The Autobiography of Alice B. Toklas* and *Four Saints in Three Acts*. Despite this prolonged exile from her native country, Stein promoted herself and her writing, especially in her later years, as being quintessentially American and intimately connected to the American landscape. Her self-staging was stunningly convincing: she and her plays have fascinated avant-garde directors and their American audiences for seventy years; productions of Stein's plays throughout the twentieth century have illuminated this expatriate playwright's leading role in the making of American theatrical and cultural history.

A VIEW FROM AFAR: LANDSCAPING AN ALTERNATIVE AMERICAN DRAMA

From the Hotel Lowry in St. Paul, Minnesota, Stein wrote to her new friend, Thornton Wilder, about her flight from Madison, Wisconsin, one of her tour stops in December of 1934: "We had a marvelous flight in a tiny plane over the snowed prairie. I am still all filled up with the xtraordinary [*sic*] symmetry of it, as a whole and in detail."[2] She was so filled up in fact, that she also wrote to her longtime friend Carl Van Vechten, the man whose organizational skills and sense of Stein's tastes had ensured a wonderful visit to the United States: "We had a wonderful time flying from Madison here, we went in a little moth plane just the two of us[3] and the pilot, no stewardesses no nothing and we flew low over the snow covered country and I never felt anything like it, I am still filled up with emotion about it, oh Carl bless you for everything but bless you most perhaps for making us fly, it is wonderful, wonderful wonderful."[4]

Stein was clearly enthralled by the airborne perspective that granted her a clear vision of the broad patterns and shapes of the Midwestern topography and a sense of vast distance. Perhaps the flight offered a more intense and concentrated version of the distant viewpoint she had maintained on the United States all her adult life. Despite her thirty-year expatriation, Stein's literary gaze often lingered on explicitly American subjects, finding ways to repattern them so her reader could see and hear them afresh. Further, she always yearned for a particularly American audience, whether in the form of the American theatre-going and reading public, the American expatriate community in Paris, or American soldiers during both of the twentieth century's world wars.[5]

Nevertheless, Stein's captivating airplane ride stimulated, rather than started, her fascination with the concept of landscape, and its relation to dramatic activity. Before boarding the S. S. Champlain in Le Havre for New York City on October 17, 1934, Stein had already completed the lecture, "Plays," that she would deliver at various U.S. universities, colleges, and clubs. In this talk, she told the story of the composition of her first play, *What Happened*, in 1913. Stein explained to her sold-out audiences[6] that the she had always been nervous in the conventional theatre because her "emotional time" as an audience member was never synchronized with the emotional time of the play.[7] She thus wanted to create works radically different from any her audiences had previously encountered, so they would not be plagued by a similar nervousness. Her solution to the "emotional syncopation" between things seen and heard on stage and the audience's reaction to them, was to reconfigure drama as a landscape, "because the landscape does not have to make acquaintance. You may have to make acquaintance with it, but it does not with you, it is there and so the play being written the relation between you at any time is so exactly that that it is of no importance unless you look at it."[8] Stein envisioned a kind of theatre in which everything was immediately and perpetually present. Instead of relying on linear narrative, which is never fully comprehensible until one has moved through it and arrived at some final textual destination, the landscape relies on the principle of simultaneous relation—"the trees to the hills the hills to the fields the trees to each other any piece of it to any sky and then any detail to any other detail."[9] Unlike narrative, the relation of trees to hills to fields to sky is instantly and immediately knowable in a single glance. It does not progress through time or demand acquaintance; it simply "is" perpetually present. The inspiration for this un-syncopated geographic relation was, Stein reports in her lecture, Bilignin, where she often spent her summers: "The landscape at Bilignin so completely made a play that I wrote quantities of plays."[10]

But "Plays" was not the culmination of Stein's theorizing about the relationship between geography and her dramatic writing. She wrote her longest and most sustained meditation on these vital matters in 1936, after she returned from her American tour and after she had taken her airplane ride over the Midwestern prairie. In *The Geographical History of America or The Relation of Human Nature to the Human Mind*, Stein frequently alludes to her airplane ride in 1934 as she attempts to map the distinctions between her fundamental philosophical categories. Throughout the course of *The Geographical History of America*, Stein gives several examples of the differences between the two: human nature is that which cannot play or write, but which always remembers, and is that which is divorced from the land and scenery. Human nature on the other hand, is that which writes, plays, is unencumbered by memory, history, and events and that which is connected to land and scenery—"the human mind knows what it knows it has nothing to do with seeing what it remembers, remember how the country looked as we passed over it, it made designs big designs like human nature draws them because it knows them without ever having seen them from above."[11] Stein then connects scenery—which is implicitly American scenery, given the airborne perspective—back to plays: "What is a play. A play is scenery. A play is not identity or place or time but it likes to feel like it oh yes it does it does wonderfully well like to feel like it. That is what makes it a play."[12] Stein's travel above the American landscape helped her restate her Bilignin-inspired theory of what makes a play.

When she resumed writing her plays after her American tour and after the composition of *The Geographical History of America*—including two of the most often-produced works of her oeuvre, *Doctor Faustus Lights the Lights* (1938) and *The Mother of Us All* (1946)—she made her new texts more accessible than her early work in terms of character, story, and structure,[13] but she continued to employ her fundamental dramatic strategies in modified form. Though her texts now regularly featured discernible, named characters, she continued to scrap narrative and psychological motivation. Other conventional trappings of theatre—clearly differentiated lines of dialogue, linear plots, and specifically articulated stage directions—remained stripped from the Steinian stage as well. Thus, her unique dramatic landscapes—both the early ones stimulated by the French countryside and late ones motivated by airborne American scenery—rely on the absence of many landmarks of traditional theatre.

Absence is, however, a very difficult thing to stage. Iconoclastic directors and production teams—including Virgil Thomson and John Houseman, Judith Malina and Julian Beck, Al Carmines and Lawrence Kornfeld, The Santa Fe Opera, the Glimmerglass Opera, the Wooster Group, Robert Wilson, Anne Bogart, Frank Galati and Heiner Goebbels—have ardently roamed Stein's spare dramatic terrain, but even these most imaginative and convention-defying of theatre artists had to fill some of her scenic absences in order to bring the texts to life on the stage. Inevitably contemporary culture and its obsessions infiltrate Stein's pristine topography via these extratextual additions, transforming the landscape in ways virtually unimaginable when the reader encounters *Four Saints in Three Acts, Doctor Faustus Lights the Lights, The Mother of Us All, In Circles,* "Melanctha," or *Making of Americans* on the printed page.

During the course of this study, I demonstrate that the spectator's reception and the critic's most nuanced interpretation of Stein's work are dependent not just on a perpetually present tense interaction of sight and sound as her theory on the page intimates, but also on text and context as the history of her writing in performance reveals. It is only by mapping the simultaneous intersections of sight and sound, and text and context, that have occurred in several productions of Stein's work that one can gain a full appreciation of what her dramatic writing has meant at various historical moments and how that writing has transformed the landscape of the American alternative theatre.

MAPPING THE LANDSCAPE OF STEIN PRODUCTIONS

After surveying the accumulation of twentieth-century stagings of Stein's works in the United States, I have carefully selected works by major directors and companies that indicate both the range of representational strategies and the concerns that appeared across the broad spectrum of productions of her work. Four dominant identity issues emerged from these performance texts: artists have used Stein's texts and her image as a prism for constructing definitions of African American cultural identity; artists have taken Stein's texts, theory, and part of the persona that seems to emerge from them as mechanisms for rebelling against the constraints of mid-century mass culture and for constructing alternative artistic identities; producing agencies have co-opted Stein's texts as tools for shaping definitions of national identity and its relationship to feminism; and artists have appropriated Stein's sexual identity as a lens through which to view and interpret her texts.

These four identity issues are the thematic centers around which I have organized the study. Like the very texts from which they emerge, however, these identity issues do not unfold in a tidy, linear, or chronological fashion. Instead they appear, disappear, and reappear from public consciousness in perceptual flashes. Rather than trying to force these issues into an artificial narrative, a device contrary to Stein's theoretical and dramatic strategies, I have arranged my study like one of Stein's theatrical landscapes. Each issue simply provides a new angle and a distinct perspective from which the reader can "make acquaintance" with the geography of Stein's fissured texts as they exist in performance and her cultural persona as it has been refashioned at particular moments.

Before I introduce the reader to Stein's texts and their history in production, I aim to reconstruct the persona that shaped that history in so many ways as it was, in some sense, the first staging of Gertrude Stein. Since Stein formed her image in relation to the landscape, I traverse the geography of her life— the literal places where she performed herself and where she gathered new material to re-script that performance. As I trek across Stein's childhood and adolescence, I take the reader with Stein from Allegheny, Pennsylvania to Paris to Baltimore and to Oakland, California. As she becomes a young woman, we travel to Cambridge, Massachusetts and back to Baltimore before we feel her taking flight as an artist and a person in bohemian Paris. We also accompany her through the French countryside in both world wars and stow away on her whirlwind celebrity tour of American college towns and cities in the 1930s. This biographical expedition charts the remarkable character that future generations of groundbreaking theatre artists will long to perform.

Chapter 2 begins with an analysis of the first public staging of any of Stein's dramatic works, the 1934 production of *Four Saints in Three Acts*. This was a landmark production for a whole host of reasons, but perhaps most notably, it involved an entirely African American cast in a play not about African American life, but about the lives of Spanish saints. The production was a tremendous success, due in part, I argue, to the production's many references to the codes of primitivism. These characteristics were used to make sense of both Stein's text and the place of the performers in that text. When Virgil Thomson, the composer of the opera and the person who cast the first production, chose to remount the opera in 1952, he attempted to reproduce the 1934 staging exactly. The thing he failed to realize, and the issue I am most interested in exploring, is that notions about African Americans were in flux in the years following World War II and preceding the American Civil Rights Movement. The codes of primitivism that seemed appealing to the white, upper-class audience in 1934 were being contested in the early 1950s. Primitivist ideas could no longer fill the spaces of Stein's text successfully. I then look at the relationship between Stein, her work, and African American identity in the mid-1990s. As I analyze Frank Galati's 1995 adaptation and direction of *Each One As She May*, I explore the ways he revisited the codes of primitivism in order to critique them.

In chapter 3, I investigate The Living Theatre's first public production, the 1951 *Doctor Faustus Lights the Lights*, and one of the Judson Poets Theatre's most successful and long-running productions, *In Circles*, from the 1967–8 season. I explore the ways that both theatre companies sought to emulate a particularly romantic, and not altogether accurate, image of Stein while embodying her aesthetic theory and practice in order to escape the stultifying constraints of mid-century mass culture. I demonstrate that although both Stein's texts—a revision of the Faust myth and one of her early, abstract "lang-scapes"[14]—and the production strategies privileged abstraction and openness, the concerns of Cold War culture crept into the spaces in the plays, thereby figuring prominently in both stagings.

In chapter 4, I analyze the Santa Fe Opera's 1976 production and the Glimmerglass Opera's 1998 production of *The Mother of Us All*, Stein's opera about Susan B. Anthony. I suggest that the Santa Fe production, conceived as the company's participation in the national bicentennial celebration, worked to conceal the politically and ideologically subversive potential present in Stein's libretto (that would have called into question various aspects of the bicentennial celebration) through the use of Virgil Thomson's highly nostalgic and patriotic music and through the set and costume designs created by Pop artist, Robert Indiana. While Stein's libretto seems bent toward revealing inconsistencies between the American national ideal and women's experience of the nation, Thomson and Indiana sought to protect and preserve popular images of American identity. I contrast the style of the Santa Fe Opera production—generally considered the standard by which all other productions of the opera must be measured—with the Glimmerglass Opera's 1998 staging. This highly acclaimed production, which later moved on to the New York City Opera, also coincided with a celebration of national significance—the sesquicentennial of the Seneca Falls Convention. In this production, the set and light designs, the characterization of the opera's protagonist, the inclusion of homosexuality as a motivating factor in several of the characters' behavior, and the use of the historical pageant as production metaphor, were all directed toward forcing audience members to examine the issues that continue to haunt the struggle for women's rights.

In chapter 5, I examine the tensions caused by a simultaneous celebration and repudiation of homosexual desire in the 1990s and the ways these tensions were manifest in Robert Wilson's 1992 *Doctor Faustus Lights the Lights*, the Wooster Group's 1999 *House/Lights*, an amalgamation of the B-film *Olga's House of Shame* and Stein's *Doctor Faustus Lights the Lights*, and Anne Bogart's 1999 *Gertrude and Alice*, a collage of Stein's writings in several genres that pieces together her life with Alice B. Toklas. During the 1990s, several critics sought to uncover images of desire lying just below the surface of Stein's texts, in a kind of empowering, critical, coming out. At the same time, various cultural injunctions made speaking homosexual desire and identity dangerous. Several theatre artists who sought to produce Stein's texts ended up staging this critical and cultural conundrum at once seeming to draw from Stein's sexual relationships for textual filling, while at the same time creating stage pictures lacking a high degree of eroticism.

In my final chapter, a kind of coda to the study, I begin to imagine where productions of Stein might go in the early twenty-first century. Heiner Goebbel's musiktheater adaptation of Stein's novel, *Making of Americans*, *Hashirigaki*, will serve as a case study for the ability of Stein and her work to cross and fuse cultures, genres, and media, thereby redefining the possibilities for her textual space and persona in performance at the dawn of the new century.

1. Gertrude Stein: Living and Writing the American Landscape ⌒

After all America is where we had been born and had always been even though for thirty years we had not really touched it with our feet and hands.

Everybody's Autobiography

When Gertrude Stein arrived in New York in October of 1934, touching her native land for the first time in thirty years, the Rockefeller Center was under construction. During the course of her seven-month lecture tour of the United States, she stopped through New York on several occasions. Recounting her journey in *Everybody's Autobiography*, Stein wrote,

> It was the Rockefeller Center building that pleased me the most and they were building the third piece of it when we left New York so quietly so thinly so rapidly, and when we came back it was already so much higher that it did not take a minute to end it quickly. It is not delicate it is not slender it is not thin but it is something that does make existence a non-existent real thing. Alice Toklas said it is not the way they go into the air but the way they come out of the ground that is the thing. European buildings sit on the ground but American ones come out of the ground.[1]

Stein seemed to hope that the same might be said of her. Before several generations of the American avant-garde staged Stein's writings, Gertrude Stein took great pains, particularly in her later years as she composed her three auto-biographies—*The Autobiography of Alice B. Toklas*, *Everybody's Autobiography*, and *Wars I Have Seen*—to stage herself as an archetypically American writer and figure. In Stein's self-dramatization, the character Gertrude Stein and the masterpieces she created, figure as unique products of the American landscape, coming out of this particular piece of ground. Motivated both by this persona and the connections she made between theatre and landscape, I try to "make acquaintance" with Gertrude Stein, the character and the dramatist, by navigating the spaces of her life's story. In *ThirdSpace*, Edward Soja overhauls the practice of biography through the "attempt to spatialize what we normally think of as biography, to make life-stories as intrinsically and revealingly spatial as they are temporal and social."[2] Following Soja's lead, I attempt to spatialize Gertrude Stein's life story in order to reconstruct her first staging.

AN AMERICAN BEGINNING: ALLEGHENY, PENNSYLVANIA

Stein made her first entrance onto the American landscape on February 3, 1874, a little after 8 A.M., in Allegheny, Pennsylvania, then a suburb of Pittsburgh. Pittsburgh was growing rapidly at the time: its population tripled between 1850 and 1880, becoming the nation's eleventh largest city by 1900. Because of this swift expansion, industrialists began gobbling up cheap land in neighboring towns: Allegheny was prime real estate in this regard, and was eventually incorporated into Pittsburgh in 1907.[3]

In the 1870s, Allegheny was hardly a cosmopolitan setting. Maps of the day show a single public school, a horse car railway, a railroad depot, an orphan asylum, a brewery, a linseed oil mill, cotton mills, a woolen factory, a keystone foundry, several churches, and the Western Theological Seminary in addition to residential property.[4] That said, conditions in Allegheny were considerably brighter than those in many areas of Pittsburgh proper—cleaner, with more green space, and more privacy—so it was the kind of spot where young middle-class household heads chose to plant their families.[5]

Like Pittsburgh and Allegheny City, the Stein family was also growing rapidly. The Steins had planned to have five children, but Gertrude was the seventh child born to Daniel Stein and Amelia "Milly" Keyser after the births of Michael, Simon, two children who died as infants, Bertha and Leo. Though both Gertrude and Leo were conceived as "replacements" for their dead siblings, a fact that biographer Janet Hobhouse notes, "both bound and haunted Gertrude and Leo throughout their lives,"[6] Gertrude was the center of her family's attention, even as family life and location changed radically. She retained the nickname "Baby," long past infancy, marking the position of privilege in the family's landscape that would continue to shape her relationships as an adult. Stein always expected care, devotion, and protection, as attested to by one of her adult nicknames, "Baby Woojams" (in relation to Alice's "Mama Woojams" and Carl Van Vechten's "Papa Woojams").

As one might expect given the era and Daniel Stein's notorious capriciousness, the family's patriarch motivated the changes in the family's geographical circumstances. During the Civil War, Daniel and his brother Solomon moved their respective households from Baltimore to open a Pittsburgh branch of the family's wholesale wool business. By the time Gertrude was born, the brothers' relationship had deteriorated terribly. Since Daniel's temperament drove away customers, Solomon was forced to expend a large part of his energy chasing them down and then winning them back. And as bad as matters were in the business sphere, conditions in the domestic sphere were no better. The Daniel Steins and the Solomon Steins lived next door to each other in matching brick houses on fashionable Western Avenue, but the harmony of the houses' exteriors belied the turmoil inside as Milly, Gertrude's mother, and Pauline, Gertrude's aunt, bickered constantly. The brothers decided to go their separate ways: Solomon moved to New York to pursue banking; Daniel sailed to Vienna.

LEAVING HOME THE FIRST TIME:
A EUROPEAN INFANCY

In late 1874, by the time Gertrude was eight months old, she was uprooted from her native soil, and experiencing her first expatriation. Daniel cited a desire for his children to receive a European education as the driving force behind the family's move. Having completed just three winters of schooling, an academic career that outlasted that of his wife, it is not surprising that he hoped for a different experience for his children. Language acquisition was of particular interest to Daniel, for whom, like his wife, English was a second language. Sometimes he would declare that the children would speak only French and German at home; at other times they could speak only English. Despite the frustration of trying to obey Daniel's shifting edicts, this early exposure to a variety of languages and the need to shift in and out of word systems was surely influential on Stein's adult work, characterized as it is by linguistic play. Furthermore, as Michael North has argued, Stein's literary experiments revealed "the strangeness of the ordinary."[7] From her earliest years, language made the performance of the most everyday activities like a family dinner at home, plenty strange.

In *The Autobiography of Alice B. Toklas*, Stein claims to remember very little of her time in Vienna. This is certainly not surprising given her age during the stay, but one may reasonably suppose she is being selective as she records these memories from the vantage point of the 1930s. By the time she was writing the book, Stein had been performing herself as a public persona for some time, and no doubt the experiences she chose to record are aimed at burnishing this particular image.

Among those few memories she did choose to record are listening in as her brothers receive instruction from their tutor—with a particularly exciting moment coming during the description of "a tiger's snarl that both pleased and terrified her"[8]—and "also she remembers that they used to play in the public gardens and that often the old Kaiser Francis Joseph used to stroll through the gardens and sometimes a band played the Austrian national anthem."[9] Both memories are significant to the spatial construction of Stein's persona. In the first memory, Stein positions herself as a narrative outsider. Her brothers' lesson was not intended for her, yet her transgression of defined roles or social spaces—assuming the place of the (male) student before she was deemed ready or worthy—was a pleasurable and frightening experience. This was, she claims, her first memory of the act of storytelling. The second memory also has significant spatial resonance. Kaiser Francis Joseph modeled for her the power that can be exerted by physically moving through a space marked with particular cultural significance, and how such a journey can perform a national identity, as suggested by the playing of the national anthem. Thus in *The Autobiography*, Stein suggests that though she was quite young, some of the patterns she would repeat as she performed herself as an iconoclastic American writer were already set.

When Daniel Stein was called home to Baltimore to deal with the family business, Milly Stein became even more lonely and homesick than she had been previously. Eventually becoming fed up with life alone with five children, she packed up the house and moved to Paris in November of 1878, where she and the children stayed for a few months. What Stein ate—soup for breakfast, spinach (which she liked) and mutton (which she didn't) for lunch[10]—dominate her memories of this period. Daniel soon reclaimed his family, taking them to London so they could see another important city—and Stein's first theatrical production: Gilbert and Sullivan's *H.M.S. Pinafore*[11]—before sailing back to Baltimore.

Gertrude spent the winter of 1878–9 in Baltimore at her maternal grandparents' house, basking in the attention of her extended family— "cheerful pleasant little people"[12]—and as she reports in *The Autobiography of Alice B. Toklas*, feeling emotions in English for the first time.[13] Though Stein lived her adult life in France, she always wrote in English, presumably because she continued feeling emotions in her native tongue. So in America Stein acquires her most fundamental writing tool. Furthermore, the space in which she acquired this linguistic instrument is quite significant. It was when she returned to the States, and when she was surrounded by domestic tranquility and security—as opposed to her time in Vienna and Paris—that she made this vital connection between emotion and language. Stein would restage these conditions in Paris when she became an adult. Once Alice Toklas ousted Leo from the Steins' apartment, and the domestic arrangement she would maintain to the end of her life was established, Stein would be able to take flight as a writer, once again forging unexpected connections between language and emotion.

While Gertrude was feeling in English and she and her siblings were exploring the waterfront, markets and museums of a new city, her father, after failing to find meaningful employment in Baltimore, headed West, ever in search of financial prosperity and the ideal spot to plant himself and his family. Having first scouted out Los Angeles and San Jose, Daniel settled on Oakland, California as his family's new home. While Gertrude, through the end of her life, seemed to regard Daniel as a negative force,[14] he still provided the precedent of radical spatial relocation when one's state— emotional, financial, or just geographical—was found somehow wanting.

CHILDHOOD AND ADOLESCENCE:
OAKLAND, CALIFORNIA

Daniel returned to Baltimore in 1880, collected his family, and boarded the train for California. Stein's first cross-country train ride merits a paragraph in *The Autobiography*:

> The only thing Gertrude Stein remembers of this trip was that she and her sister had beautiful big Austrian red felt hats trimmed with a beautiful ostrich feather and at some stage of the trip her sister leaning out of the window had her hat blown off. Her father rang the emergency bell, stopped the train, got the hat to the awe and astonishment of the passengers and the conductor. The only other she remembers is that they had a wonderful hamper of food given them by the aunts in Baltimore and that in it was a marvelous turkey. And that later as the food in it diminished it was renewed all along the road whenever they stopped and that that was always exciting. And also that some-where in the desert they saw some red Indians and that somewhere else in the desert they were given some very funny peaches to eat.[15]

Here Stein repeats some of the patterns she followed when telling the story of her first time in Paris: she both claims a degree of non-memory and shifts what she did remember to what she ate. In these moments of transition, as she and her family underwent a significant change in the domestic spaces they inhabited, Stein retreats to the very private physical space of the body, and most especially the stomach. Though she doesn't emphasize this psycho-physical strategy when telling the story of her lecture tour of America in 1934–5, she used food to calm her anxiety again. In *The Alice B. Toklas Cookbook*, Toklas reports, "When during the summer of 1934 Gertrude Stein could not decide whether she did or did not want to go to the United States, one of the things that troubled her was the question of the food she would be eating there."[16] Her concerns were alleviated when a friend sent the menu from one of the hotels at which they would be staying. "Consolingly," Alice writes, "there were honey-dew melons, soft-shell crabs and prime roasts of beef. We would undertake the great adventure."[17]

Though it did not boast miraculously replenished food hampers like the train that brought Stein there, Oakland was still a very interesting place by the 1880s. In 1859 the city created a deep-water port by dredging the San Antonio Bar; in 1869 the Central Pacific Railroad chose Oakland as the terminus for its California line instead of San Francisco. Thus Oakland was in the process of becoming a commercial, industrial, and communications center. The population responded. In 1860, 1,500 people resided in Oakland. By the 1880s, that number jumped to 67,000.[18]

The geography of Oakland helped foster this boom, and helped feed its inhabitants' spirits in addition to filling their pockets. L. Eve Armentrout Ma describes Oakland's early landscape:

> Located on the eastern shore of San Francisco Bay, intersected by several waterways, with tidal flats, the estuary and marshes along its western edge and the hills of the coastal range to the east, it was also a pretty place. In the hills to the north and east of the city, there were beautiful redwood groves. The valley surrounding the city contained large cattle ranches, grain farms planted with wheat and barley, and cherry orchards.[19]

After brief stays at the Tubbs Hotel and a rented house on East Twelfth Street, the Steins settled into the place that would really become home in April of 1881. It was then that the family took up residence in what was known as "The Old Stratton Place." Perched atop a hill, the rented house presided over ten acres of orchards, eucalyptus trees and a swimming hole. Here Gertrude played as a child, and here she returned imaginatively when she began writing her massive novel, *Making of Americans*, in Paris in 1903. She remembered the sensual and spatial pleasures of these days, bequeathing them to the Herslands, a family with a particularly geographical name, which bore a striking resemblance to her own.[20] She thus transposed her lived spatial experiences into the field of representation. A century later, Heiner Goebbels would transpose these experiences once again, transforming them from the literary into the theatrical in his production, *Hashirigaki*.

While the Oakland landscape was bucolic, its inhabitants were quite cosmopolitan. In the 1880s, Oakland in general had a diverse population, and the Stein's neighborhood in particular, was home to children from several countries. Stein's remembered in *Wars I Have Seen*, "California meant knowing lots of nationalities. And if you went to school with them and knew about their hair and their ways and all you were bound later not to be surprised."[21] California was like a theatre for Stein, bringing together a cast of diverse characters with whom she could make acquaintance. In her adult writing, Stein first tried to make acquaintance with people through her portraits—sorting through their hair, and their ways, and their general features physical, emotional, and verbal. She had, she claims, "been enormously interested all my life in finding out what made each one that one so I had written a great many portraits."[22] Eventually she rejected verbal portraiture as the best way to capture her sitters:

> I came to think that since each one is that one and that there are a number of them each one being that one, the only way to express this thing each one being that one and there is being a number of them knowing each other was in a play. And so I began to write these plays.[23]

So while the subject of Stein's plays was never literally the international cast of characters she came to know as a child, her interest in classifying people and capturing their essences through nonnarrative means, was still central to her dramatic writing.

Stein's childhood in Northern California was also important for providing the theatrical landscape she would rebel against as an adult. As a child she read avidly and precociously—Shakespeare, Wordsworth, Burns, Bunyan, Fielding—and found she preferred these literary experiences to the ones she had in the theatre, because she remembered, the theatre "goes too fast, the mixture of the eye and the ear bothers her and her emotion never keeps pace."[24]

From the theatre of her childhood that went too fast, she tells her audience in the lecture "Plays," she remembered only Eliza's escape across the ice in *Uncle Tom's Cabin*, Booth's Hamlet lying at his mother's feet, the fight in *Faust*, the Indian attack in *Buffalo Bill*, the boy being changed into a swan in *Lohengrin*, and an English actor of Bulwer-Lytton's *Richelieu* calling out, "Nemours, Nemours," which was according to Stein, in "Plays," the first thing she ever remembers hearing at the theatre as all her other memories were purely visual.[25] Her two best experiences in the theatre were seeing Sarah Bernhardt when she was sixteen, "It was all so foreign and her voice being so varied and it all being so French I could rest in it untroubled"[26] and seeing William Gillette's *Secret Service* because she admired the fact that "Gillette had conceived a new technique, silence stillness and quick movement. . . . And it made the whole stage this technique. . . . And one was no longer bothered by the theatre, you had to get acquainted of course but that was quickly over and after that nothing bothered."[27] As a child, Stein tells her audience, she had already identified the fundamental dramatic problems that she would explore in her more than eighty plays: could she see and hear at the same time, and how did emotion affect these perceptions. Emulating Bernhardt, she would seek to transform dramatic language so she could rest in it "untroubled," and like Gillette, she would reimagine the movement of the stage picture so that it exhibited a principle of simultaneous relation—or one in which the viewer would no longer be quite so bothered by making acquaintance.

The defining features of Stein's psychological landscape also developed during this period. Stein and her brother Leo had always been close—perhaps because of their shared status as replacement children, a fact with which their elder sister Bertha liked to taunt them—but their bond grew tighter during these years. The two youngest Stein children shared a love of literature and art then alien to the rest of their siblings.[28] The isolation they cultivated from the rest of the family was exacerbated by losing their mother to cancer, an occurrence that Gertrude claims in *Everybody's Autobiography* was less than earth shaking—"we had all already the habit of doing without her"—but that biographer Linda Wagner-Martin sees differently, suggesting that "her denial of the centrality of her mother doesn't mask her real feelings"[29] of loss and abandonment. In 1891, just two and a half years after the death of their mother, the children lost their unpredictable father when one morning they were unable to wake him up. Gertrude describes the effect of her father's death in *Everybody's Autobiography*: "Then our life without a father began a very pleasant one." Despite her protests to the contrary, the trauma of losing both parents at a young age motivated Gertrude to depend on a single strong external figure. For the next several years, Leo would inhabit that space in her life.

Life without a father also led to a change in financial circumstances. Gertrude's oldest brother, Michael, was employed by Omnibus, a streetcar company owned by his father. Finding it impossible to support himself and his four siblings on his salary, and discovering his father's assets had been limited to real estate in Baltimore and Shasta County, Michael needed to do something drastic. Realizing the uniqueness of the vision Daniel had had about consolidating the separate lines of the San Francisco street lines, Michael drafted his father's plan and sold it as well as the Omnibus franchise to railway magnate, Collis Huntington. The money from this deal was then invested in real estate—developing some of the first duplexes in San Francisco. Michael's wherewithal in defining the spaces of modern urban life created the Stein family trust, thereby giving Gertrude the income she would need both to attend college, and later to live abroad without working.

COLLEGE: CAMBRIDGE, MASSACHUSETTS

Before going off to college at the Harvard Annex, as Radcliffe was then called, she, Leo and Bertha lived with Milly's younger sister in Baltimore. While Michael had no trouble managing the family's financial circumstances, he quickly tired of playing parent to his siblings and re-cast Fanny and David Bachrach in the part. The manners of the less wealthy California Stein cousins did not blend easily with the society frequented by the upwardly mobile Baltimore Bachrachs. One of Gertrude's traits considered particularly troubling by her aunt was her habit of taking long walks through various, not always seemly, Baltimore neighborhoods, and stopping to talk with whomever she found interesting. While these excursions expanded her sense of the city's geography and gave her the opportunity to study the language patterns of the city's inhabitants, such outings were not considered appropriate for a young lady of Stein's station. Stein's transgressive walks around Baltimore anticipate and enact de Certeau's ideas in "Walking in the City." Rather than obeying the logic of urban planners or the social proscriptions of her class, Stein created a "pedestrian rhetoric" or "urban text" of her own, "cruising" new people, places, and possibilities.[30]

Fanny's desire to find suitable spouses for her nieces and nephew exacerbated the domestic unrest. If Gertrude was positioned in the clear (and confining) social space of the upper-middle-class wife, her defiant wandering might be curtailed. But while docile Bertha showed no resistance to Fanny's plan, Gertrude and Leo had other ideas. Leo escaped to Harvard in August 1892 to pursue the degree he had left without finishing at Berkeley; Gertrude joined him in Cambridge the next year.

Gertrude's time in Cambridge introduced her to a new piece of the American landscape—the Northeast—but even more importantly it gave her a particularly vibrant intellectual landscape within which she might orient herself. Among her professors were George Santayana, William James, William Vaughn Moody, Hugo Munsterburg, and George Pierce Baker. Of these notable thinkers, the one to have the greatest influence on Stein's life and early writing was William James.

In her freshman year at Radcliffe, Stein took Philosophy I, a course featuring lectures by George Herbert Palmer, George Santayana, and

William James. James was a gifted performer in the classroom—humorous, unconventional, open to and respectful of his students—and thus an extremely popular teacher and Stein's favorite.[31] Stein's affection for him is clearly evident in one of the essays she wrote for William Vaughn Moody's English Composition course: "Is life worth living? Yes, a thousand times yes when the world still holds such spirits as Prof. James. He is truly a man among men."[32]

Beyond James's personal charm in the classroom, Stein was, Lisa Ruddick argues, attracted to his philosophical ideas as a way of dealing with her ambivalent feelings about her emerging lesbian sexuality. In *Reading Gertrude Stein: Body, Text, Gnosis*, she writes:

> As James's student in college, Stein was drawn to his theories because they gave her a way of rethinking a conflict she perceived in herself, between sexual desire and sexual self-loathing. James's psychology views the tension between promiscuous and conservative mental habits—specifically habits of attention—as an essential feature of a healthy mental life. Stein easily projected her sexual conflict onto what in James were issues of attention, and thereby found a way to see her own conflict as creative rather than paralyzing . . . . Her mapping of sexual issues onto James's psychology helped to produce "Melanctha."[33]

As important as James and his ideas were in her college years and early writings, Stein found herself battling against simplistic equations of her style with Jamesian philosophy later in her career. Part of this confusion likely arose from the work she did in one James's graduate seminars. Because she had done so well in a course taught by Munsterberg, he recommended that James allow her to enroll in his graduate seminar, despite her undergraduate status. There she met Leon Solomons, with whom she worked on the question of "normal motor automatism."

Solomons and Stein used themselves as subjects as they explored whether a person's subconscious might control his or her movements when he or she was distracted or fatigued. The experiment, though it used planchettes, and later regular pencils and paper, was not designed to study automatic, or in the terminology most associated with Jamesian philosophy, stream of consciousness, writing specifically. Stein recorded her experience in one of the experiments as follows:

> Next she finds herself with a complicated apparatus strapped across her breast to register her breathing, her finger imprisoned in steel machine and her arm thrust immovably into a big glass tube. She is surrounded by a group of

earnest youths who carefully watch the silent record of the automatic pen on the slowly revolving drum. Strange fancies begin to crowd upon her, she feels that the silent pen is writing on and one forever. Her record is there she cannot escape it and the group about her begin to assume the shape of mocking fiends gloating over her imprisoned misery. Suddenly she starts, they have suddenly loosed a metronome directly behind her, to observe the effect, so now the morning's work is over.[34]

Stein's unpublished report makes clear that she did not enjoy this experience. What she found much more interesting when some of the experiments expanded to include fifty female and forty male college students, was her ability to catalogue the various personalities she encountered. This observation and classification of people was more central to her later writing than the subconscious movements of her hand or what might be called automatic writing. At the conclusion of their work, it was Solomons who wrote up the findings from the experiments, publishing them under both their names in *The Harvard Psychological Review* in 1896.

In 1934, B. F. Skinner relied on this article, Stein's first published work, when he made his claim, in *The Atlantic Monthly* under the title "Has Gertrude Stein a Secret," that Stein had used automatic writing in composing her mature, and now famous works. Skinner's piece, obviously derisive of the innovations and achievements she had made while misrepresenting the precise nature of her early scientific experiments, rankled Stein. She corrected Skinner on the facts of the experiment and dismissed his evaluation of her writing method in *Everybody's Autobiography* concluding, "Writing should be very exact and one must realize what there is inside in one and then in some way it comes into words and the more exactly the words fit the emotion the more beautiful the words that is what does happen and anybody who knows anything knows that thing."[35]

While Skinner's article popularized a misperception about Stein's writing and the nature of its debt to William James, she remained fond of her college mentor and grateful for his early influence. In an interview with Robert Haas in 1946, the year she died, Stein said,

I like a thing simple but it must be simple through complication. Everything must come into your scheme, otherwise you cannot achieve real simplicity. A great deal of this I owe to a great teacher William James. He said, "Never reject anything. Nothing has been proved. If you reject anything, that is the beginning of the end as an intellectual." He was my big influence when I was at college. He was a man who always said "complicate your life as much as you please, it has got to simplify."[36]

MEDICAL SCHOOL: BALTIMORE, MARYLAND

Before he influenced "Melanctha" and Stein's writing more generally through a complicated simplification of language, structure, and idea, James influenced where Stein would next land on the American landscape: his urging spurred Stein to go to medical school and his letter of recommendation gained her admittance to Johns Hopkins in Baltimore. Though Stein's marks at Harvard had been stellar—she graduated magna cum laude in philosophy—they were low enough at Johns Hopkins that a committee of the medical school faculty met and decided that Stein would not be granted a degree with her class, despite suffering through four years of school.[37] In *Favored Strangers*, Wagner-Martin attributes some of Stein's problems to the sexism and anti-Semitism at Johns Hopkins,[38] but equally important, as she notes, in her declining academic interest was the change in her personal life and her awakening to a new part of the sexual landscape.

During her third and fourth years of medical school, Stein had a relationship with May Bookstaver, a Bryn Mawr graduate rooming with another Johns Hopkins Medical School student, Emma Lootz. The relationship is difficult to outline with certainty because the letters exchanged between Stein and Bookstaver were burned by, or at the behest of, Alice B. Toklas. The relationship is also one Stein chose not to spotlight in her autobiographies. Whatever the precise details, it seems that Stein was far more devoted to Bookstaver than Bookstaver was to Stein. Either in an effort to gain distance from Bookstaver or in an attempt to get closer to her once again, the next few years were Stein's most nomadic, as she wandered across Europe and occasionally back to the United States. In summer 1901 she traveled with Leo in Spain; in summer 1902 she stayed in Florence, then England—London and the Lake District; fall 1902 took her back to London. Gertrude then stayed by herself for six weeks before sailing back to New York where she stayed with Mabel Weeks, Estelle Rumbold, and Harriet Clark, occasionally traveling to Baltimore to see Bookstaver and Bertha and her children; summer 1903 Leo invited her to move to Paris (that summer they also traveled in Italy during which time Stein met up with Bookstaver and her lover and Stein's rival Mabel Haynes); four months in 1904 feature a return to the United States, again lured by the chance of seeing Bookstaver; permanent residence in Paris follows thereafter.

In this period of Stein's life, the volatility of her emotional landscape translated into a peripatetic encounter with the world's geography. Stein's drifting embodied her romantic difficulties without resolving them. When this marking of literal physical space failed her, Stein tried marking literary space, using writing to work through her complex emotions. In fact the tumultuous relationship with Bookstaver fueled early works like *Q.E.D.*, which she then reworked again as "Melanctha," the most well known of the three novellas comprising *Three Lives*. "Melanctha" also became significant to the history of Stein's work in production, even though it is not a dramatic work, because Frank Galati adapted it for a 1995 staging at Chicago's Goodman Theatre.

ADULTHOOD: AN AMERICAN (IN) PARIS

Biographers and critics tend to read Stein's expatriation to Paris much as critic Shari Benstock does in *Women of the Left Bank*: "separation from America liberated Stein's personal and professional lives."[39] While it is indisputable that Left Bank mores permitted Stein to create a life and home with Alice B. Toklas that would have been allowed very few places in the sexually conservative United States of the early twentieth century, and that all of Stein's major mature work was written while she lived abroad,[40] what is less clear is how un-American her years in France really were, as she surrounded herself with a shifting constellation of American admirers—from members of her own family, to her lover, to American writers and artists who visited her salon, to American G.I.s at the close of World War II. In Paris, Stein created a simulated America, eventually restaging her native country with French bohemian embellishments that gave her control over domestic, sexual, and creative space, and gave her the backdrop against which she could star as an American literary genius.

Stein's earliest years in Paris were spent in the company of her family. After Leo had rented the apartment at 27 Rue de Fleurus, he invited his sister to join him there. She had doubts about leaving her native country permanently, and when she first arrived she was homesick, writing to friends about the foods she missed, yet again retreating to the interior spaces of the body when spatial anxiety hit. She also insisted to her brother that though she was willing to pool their two incomes, she would need funds to return home to the United States for an annual visit. She did so in 1904; she never wanted to again. Biographers speculate on whether her change of heart might have been caused by the final demise of her relationship with Bookstaver, her progress on *Making of Americans*, or both.[41] No doubt some of her homesickness was soon abated by the arrival of her brother Michael, his wife Sally, and their son Allan. The Michael Steins set up house at 58 Rue Madame. Leo and Gertrude ate daily with Mike and his family and more important than the sharing of meals, was their sharing of love for the new painting in Paris. Mike and Sally purchased a Matisse at the Autumn Salon.

Afterward, Leo took them to meet Henri Matisse, beginning an important patronage for Matisse as well as a lifelong friendship for Sally. Both sets of Steins soon gained a reputation as collectors, and to some extent eccentrics, for buying art that Paris critics of the day found laughable. As the various Steins' fame spread, more and more people wanted to meet them and see their collections. Thus began the Saturday salons, Mike and Sally's usually beginning at 9 P.M. and ending fairly early, Leo and Gertrude's taking up where their brother and sister-in-law's left off, sometimes lasting until dawn.

Leo may have made another very important introduction: he may have introduced his sister to Pablo Picasso. The stories recounting Gertrude's meeting with Picasso differ. One has it that Picasso spotted the famed brother and sister (who were frequently mistaken for husband and wife) at Clovis Sagot's gallery. Attracted by what he presumed to be their wealth, given their reputation as collectors, he asked Sagot to arrange for him to paint Gertrude. The other story suggests that after Leo purchased "Acrobat's Family with a Monkey" and "Young Girl with a Basket of Flowers," he wanted to meet the artist, as was his habit whenever he bought new work. After a visit to Picasso's studio, the Steins invited Picasso and his lover, Fernande Olivier, to dinner. There, bored with Leo's prattling on about Japanese prints, Picasso asked to paint Gertrude.

While Picasso would prove to be a positive force on Gertrude's writing—she would later claim that during her more than eighty sittings for Picasso's portrait of her she discovered a new direction in literature and her late-twentieth-century critics would widely agree that Cubism was tremendously influential on her writing, dramatic or otherwise—Leo was far less positive. His curt criticism of her early work led her to stop sharing her efforts with him and drove her to write late at night after he had gone to bed. In Stein's early years in Paris, the domestic space of 27 Rue de Fleurus was clearly governed by Leo's will, and the dependence that had seemed comforting in her adolescence in the States was starting to chafe. In addition, during the early salons, visitors to the apartment like Alfred Stieglitz remarked on how very quiet Stein was—a quality previously and later alien to her.[42] These early years in Paris with Leo might be read as a kind of rehearsal in which Stein learned what kind of domestic space she did not want and what position she did not want to occupy within it. What she needed, to bring her new vision to life, was a willing supporting player to animate the space she had crafted.

Surely the most important American to touch the life of Stein in Paris, was sister Californian, Alice Toklas. If Leo was a negative influence on Stein's writing, Alice was in almost every way positive, loving her, body and soul, as she created the sensual, sexual domestic landscape that Stein had so long craved. Stein met Alice Babette Toklas in September of 1907. In the one spatializing move that biographers conventionally make when telling Stein's life story, several have noted the relationship between Alice's visit to Paris and the great San Francisco earthquake of 1906, bandying about various metaphors of seismic tremors and forces of nature.[43] Anne Bogart would direct an ode to this earth-shaking love more than ninety years after their meeting under the title *Gertrude and Alice: A Likeness in Loving*. After the earthquake, Mike and Sally returned to California to check on the welfare of Simon Stein. While Sally was home she reconnected with several old friends—including Harriet Levy and Alice Toklas—and sang the praises of Paris, urging her friends to see it for themselves. When Alice and Harriet took Sally's advice, it was Sally who introduced Alice and Gertrude. Apparently Gertrude was so immediately taken with Alice that she invited her to go walking in the Luxembourg Gardens the next day. When Gertrude tells of Alice's reaction to meeting her in *The Autobiography of Alice B. Toklas*, Stein has Alice claim that this was one of three times in her life when she heard a bell within her ring.[44]

Alice returned to California in the winter of 1907–8, but Stein's courtship of her resumed in earnest during the summer of 1908 in Italy. Mike and Sally rented a villa in Fiesole large enough to accommodate Leo and Gertrude as well; nearby, Harriet and Alice rented the Casa Ricci. There Alice assumed one of the many tasks that would serve Stein throughout the rest of their lives together: she began typing Stein's manuscript of *Making of Americans*, thus becoming Stein's first and most privileged audience. Rather than returning to San Francisco in the fall of 1908, Alice and Harriet rented an apartment on the Rue de Notre Dame des Champs. Though Alice had her own address, she spent more and more time at the apartment of Leo and Gertrude. In the winter of 1909–10, Alice finally moved Harriet back to the States and herself into the flat at 27 Rue de Fleurus.

This change in living arrangements was not one that Leo welcomed. Leo was uncomfortable with Gertrude's sexual relationship with Alice, a discomfort nearly matched by Gertrude's disapproval of Leo's relationship with the woman who would become his wife, artists' model Nina Auzias. Complicating matters further was Leo's continued lack of support for his sister's writing. Even when Gertrude received positive reviews for *Three Lives*, Leo was unable to celebrate her achievements, publicly mocking her style and doubting her talent. As Leo's jealously mounted, the final straw seems to have come when he sold one of Gertrude's beloved Picasso's hanging on the studio room wall so he could buy a Renoir. Finally brother and sister decided to split up their art collection and their lives, establishing separate homes in 1914.

Alice's ousting of Leo, both psychologically as the person on whom Gertrude was most dependent and physically from the apartment, was a strategy she would repeat with others. A notable example from this era in Stein's life was Mabel Dodge. Dodge would prove very helpful in constructing Stein's persona in America. First, Dodge had been so pleased with Stein's "Portrait of Mabel Dodge at the Villa Curonia," that she had 300 copies bound, which she distributed to her avant-garde friends. More important was Dodge's essay, "Speculations, or Post-Impressionists in Prose," a piece that compared Stein's writing to Picasso's painting, which she wrote as a publicity piece for the famous Armory Show of 1913 that was later reprinted in *Camera Work*. Overwhelming these virtues, was the sin Alice felt Dodge had committed in 1912 when Dodge seemed to have attracted Stein's sexual attention.[45] Stein and Dodge's relationship would never recover, with Toklas maneuvering to keep Dodge far removed from Stein.

World War I disrupted Paris life with Alice. In February 1915, Alice and Gertrude decided to leave the city for Majorca where they stayed until the summer of 1916 when they returned to Paris. There they soon learned of the American Fund for the French Wounded, and signed up as delegates. In order to serve, the women had to provide their own transportation, which some of Stein's American cousins acquired through their own funds and those they solicited from friends. They sent Stein a Ford, which she promptly named "Auntie" in honor of her level-headed Aunt Pauline. In Auntie, Stein and Toklas delivered supplies to Saint-Cloud, Perpignan, and Nimes, and also helped transport sick and wounded soldiers. Their experience of World War I was thus very mobile and proactive, and completely different from what they would face during World War II. When *Vanity Fair* published Stein's poem, "The Great American Army" in its June 1918 issue, it was accompanied by a lithograph captioned, "Gertrude Stein has, since the outbreak of the war, been living in France and working in war relief as an ambulance driver. Few American women have taken a more active part in the conflict than she."[46] Such publicity, regardless of its inaccuracies, contributed to the fascination Americans, both at home and abroad, would have with Stein in the years between the wars.

While the prewar salons, especially those while Leo still lived at 27 Rue de Fleurus, were dominated by painters, collectors, and Leo's conversation, those between the wars were dominated by writers enticed by Gertrude's reputation and her writings, rather than the collection of art that Leo seemed to regard as primarily his. The visitors in the 1920s, most often hailing from America, were in search of the American icon in Paris. They became the audience for some of Stein's most fascinating performances.

Since these performances at the Stein atelier were metaphorical rather than literal, those wishing to attend could not just walk up to the box office and purchase a ticket; instead they needed a letter of introduction. Frequently Sylvia Beach, the American woman who opened the bookshop, Shakespeare and Company, in 1919, provided this hybrid ticket/passport. Beach herself was an important landmark on the American expatriate map of Paris. Because it had been very difficult to acquire works of literature written in English in Paris, Beach stocked her shelves with English-language classics, but she also had long rows of work by new talents like Gertrude Stein. Beach's shop thus drew English-speaking, and especially American, readers. She then directed the worthy visitors to the next important destination in literary Paris: Gertrude Stein. This practice lasted while the Beach/Stein friendship endured. It ended when, in Stein's opinion, Beach betrayed her by publishing her rival, James Joyce's, *Ulysses*.

Before that break, Beach guided Sherwood Anderson to Stein's door. Anderson proved an important part of the American/Parisian landscape as he was one of the most talented and already well-known young men eager to sit at the feet of Stein for literary instruction. He repaid this debt through his essay of introduction to Stein's *Geography and Plays*.[47]

It was Anderson who introduced Stein to Ernest Hemingway, the American writer with whom Stein had the most volatile relationship. When Hemingway first arrived in Paris with his wife Hadley in 1922, he asked Anderson to write him a letter of introduction so that he might meet the now legendary Gertrude Stein. Gaining admission to the Stein salon, Hemingway brought with him his short stories, all of which Stein liked with the exception of "Up in Michigan," which she found too blatantly sexual to be published. She encouraged his writing, urging him to look inward, to heighten visual motifs, and to learn the difference between realistic literary conversation and conversations as they spin out in real life. Stein continued to encourage him as he worked on his first draft of *The Sun Also Rises*. He returned the favor by getting Ford Maddox Ford to publish parts of *Making of Americans* in the *Transatlantic Review*. During these days Hemingway brought other young Americans to the Stein home including John Dos Passos, Archibald MacLeish, David Ogden Stewart, Nathan Asch, Evan Shipman, Ernest Walsh, and F. Scott Fitzgerald, a particular favorite of Stein's who made Hemingway very jealous. In general, Hemingway's strategy in visiting the Stein salon was to bring with him a supporting cast not likely to upstage him in his own performances for and with Stein. Hemingway's relationship with Stein quickly soured. This may have been due in part to Edmund Wilson's review of Hemingway in *The Dial*[48] that called him Stein's pupil—a public appellation he couldn't stomach—and his lingering discomfort with Stein's sexuality. He ended their friendship quite publicly by mocking both Stein and Sherwood Anderson in *The Torrents of Spring.*

Carl Van Vechten's relationship with Stein was as long and steady as Hemingway's was short and tumultuous. Van Vechten met Stein in the summer of 1913 and from the outset, he became a champion of her work. It was he who worked tirelessly to find her publishers, to arrange the American tour, and it was he who became the Papa Woojums to Alice's Mama and Gertrude's Baby. He also enriched the lives of Stein and Toklas by the visitors he brought to their salon, most notably Blanche Knopf, Nora Holt, Nella Larsen, and Paul and Essie Robeson. His influence on Stein's work and legacy continued even after her death. For example, he advised the Living Theatre during their 1951 production of *Doctor Faustus Lights the Lights* and preserved their work in photographs for future generations of theatre historians.

Stein's visitors helped construct the salon as an American enclave within bohemian Paris; Stein and Toklas's behavior within the apartment used the space to perform their relationship in a way that was radical in what it was willing to reveal to the discerning spectator. In "Queer Sites of Modernism: Harlem/The Left Bank/Greenwich Village," Joseph Boone argues that "the appropriation of public social space—the park, the café, the store window, the subway, the bathhouse—often radically reorganizes what is considered public and private space, in ways that become especially constitutive of modern gay male identity."[49] Stein and Toklas seemed to do the reverse of what Boone describes: they made their private, lesbian domestic space public. And, rather than concealing their sexual roles in the relationship, they used the space of the apartment to reveal it, publicly performing the roles of husband and wife, although many of their visitors may have been unable to read the spatial text their bodies were writing. During the salons the husbands/artists sat in one room with Gertrude, while in a separate room the wives sat with Alice.[50] A play written in 1920, *A Circular Play A Play in Circles,* which would be produced by the Judson Poets Theatre in 1967 as *In Circles,* reflects Stein's convention defying sexual–social landscape. As Ulla Dydo has said of *A Circular Play,* "There is no imperial, sexual or grammatical authority. Sexuality and language surge in play about the creative process."[51]

After Hemingway's stinging betrayal, the visitors to the salon changed. Later in the 1920s the visitors were less often heterosexual males. In these years Stein's visitors included Hart Crane, Paul Bowles, Janet Flanner, Bryher, Jane Heap, Kay Boyle, and Natalie Barney. A particularly important American visitor to the Stein apartment during the mid-1920s was the young homosexual composer, Virgil Thomson.

Like many of her visitors earlier in the decade, Thomson had been sent, though somewhat indirectly, by Sylvia Beach. Thomson tells the story of his meeting with Stein in his memoirs. He says, "though addicted from Harvard days to 'Tender Buttons' and to *Geography and Plays*, . . . I still had made no effort toward the writer."[52] He had believed their meeting would happen naturally, and so indeed it did in 1925. Thomson's friend, George Antheil, was all the rage that year. Stein asked Beach to arrange a meeting, and Antheil brought Thomson along, for as Thomson puts it, "intellectual protection,"[53] from the American lioness.

Shortly after this first meeting, on New Year's Day 1926, Thomson left a gift outside Stein's door: the manuscript for his musical accompaniment to her poem, "Susie Asado." Thomson wrote of his creation in his memoirs,

> My hope in putting Gertrude Stein to music had been to break, crack open, and solve for all time anything still waiting to be solved, which was almost everything, about English musical declamation. My theory was that if a text is set correctly for the sound of it, the meaning will take care of itself. And the Stein texts, for prosodizing in this way, were manna. With meanings already abstracted, or absent, or so multiplied that choice among them was impossible, there was no temptation toward tonal illustration, say of birdie babbling by the brook or heavy heavy hangs my heart. You could make a setting for sound and syntax only, then add, if needed, an accompaniment equally functional. I had no sooner put to music after this recipe one short Stein text than I knew I had opened a door. I had never had any doubts about Stein's poetry; from then on I had none about my ability to handle it in music.[54]

Just as the "Susie Asado" composition opened a door for Thomson, so too did it open one for Stein. As Stein's comments about her childhood experiences in the theatre indicate, the visual overwhelmed the aural in her conception of theatre. Hearing her words performed, particularly to music as her staged works would so often be in her lifetime and after, was surely a revelation. The dramatic scenery she had envisioned now had an American soundscape to match. Furthermore, it would be the collaboration with Thomson that would provide one of only two opportunities she had during her lifetime to see her work fully mounted: *Four Saints in Three Acts* during her tour of the United States.[55] After this successful project, she and Thomson would collaborate on her last opera, *The Mother of Us All*, though she never saw it staged.

And whether future directors of Stein texts know Thomson's comments or not, he has in essence isolated the impulse driving many of the most interesting productions of Stein's work in the twentieth century. A Stein text, because of its abstract absence, resists the kind of illustration most typically employed in the theatre: characters need not be singular or psychological, settings need not be naturalistic or familiar, and physical action need not be indicative or even logical. Artists are freed in the presence of a Stein text to open a new door—not just musically as Thomson did, but to culture, to artistry, and to experiment with what theatrical representation can entail.

COMING HOME: THE AMERICAN TOUR

If Thomson made a stunning discovery about Stein's theatrical drama, Alice made an equally shattering discovery about her personal drama. In the summer of 1932, Alice found the "lost" novella of *Q.E.D.* Not only did the manuscript tell her about a pivotal relationship in Stein's life about which she had never heard during the twenty-five years of their life together, but she also learned that Stein had recorded the relationship for posterity, immortalizing Bookstaver in a way she believed she never had been.[56] To atone for these most grievous sins (and to make some much-needed money), Gertrude wrote a book for Alice: *The Autobiography of Alice B. Toklas*. It was the phenomenal financial, popular, and critical success of this book, coupled with the triumph of *Four Saints in Three Acts*, that lead Stein to embark on a lecture tour of the United States, returning to American soil for the first time in thirty years.

Stein's tour was extensive: during her stay she visited New York; Chicago; Madison, Wisconsin; St. Paul, Minnesota; Detroit; Cleveland, Toledo and Columbus, Ohio; Washington, D.C., Baltimore; Cambridge, Springfield, Amherst, Pittsfield, and South Hadley, Massachusetts; Wallingford, Middletown, and Hartford, Connecticut; Williamsburg, Richmond, and Charlottesville, Virginia; Black Mountain and Chapel Hill, North Carolina; Charleston, South Carolina; Atlanta; Birmingham; New Orleans; Bryn Mawr, Pennsylvania; St. Louis; Indianapolis; Memphis; Dallas, Fort Worth, Houston, and Austin, Texas; Omaha; Oklahoma City; and Pasadena, Beverly Hills, Del Monte, Berkeley, San Francisco, and Oakland, California.[57] While she seemed quite charmed by the places she had not known in her youth, writing such things as, "The size of everything in Indianapolis was different from anything in Ohio or Illinois or Wisconsin or Minnesota entirely a different size, I was tremendously interested in each state I wish well I wish I could know everything about each one,"[58] she was at best ambivalent about the places she had lived, writing of Baltimore, "After all everybody has to come from somewhere, nobody thinks about that enough to be a bother but sometimes they think about it enough to be a pleasure and sometimes not,"[59] and of Oakland, "what was the use of my having come from

Oakland it was not natural to have come from there yes write about it if I like or anything if I like but not there, there is no there there."[60]

During this reacquaintance with the American landscape, Stein became acquainted with herself in the role of the American celebrity. Though she had dreamed of fame and fortune for years, the realization of these dreams on a grand stage seemed somewhat disconcerting. In *Everybody's Autobiography*, she writes of walking along the street in New York and liking the fact that people knew her name and spoke to her on the street, but then, she writes, "we saw an electric sign moving around a building and it said Gertrude Stein has come and that was upsetting."[61] Gertrude Stein had finally become a character in a popular American drama. This bizarrely theatrical set of events had a substantial effect on her writing: first writer's block, then desire for more fame prompting the creation and publication of Stein's second autobiography, *Everybody's Autobiography*, and eventually some of the most frequently produced and most accessible dramatic writing she ever composed: *Doctor Faustus Lights the Lights* and *The Mother of Us All*.

Doctor Faustus Lights the Lights, written in 1938 with important productions by the Living Theatre in 1951, Robert Wilson in 1992, and the Wooster Group in 1999, and *The Mother of Us All*, written in 1946 with famous productions by the Santa Fe Opera in 1976 and the Glimmerglass Opera in 1998, demonstrate Stein's desire to keep an American audience once she had cultivated it. Though both texts defy conventions of dramatic form like clearly differentiated lines of dialogue and stage directions that are obviously distinct from the portion of the text that are intended to be spoken, both scripts now feature discernible characters—borrowed from literature, in the case of *Doctor Faustus*, and history in the case of *The Mother of Us All*, which has Susan B. Anthony as its central character. Furthermore, these late texts stray into the realm of narrative. *Doctor Faustus Lights the Lights* tells the story of the title character's quest to discover electric light and the price he pays for this discovery, while *The Mother of Us All* meditates on Anthony's struggle to enfranchise women. The post-tour works reveal a changed Stein, one who was willing to temper the intensity of her textual innovation, in order to keep or expand the warm and eager audiences she found awaiting her around the country.

STAYING OVER THERE: THE SPACE OF WORLD WAR II PERFORMANCE AND AMERICAN G.I.s

Though Stein had been given star treatment during her lecture tour, she did not want to return to the United States to seek refuge during World War II, despite the pleadings of many friends and the general advisories given by the American ambassador that U.S. citizens should return home. That a Jewish lesbian intellectual from the United States remained safe in occupied France is a miracle—one likely engineered in part by Stein's longtime friend, and Nazi collaborator, Bernard Faÿ,[62] and also by sympathetic villagers in the places where she stayed. For this miracle to work though, Stein had to play "French," and abandon her beloved role as the archetypal American.

Stein left Paris in 1939, heading for the sanctuary of the French countryside in Bilignin and later Culoz. The war years were likely Stein's period of most intimate contact with the French, living a life akin to that of the villagers instead of the distinctive life of the American expatriate that she had lived in Paris. In the first year of the war, Stein seemed to have regarded her exile from Paris as something of adventure, finding pleasure in the simple existence that Alice helped create from their wartime rations with the aid of their chickens and goat. In "The Winner Loses: A Picture of Occupied France," Stein wrote,

> The country is a better place in war than a city. They grow things to eat right where you are, so there is no privation, as taking away is difficult, particularly in the mountains, so there was plenty of meat and potatoes and bread and honey and we had some sugar and we even had all the lemons and oranges we needed and dates; a little short in gasoline for the car, but we learned to do what we wanted with that little, so we settled down to a comfortable and pleasantly exciting winter.[63]

When Italy entered the war, however, Stein and Toklas began to question their decision to remain in France. Stein wrote, "I was scared, completely scared, and my stomach felt very weak, because—well, here we were right in everybody's path; any enemy that wanted to go anywhere might easily come here."[64] They prepared to make an escape, having been told by the American consul in Lyon that they should get out immediately, but at the last minute they changed their minds, deciding it was safer to stay amongst the friends they had than to cast their lot among strangers, despite the fact that she had come to regard wartime life as "medieval,"[65] a sentiment she repeats in Denise's opening lines in her 1945 play, *Yes is for a Very Young Man*.[66] The evidence of the villagers' friendship for Stein and Toklas comes from the fact that their presence was never reported, something easy enough to do as German soldiers were frequently billeted in Bilignin, even staying in the house that Stein and Toklas rented on more than one occasion.

From time to time, Stein broke character. She never learned to speak accent-less French, and her raucous laugh was considered a distinctly

American trait. She also found it impossible to forego her celebrity completely. In a German-occupied train station, she gleefully fulfilled a French guard's request to inscribe his copy of *The Autobiography of Alice B. Toklas*.[67] Perhaps Stein's most foolish move was attempting to sue their landlord when she evicted Stein and Toklas so her son could live in the house instead. This legal proceeding, more typical of an American celebrity than a French villager, attracted attention, but once again, when they were warned by the sous-prefet of Belley to leave for Switzerland immediately lest they wanted to find themselves shipped off to a concentration camp, they started over in Culoz, in Le Colombier manor house. This move was also brazen as they gave up the seclusion of Bilignin for the larger town of Culoz, which housed a busy railway center used by German soldiers.

Though the French had treated her with immense kindness during the war, Stein embraced the opportunity to reconnect with Americans and shed her French guise completely when the liberating U.S. soldiers came through Belley, an experience she recounts with delight at the end of *Wars I Have Seen*. Writing of putting several soldiers up in September of 1944, Stein says,

> How we talked that night, they just brought all America to us every bit of it, they came from Colorado, lovely Colorado, I do not know Colorado but that is the way I felt about it lovely Colorado and then everybody was tired out and they gave us nice American specialties and my were we happy, we were, completely and truly happy and completely and entirely worn out with emotion.[68]

As Stein tells the story of her reunion with America, she uses spatial terms to do so, feeling that particular places were brought home to her through the conversation and the food.

Stein and Toklas continued housing and feeding American soldiers in Culoz until they were able to return to Paris. There they did more of the same. In Paris, Stein also made good on the promise she made when the soldiers leaving the French countryside said, "Write about us they all said a little sadly."[69] This she did in her last novel, *Brewsie and Willie*.

No sooner had Stein and Toklas returned to Paris than many people seemed to be leaving: friends Donald Gallup and Virgil Thomson, and the U.S. troops. This leave-taking of Americans only briefly precedes Stein's ultimate leave taking. The "colitis" and "bowel infections" that had tormented her for years worsened. On July 19, 1946, when she was en route to the house in Bilignin that Bernard Faÿ had lent her, she had a terrible attack of stomach pain. Originally planning to go to see specialists in Paris, she was diverted to the American Hospital in Neuilly. Though doctors felt she was too weak from the cancer to operate on, Stein insisted. She never awoke from the anesthetic, dying at 6:30 P.M. on July 27, 1946.

GERTRUDE STEIN, A.D.: INSPIRING THE AMERICAN ALTERNATIVE THEATRE

Nearly all her adult life, Stein's stayed in France. So too after her death, her body remained in Paris, interred at Pere Lachaise Cemetery. But her spirit lived on in the United States, inspiring the work of new generations of artists in a variety of media.

When Stein was alive her image fascinated visual artists. Though her most famous likeness was created by Picasso, she was also painted by Francis Rose, Marie Laurencin, Felix Vallotton, Francis Picabia, Pierre Tal-Coat, and Florinne Stettheimer, sculpted by Jacques Lipchitz, and photographed by Cecil Beaton, Alvin Langdon Coburn, Man Ray, Carl Van Vechten, and many others. Long after her death, her image was re-created by such artists as Red Grooms in his 1975 three-dimensional lithograph, "Gertrude"; Andy Warhol, in his 1980 silk-screened print "Gertrude Stein," part of his series, *Ten Portraits of Jews of the Twentieth Century*; Faith Ringgold, in her 1991 story quilt, "My Dinner at Gertrude Stein's," part of her series, *The French Collection*; and Deborah Kass's 1992–8 *Warhol Project* and *Chairman MA Series*.

The literary arts have also featured Gertrude Stein. Most recently, Monique Truong's best-selling 2003 novel, *The Book of Salt*, tells a fictionalized account of Stein and Toklas's Vietnamese cook, but the numbers of biographies, collections of letters, and critical studies are too numerous to mention. Also important are the reprints of Stein's works. Though most all of her work had gone out of print by the 1970s, almost all of it was back in print by the 1990s, from a variety of presses from major university presses to small, alternative publishing houses.

But one of Stein's greatest areas of influence after her death, and this study's primary site of interest, is the American alternative theatre. In *American Avant Garde Theatre: A History*, Arnold Aronson lists four artists whose work and ideas laid the foundations for the American alternative theatre: Bertolt Brecht, John Cage, Antonin Artaud, and Gertrude Stein. As she lay on her deathbed, about to be wheeled into surgery, Stein's final words to Toklas were, "What is the answer?" When she found Toklas too overwhelmed with emotion to respond, Stein followed up with, "In that case what is the question?" Since her work was first performed for American audiences in 1934, Gertrude Stein seems to have been posing the questions that the most innovative directors working in the American theatre—Judith Malina, Lawrence Kornfeld, Robert Wilson, Frank Galati, Elizabeth LeCompte, Anne Bogart, and Heiner Goebbels, among others— have sought to answer. The next chapters showcase the queries that lead to the formation of the landscape of American alternative theatre and many provocative re-stagings of the character and dramatist, Gertrude Stein.

2. Behind the Mask of Primitivism: Untangling the Images of Gertrude Stein and African Americans in *Four Saints in Three Acts* and Frank Galati's *Each One As She May* ⤝

W hen I try to picture Gertrude Stein's face, the first image that comes to mind—despite the multitude of images of her made during and after her lifetime—is Pablo Picasso's "Portrait of Gertrude Stein." Ironically it was Stein's face that eluded Picasso. After months of sittings, during which Stein was mentally composing "Melanctha," Picasso was unable to capture the qualities animating his sitter's unique persona. Eventually he became so frustrated that he simply wiped the face off his canvas. When he saw the visages of fifth- and sixth-century Iberian stone carvings, he knew that he had found the solution to his problem. Above a softly draping brown corduroy robe, lace scarf, and coral brooch and beneath the brown hair primly coiled into a high bun, Picasso painted a "primitive" mask.[1]

In *The Autobiography of Alice B. Toklas*, Stein claims that she did not think the image bore a strong resemblance to her. Picasso reportedly quipped, "It will."[2] Nearly a century later, the primitive mask has overtaken photographs and the later portraits as the repository of Stein's image (see photo 2.1). This is due in part to the frequent reproduction of the Picasso portrait, but the dominance of the image may also be related to its congruence with Stein's writing style. Composed of simple, even childlike words and sounds, driven by rhythm rather than logic, freed from the stultifying constraints of generic convention, and gleefully indulging in sensual and sometimes

Photo 2.1   Gertrude Stein with Picasso's portrait (photograph by Man Ray, 1922; Yale Collection of American Literature, Beinecke Rare Book and Manuscript Library)

erotic play, Stein's texts might reasonably be regarded as a kind of literary primitivism.

It is, however, extremely unusual for literary critics to affix this term to Stein's dramatic writing. Though primitivism is regarded as a tremendously important impulse in the history of modern art, it is a highly problematic and nearly unsavory term. First, primitivism suggests a comparison between the supposedly advanced and sophisticated culture from which the artist comes, and the theoretically naive and less civilized world from which the object of the artist's inspiration has been appropriated. When the artist pillages the iconography of another culture, he is subject not only to charges of cultural imperialism, but also to the claim that he lacks originality.[3]

The issues surrounding primitivism get even stickier when the race of artist and subject are taken into consideration. When Picasso used Iberian iconography to represent Stein, or when Stein used her playful, childlike language to construct her abstract plays, these choices were not read as indicators of the lack of artistic skill or intellectual acuity possessed by the artist, the subject, or white people in general. As Richard Dyer argues in *White*: "There is no more powerful position than that of being 'just' human. The claim to power is the claim to speak for the commonality of

humanity. Raced people can't do that—they can only speak for their race."[4]
While Dyer's statement is perhaps becoming less true of some aspects of
contemporary culture—African American athletes transform shoes into hot
commodities, an African American talk show host's book club dictated what
topped the *New York Times'* Best Sellers List for years, and African American
musicians articulate teenage suburban angst—when "raced" artists used
primitivist techniques or when the tale was about a "raced" subject in Stein's
day, these choices were rarely perceived as insignificant.

During the Harlem Renaissance, for example, black artists were frequently encouraged by white patrons to use primitivist modes, while several
white artists used the language of primitivism to depict black characters.
These representations contributed to a body of stereotypes that had a wide
circulation. Notions that African Americans were exotic, naturally gifted
musically and rhythmically, childlike, unspoiled by education, innately
mystical or religious and thus spiritually elevated, and by contrast physically
dominated or sexual, were all by-products of primitivist depictions.

As Paul Gilroy eloquently puts it, during the Harlem Renaissance,
"Negrophilia and Negrophobia were mutually entangled in some surprising
patterns."[5] The stereotypes generated by and through primitivism were
simultaneously complimentary, in the sense that they praised qualities that
whites believed that modern society had corrupted out of them and that
they desired to reattain, and derogatory, in the sense that they are a clear
form of othering and essentialism.

The first staging of Stein's *Four Saints in Three Acts*, produced in 1934,
follows close on the heels of the Harlem Renaissance, and as such the ideas
of that period continued to be influential for the creators and audience of
the first production of Stein's opera. I demonstrate that producers of the
performance text held attitudes toward African Americans typical of those
generated by primitivism, that these attitudes led to the decision to employ
an entirely African American cast in the opera, and that the ambivalent attitudes the white audience had to the cast colored their perception of the
other elements of the performance text, creating from a disparate array of
visual and aural signs, a synergistic whole dependent on the individual audience member's perceptions of African Americans. In short, the attitudes and
ideas of primitivism filled the spaces in Stein's libretto in 1934.

In 1952, Virgil Thomson attempted to reproduce the 1934 *Four Saints
in Three Acts* exactly. He found it an impossible task because the entwined
patterns of negrophilia and negrophobia that had unified the 1934 production had changed. Most importantly, the burgeoning civil rights movement
had problematized the primitivist notions that were culturally prevalent in
1934. It was no longer possible to read a production of *Four Saints in Three*

Acts performed by African Americans through a single cultural lens that relied on the spectators' perception of the performer as a kind of noble savage. Primitivism no longer satisfactorily filled the spaces in Stein's libretto by 1952. The conflicting, unstable readings of the performance text produced in the critics' appraisal of the production reflect the sharpening struggle to define not only the place of African Americans in the landscape of American society, but who got to define and depict this place.

The 1990s also provide another important vantage point from which to view the relationships entangling primitivism, constructions of African Americans and the texts of Gertrude Stein. In 1995, Frank Galati staged his adaptation of Stein's short story with all African American characters, "Melanctha," at the Goodman Theatre in Chicago. In this production Galati tried to confront some of the same stereotypes that had infiltrated the 1934 and 1952 *Four Saints in Three Acts* making it possible to explore their influence on racial issues in the 1990s. Galati interrogated the codes of primitivism, the old ideas used to fill the spaces in Stein's texts, demonstrating that when these ideas are reinscribed, they have the potential to express in an ambiguous, ambivalent, and critical fashion the transracial space inhabited by and localized in Stein's texts.

In investigating the ways that primitivist notions have figured prominently in productions of Stein's work, I do not suggest that the method in which the producers of the 1934 staging of *Four Saints in Three Acts* both con-structed and capitalized on existing constructions of African Americans pre-determined the constructions of African Americans in later works and productions by Stein. Instead I highlight the significant ways that images constructing racial identity, changed radically, or descended differently due to the evolving cultural environments in which they were created and the dramatic space Stein provided for such a changed landscape.

FOUR SAINTS IN THREE ACTS IN 1934

The story of the success of the first *Four Saints in Three Acts* begins with Virgil Thomson's decision to cast African Americans in his opera. Recounting the history of the show and the casting decision seems straight-forward enough until one discovers that there are actually two distinct sto-ries about how Thomson seized upon the idea. The first story, published in the foreword to the 1934 edition of the libretto of *Four Saints in Three Acts* and in the program for the 1934 productions, comes from Carl Van Vechten, a friend of both Stein's and Thomson's, and a popularizer of the primitivist Negro Vogue of the Harlem Renaissance through his novel

Nigger Heaven. Van Vechten writes:

> [An] important detail about the performance was decided in my presence. Virgil had accompanied me to the performance at the Lyric Theatre in New York of *Run Little Chillun*, Hall Johnson's choral play enacted by Negroes. It was, I think, during the intermission that Virgil turned to me and said, "I am going to have *Four Saints* sung by Negroes. They alone possess the dignity and the poise, the lack of self-consciousness that proper interpretation of the opera demands. They have the rich, resonant voices essential to the singing of my music and the clear enunciation required to deliver Gertrude's text."[6]

The other story comes from Thomson himself. This one also involves his appreciation of the vocal talents of a particular African American performer, and especially the ability of this singer to enunciate clearly. But instead of taking place in the Broadway theatre, Thomson's story takes place in the Hot-Cha Bar and Grill in Harlem, the club where Billie Holiday was discovered. Thomson claims the source of his inspiration was tenor Jimmie Daniels's performance of "I've Got the World on a String." Thomson's memory of the event went as follows: "I had a brain wave. It suddenly hit me that he was singing so clearly and I could understand everything he said. He wasn't just vocalizing and adding a few consonants here and there, he was singing the *words*."[7]

The double site of Thomson's "brain wave" tallies with the double vision with which the critical audience in 1934 viewed the opera's African American performers. If the idea formed while Thomson watched *Run Little Chillun*, a musical that constructed its African American performers as naively spiritual, natural, and simplistic, as Barbara Webb has suggested,[8] it is not surprising that these same stereotypes might have been brought to bear in production and used by audiences as they tried to interpret the actors' place in the opera. If, however, Thomson's casting idea developed in Harlem against the backdrop of the New Negro Chic of the Harlem Renaissance,[9] this set of characterizations—that fashioned African Americans as sophisticated, sensual, and exotic—might have dominated the production. Regardless of where the decision was actually made, the stereotypes native to both sites meet in the notion of primitivism. With the culturally prevalent tools of primitivism, it was possible for 1934 audiences to construct the African American performers as both simple and sophisticated, spiritual and sensual, natural, and exotic. The richly varied critical response to the production reveals that at least these specialized audience members sometimes borrowed elements of their interpretive grids from both extremes of primitivist depiction. I am interested in investigating the ways that the other elements of the performance text facilitated the simultaneous existence of these ambivalent and highly personal reactions.

In order to analyze these specific elements of the performance text, the reactions of the artists who crafted these elements to African Americans in general, and the cast in particular, need to be explored, as these attitudes surely affected the artists' choices in production. My point here is not to deride the artists for these expressions of opinion, but to comb through the tangle of contradictory perceptions that white, upper-middle to upper-class Americans had about African Americans at the time of the production.

Thomson's statements regarding African Americans are the best place to begin this investigation since the casting decision was his. Looking back on this choice in his 1966 autobiography, Thomson wrote:

> The Negroes proved rewarding in every way. Not only could they enunciate and sing; they seemed to understand because they sang. They resisted not at all Stein's obscure language, adopted it for theirs, conversed in quotations from it. They moved, sang, and spoke with alacrity, took on roles without self-consciousness, as if they were the saints they said they were. I often marvelled at the miracle whereby slavery (and some crossbreeding) had turned them into Christians of an earlier stamp than ours, not analytical or self-pitying or romantic in the nineteenth-century sense, but robust, outgoing, and even in disaster, sustained by inner joy.[10]

Thomson's memory of his success is sharp. Equally clear is his admiration for his cast, though his affection seems to be entangled with reductive, essentializing notions. On the one hand, Thomson praises the performers for their technical execution of the work, noting their ability to sing, speak, and move within Stein's difficult text. But on the other hand he seems to see their success in execution (beyond his abominable remark about crossbreeding) as being related to their lack of cognition either about themselves or the text—they are described as being naturally suited to *Four Saints in Three Acts* due to various innate spiritual qualities, rather than accomplishing a complicated analytical feat. Not surprisingly the actors' memories about their relationship to the text were different than Thomson's. No doubt this was in part due to the fact that the singers and dancers provided Thomson with what he expected and wanted to see—at least one level of their performance was opaque to him. Chorus member Kitty Mason said, "You go through this thing day after day, and day after day you get something out of it—it wasn't altogether nonsensical."[11] Furthermore, any lack of understanding the performers may have had about the proceedings was not a result of their lack of analytical skills as Thomson suggested, but was more likely due to the fact that Thomson, Ashton, and Houseman would speak to each other in French whenever there was something they did not want the cast to hear.[12]

Frederick Ashton, the production's choreographer, also made a comment indicative of his attitude toward the cast. Ashton said, "None of them was trained, but naturally like all Negro people they knew how to move."[13] Here Ashton perpetuates the stereotype, derived from primitivism's emphasis on the power of native rhythms, that African Americans are naturally gifted dancers. The comment may also reflect the primitivist perception that African Americans have a strong physical or sensual connection to the world instead of a cognitive one.

Perhaps more telling than this brief comment is a photograph of Ashton and his male dancers taken by George Platt Lynes. In the photograph Ashton, dressed in a dark suit and striped tie, kneels. Ashton, in profile, looks down rather benevolently on one of the three nude male dancers who reclines around him. One of his hands rests on the shoulder of the man he looks at, while the object of his gaze looks down. Ashton's other hand rests on the neck of another dancer who also does not meet his gaze. The third dancer, propped up on one elbow while the other arm drapes across the leg of another dancer, looks up at Ashton. On the wall behind the scene the oversized and somewhat indistinct shadows of three of the men are visible.

The exact occasion for this photograph is not known. It is, however, known that Ashton had a sexual relationship with at least one, and possibly two, of the dancers. The photograph gives the simultaneous impressions of a sultan surveying the jewels of his harem, thanks to the languid intertwined poses of the nude dancers, and a proprietary father gathering his children, thanks to Ashton's elevated position above his flock, the protective placement of his hands on the dancers' bodies, and his facial expression. The staged image suggests that the man at its center saw these African Americans as sexual objects available for his sensual gratification and as children or subjects for whom he might want to care and provide—more notions congruent with the tenets of primitivism.

There is little evidence about costumer and set designer Florine Stettheimer's attitudes toward African Americans in general or the cast in particular. The only potentially suggestive information comes from her reactions to the variation in skin tones among the cast. In his memoirs, the production's eventual official director, John Houseman, reports that Stettheimer was dismayed to discover that all African Americans did not have the same color skin. Stettheimer considered painting the faces of the cast white or silver so that she could achieve the uniformity she desired. When Thomson rejected this idea, she was pacified with the alternative of requiring all the performers to use the same medium-toned base. She also achieved what she deemed a small victory in getting the actors to wear white gloves so that their variously colored hands would not distract further attention from the color of her costumes.[14] In short, Stettheimer sought to construct a stage picture that reflected her uniform image of African Americans. Though her attitudes are not direct derivatives of primitivism, her desire to make the physical differences among the performers invisible does coincide with primitivism's general effect of erasing the complexities of the different groups of people who are regarded as "primitive" by the mainstream culture.

Stein created her portion of the performance text long before Thomson decided to employ an African American cast. As such, her opinions regarding African Americans are not likely to have figured in the libretto, but they are still worthy of consideration because Stein's perceptions of African Americans and their relationship to modernism's interest in primitivism seem to be more complicated in some ways than the artists involved in the production of the opera, and more complex than her critics have sometimes acknowledged.

When Thomson first approached Stein with the idea of the African American cast, he did so by letter. In that same letter he also explained that Florine Stettheimer was contemplating clothing the actors in transparent robes. Stein, through her agent, William Bradley, replied in a letter:

> I suppose they have good reasons for using negro singers instead of white, there are certain obvious ones, but I do not care for the idea of showing the negro bodies, it is too much what the English in what they call "modernistic" novels call futuristic and does not accord with the words and music to my mind.[15]

Stein does not make clear what the "certain obvious" reasons for using African American singers might be, although Thomson's recent biographer, Anthony Tomassini, speculates that the remark might be a snide reference to Thomson's sexual forays in Harlem.[16] Stein is not much more specific in the letter about why using African American singers would make the opera futuristic. If by "modernistic," Stein means modernist, her comment seems to suggest that she sees the words and music of her opera as resisting the tenets and topics of modernism. Perhaps Stein felt that modernism's interest in primitivism, African American subjects, and forms, like jazz, to which African Americans made tremendous contributions, were antithetical to those held by her Spanish saints, despite her own use of modernist writing techniques. It is possible that Stein liked the tensions created by the differences between her subject matter and her style and felt that casting actors already contaminated by modernist assumptions would force her work into a kind of alignment she sought to avoid.

Stein is concerned with some similar issues in *The Autobiography of Alice B. Toklas*. In one passage, she, through the narrative voice of Alice, talks about the influence of African sculpture on Picasso's Cubism. Alice says of Stein,

> She was not at any time interested in african sculpture. She always said that she liked it well enough but that it has nothing to do with europeans, that it lacks naivete, that it is very ancient, very narrow, very sophisticated but lacks the elegance of the egyptian sculpture from which it was derived. She says that as an american she likes things to be more savage.[17]

In this commentary, Stein seems to reject notions of primitivism almost entirely. Instead of seeing "african" forms as naive and savage, she suggests the very opposite. Though she rejects the notions of primitivism, she is clearly aware of them and their associations with African Americans.

A much more frequently cited passage from the *Autobiography* is one in which Alice discusses the occasions on which Carl Van Vechten brought Paul Robeson to the Toklas/Stein home:

> Gertrude Stein concluded that negroes were not suffering from persecution, they were suffering from nothingness. She always contends that the african is not primitive, he has a very ancient but a very narrow culture and there it remains. Consequently nothing does or can happen.[18]

This passage is the one usually used to document Stein's racism, and clearly there are reductive elements in it, but instead of vilifying Stein for these comments instantly and finally, it is worth exploring the things she says closely.

The idea that African Americans were not suffering from a variety of forms of persecution in the early twentieth century is either insensitive or naive. Stein's next idea, that African Americans were suffering from nothingness, is more intriguing. In the following sentence, Stein identifies an ancient, albeit in her opinion, narrow culture that belong to "negroes." The nothingness that has theoretically caused the suffering, cannot, it seems, result from a lack of cultural identity. Instead the problem seems to be in the static condition of the culture—that there is no change. Despite Stein's earlier repudiation of primitivism and its reductive vision of African Americans, this idea is one of the notions under-girding the movement. When a Western artist mines the iconography of an African culture for import into his own work, he generally does so without regard to the precise context from which it came. What seem to matter are only its "exotic" and "tribal" qualities. This mind-set reveals a lack of interest in the evolution of the culture from which the object or image has been taken.

Colin Rhodes notes this orientation in an institution so august as the British Museum:

> Until very recently rarely have attempts been made to establish or to provide dates of production—or even acquisition—of primitive art. Implicit here is a belief that objects made relatively recently, such as the Brighton Ibo mask (collected between 1905 and 1910, but probably dating from the late nineteenth century) [and now housed in the British Museum] are probably little different to lost objects of greater antiquity. Viewed as the material culture of long-standing traditions, primitive art is thus cast as static and isolated from history.[19]

Stein's primitivist perception of African Americans as unchanging, inactive, and therefore mired in nothingness, resonates with what she claimed that she had attempted to do in writing an opera about saints. In *Everybody's Autobiography*, Stein writes:

> A saint a real saint never does anything, a martyr does something but a really good saint does nothing, and so I wanted to have Four Saints [*sic*] who did nothing and I wrote the Four Saints in Three Acts [*sic*] and they did nothing and that was everything.[20]

If Stein had had a truly coherent theory of race at this time in her life, she might have thought that African Americans would have been the ideal performers for her opera, since in her mind saints and African Americans both did nothing, unless she did hope to achieve a kind of dissonance between her subject matter and the presentation of it. In any case, Stein seemed to possess a complicated morass of perceptions about African Americans. Through her comments we see her imagining African Americans as sexual, futuristic/artistically innovative, sophisticated while artistically inelegant and narrow, and suffering from some not clearly defined nothingness.

Stein also made many direct comments about African Americans in *Everybody's Autobiography*, published in 1937. In this work, Stein speaks in her own voice and continues her story where the *Autobiography of Alice B. Toklas* left off, discussing the effect of the *Autobiography* on her career and self-image as well as her experiences during her 1934 lecture tour of America. On the tour Stein seemed to have had more encounters with African Americans than she had in the rest of her life, except during her career as a medical student at Johns Hopkins when she delivered African American babies in Baltimore. During the tour Stein saw a performance of *Porgy and Bess* in Fort Worth. Stein made no substantial comment on her opinion of the African American actors' performance of her opera in

Everybody's Autobiography (she mentions liking St. Therese and signing the actors' programs in Chicago) but she did comment on her perception of the actors in *Porgy*:

> Any Negro actors act anything so naturally that it is natural that it should be done very well and why not since they might be any one as they are never any other one that is with Negroes such a natural thing, with many of them with most of them, publicity does not hurt them because they can be what anything makes them and it does not make anything else of them because they are the thing they are then. So it is not acting it is being for them, and they have no time sense to be a trouble to them.[21]

In this passage, Stein praises the skill of the African American performers, yet seems to attribute it to a neutrality—"they might be any one as they are never any other one" and "they can be what anything makes them"—or again, a kind of nothingness. Stein seems to see African American performers as blank slates onto which any image can be projected. Quite miraculously, at least in Stein's perception, the performer is then actually transformed into this image, as he or she is not "acting" but "being."

The images that were projected onto the surface of the cast during the course of performance were constructed by contemporary culture, and simultaneously reinforced by the images and sounds that surrounded them on stage. Many of the elements of the performance text, both visual and aural, were composite constructions. Assembled from a variety of sources or simply involving the juxtaposition of unusual sights or sounds, the libretto, score, choreography, scenario, set, and costumes all seemed to invite references to a variety of cultural stereotypes about African Americans simultaneously.

Stein's open libretto was one of the elements of the performance text most responsible for allowing a variety of cultural stereotypes to circulate. When John Houseman first agreed to "direct" the production—Thomson hired him to coordinate the elements of the production about which Thomson had already made all the artistic decisions—he began by reading Stein's libretto, ostensibly about the lives of Spanish Saints Therese and Ignatius and their friends. Houseman remembers his experience with the libretto in his memoir *Run-Through*: "The first thing I must do, I decided, was to find out what the opera was about. I had heard it three times by now and read it zealously; the text was becoming familiar but not intelligible."[22] Houseman recalled turning to Thomson for help making sense of the libretto. Thomson told him that the opera was a metaphor for artistic life in Paris in the 1920s and that St. Therese represented Gertrude Stein, while St. Ignatius represented James Joyce or André Gide. Both writers/saints had their disciples and were creating remarkable artistic projects, thus there was competition between the two figures. Thomson's reading of *Four Saints in Three Acts* expresses the same view as many literary interpretations of the text that focus on the self-reflexivity of the libretto: those of Bonnie Marranca, Marc Robinson, Jane Bowers, and others. These analyses make a great deal of sense when the work is encountered on the page. Particularly astute spectators might have formed such an interpretation. But since there were no visual or aural cues to reinforce this reading, and since such an informed reader as John Houseman did not come to this conclusion even after hearing the text three times and reading a printed version, it seems likely this is not the interpretation most spectators would have reached.

What most spectators probably encountered, thus influencing their analysis, was a dizzying torrent of aural stimuli. Act four, of an opera that proclaims in its title only to have three acts, begins as follows:

> How many acts are there in it. Acts are there in it.
> Supposing a wheel had been added to three wheels how many acts how many how many acts are there in it.
> Any Saint at all.
> How many acts are there in it.
> Wedded and weeded.
> Please be coming to see me.
> When this you see you are all to me.
> Me which is you you who are true true to be you.
> How many how many saints are there in it.
> One two three all out but me.
> One two three four all out but four.
> One two all about but you.
> How many saints are there in it.
> How many saints are there in it.
> How many acts are there in it.
> One two three four and there is no door. Or more. Or nor.
> Or door. Or floor or door. One two three all out but me.
> How many saints are there in it.[23]

If one becomes attuned to this flood of words, instead of frustrated and dismissive, one first notices the repetition of simple words, most of which are numbers. There seems to be little logical sense in the words, beyond Stein's playing with the listener's desire to find her place within the opera, to know how many acts or how many saints there are in it, since she had probably assumed there would be four saints in three acts. Stein forces the listener to recognize the foolishness of this logical, conventional desire in the face of her sensual, aural playing. The more often these questions are asked, or the more often the desire for order is expressed, the less sensible these questions and desires seem to become. Even these simple words stop sounding the way they usually do and start to transform. Logic takes flight, leaving behind only the pleasures of sound and rhythm.

In *Everybody's Autobiography*, Stein writes about counting:

> Everybody is counting, counting is everybody's occupation. And that is because everybody is certain that there is the difference that is what makes men men and as everybody wants to be sure that men are men just now wants to have it as an affirmation everybody is counting. I always liked counting but I liked counting one two three four five six seven . . . counting more than ten is not interesting at least not to me. . . . Counting is the religion of this generation it is its hope and its salvation.[24]

As she makes her audience listen to her play with counting, she suggests, I think, that the obsession with counting is unholy, and that seeking salvation through counting is foolhardy. In her saintly play, Stein seems to hope that her audience can practice a new, less restrictive, and more abstract religion—one founded on sensual freedom and pleasure.

If one hears in Stein's libretto what I hear—an invitation to nondiscursive and irrational sensual play—one has identified components of primitivism that generated stereotypes about African Americans in the 1930s. And since the words do not make logical sense, it is likely that stereotypes about the people who sung the words might be imported into the production to add a kind of sense. One could have seen in the combination of the words and the people who sang them the height of suave, exotic sophistication, simple sensuality and joyful abandon, or both simultaneously.

Representative of the large body of commentary that saw the performers as simple is the following statement from the *Vogue* review: "Whites could never in the world have sung that opera. The very essence of the work demands primal ignorance and native awkwardness of which only the Negro people are capable."[25] Countering this view among critics in major publications was the lone voice of the *New York Times* music critic, Olin Downes, who wrote, "Where a complete injustice was done the intelligence of the singers was in the assumption that the naivete and presumptively unsophisticated minds would enable them to do more with the Stein text and be less self-conscious about it than if white singers were employed."[26]

It is well worth noting that the *Vogue* reviewer's attitude is far more derogatory toward the performers than the attitudes of the artists involved in creating the performance text, while Downes's position is more astute. In order to understand the genesis of the reactions, we must investigate what developed from the artists' perceptions—their choices for the performance text—that made both of these critical reactions possible. Thomson's biographer, Anthony Tommasini vividly describes the musical composition of *Four Saints in Three Acts*:

> The varied musical materials and styles alternate constantly. Emphatic minor-key music sung by the chorus in full-throated block harmonies makes Stein's number games ("Four saints are never three / three saints are never four") sound like delivered religious truths. A vocal quartet ("In some on some evening would it be asked") could be a slip of an English madrigal. There are foursquare marches; sequential passages with plaintive melodies; unison chants for the chorus that would echo Renaissance sacred music, were it not for the wondrously bizarre words ("There is no part parti-color in a house"). Passages of neo-Baroque recitative; bits of made-up hymns, chanteys, parlor dances, fanfares—Thomson's music is a beguiling jumble of materials. Yet the continuity and integrity of the musical line is never in doubt, and the tone, though humorous, is serene and sincere.[27]

Though Tomassini's emphasis is on the religious spirit that transforms even the most mundane of Thomson's inspirations, my interest is in the assembly of diverse musical materials. As Tomassini describes Thomson's composition, it is a kind of repetition of several clearly recognizable musical forms. Not all listeners would be likely to understand all of the allusions Thomson made. Instead, the listener could assemble his or her own text, focusing on the familiar sounds and the images they invoked. The *Newsweek* reviewer, for example, heard "Mozart, Gregorian chants, Spanish tangos, Negro spirituals, Sir Arthur Sullivan, and Jazz."[28] The *New Republic* reviewer heard, "C-major banalities, Anglican chants, 'America,' and imitations of the bim bam of chimes."[29] The *Saturday Review* critic heard intimations of "the minstrel show and *Porgy*, Italian opera, and anything else that could be made to cohere long enough for music and setting to hold together."[30] Though the reviewers recognized different influences in the score, they all heard both high art and popular sounds. Thus Thomson's score provided the space for the African American performers who produced these sounds to be imported into both these traditions. If viewers wished to construct the performers as the apotheosis of sophistication, they could do so in relation to certain portions of the music; if they wanted to imagine the performers as naive and simple they could concentrate on the parts of the score that evoked those images instead.

Frederick Ashton's choreography also combined the high art with the popular. Though Ashton's forte was ballet, he found that he could not choreograph completely balletic movements for the opera. He discovered that he "had to create something becoming and appropriate out of what they (the dancers) could do naturally."[31] There were few ballet schools in America in the 1930s in general, and opportunities for African Americans to receive classical dance training were particularly scarce. Ashton did find three women who had some very elementary training, but he could not find male partners for them. Ashton moved his search to the Savoy Ballroom on Lenox Avenue, where he found his three male dancers. Ashton decided he would blend the movement style of his own training and snippets of his most recent ballet *Les Rendezvous* with the kind of popular dance practiced in night clubs like the Savoy that he believed his dancers could "do naturally."

Two vivid examples of Ashton's technique came in the dances of the second act. In one, called "the angel ballet," the female dancers represented angels learning how to fly with the assistance of their male partners. Ashton described the dance composed of a variety of styles of lifts to a *Hartford Courant* reporter as being a combination of "snake hips and gothic."[32] While angelic flight might have represented the gothic, the dance steps used to create this illusion were largely modern and secular. The snake hips mentioned by Ashton was a popular dance created by Earl "Snake Hips" Tucker in the 1920s. In addition to the snake hips, the angel ballet also referenced the Charleston and the Lindy Hop.

The second dance that reveals Ashton's choreographic style was the Spanish tango. In this dance, the three couples danced the popular tango, but did so with a kind of exaggerated formality: "emphasizing the negative space between the partners, suspending dips and pauses so that the extended limbs and arched backs could be contemplated like the extensions and gesture of ballet, and utilizing a flat, presentational style oriented toward the proscenium that was reminiscent of Nijinsky's choreography in *L'Apres-midi d'un Faune*."[33] Once again, the dance was a hybrid of popular and high art forms (see photo 2.2).

There is little evidence about how critics read Ashton's choreography. Many reviews did not mention Ashton's contribution at all. Some, like the *New Yorker* review, mentioned his "unorthodox choreography" only in passing. The *New York Times* dance critic, John Martin, however, did devote the bulk of one of his columns to Ashton's work. Martin wrote that though the choreography suffered because of the dancers' lack of training, the "two set dances [the angel ballet and the tango] are nonetheless delightful in concept, and his mise-en-scene throughout is varied and imaginative." Martin did not comment on the snake hips, the Charleston, and the Lindy Hop,

Photo 2.2   *Four Saints in Three Acts* in 1934 (Yale Collection of American Literature, Beinecke Rare Book and Manuscript Library)

but he did see references to Mae West in the gestures of the Commere, which he thought inappropriate to operatic movement.[34] If Martin's comments are at all indicative, like Stein's text and Thomson's score, the choreography, in the spaces between recognizable forms, seemed to provide the room for audience members to imagine their own images of the performers and their movements.

Florine Stettheimer's contributions to the performance texts may also have contributed to dual images of the performers: her set may have helped construct the actors as naive, simple, or childlike, while her costumes seemed to connote sensual sophistication. Nestled beneath a proscenium arch bedecked in lace, was an extravagant cyclorama made of swathes of gathered cellophane. Center stage stood, nested one beneath the other, two arches representing the door to the cathedral made out of large glass beads or globes. The arches served as a second proscenium to frame the various tableaux staged underneath it. On either side of the arches were a single cellophane palm tree and chained stone lions. At the far ends of both sides of the stage were risers for the chorus. Stage right sat an opera box from which the Commere and Compere watched most of the proceedings.

Maurice Grosser, the scenarist for the opera, describes his interpretation of the setting in the foreword to his scenario:

> The settings, composed out of lace, feathers, gold paper, glass beads, cellophane, tarlatan, and tulle, suggested, with no attempt at actual reproduction, the tinsel and glitter, the exuberance and informality of the naive altar decorations characteristic of Latin countries.

Though Grosser references Latino rather than African American culture in this passage, his words still indicate that he believed the set had a naive quality, despite its clear meta-theatrical references.

It appears that Grosser was not alone in regarding Stettheimer's artistic style as naive. In *The Life and Art of Florine Stettheimer*, Barbara Bloemink attempts to correct misperceptions of Stettheimer's style. She writes, "Stettheimer's work has been largely forgotten, except as an example of American naïf or eccentric style. This categorization of the work—as artless and unsophisticated—could not be further from the truth."[35] Though Bloemink is advocating a reconsideration of Stettheimer's work as complex and allusive, her statement indicates that the general critical perception of the work until the mid-1990s was otherwise.

While Stettheimer's set may have read as simple and naive (thus constructing the performers in a similar light as they inhabited it), her costumes seem to have inspired a different reaction. The Compere and Commere, the master and mistress of ceremonies seated in the opera box and occasionally venturing onto the stage to get a better look at the action or even to engage in a dance, were dressed in contemporary formal wear: the Compere in black tie and tails and the Commere in a series of three full-length, elegant evening gowns. The dancers also changed costumes. In Act I, the dancers wore very short lace skirts and midriff halters that wrapped around one shoulder. In Act II the women added transparent tunics and wings to their costumes, while their male partners wore billowy, but very short, shorts, and sported bare chests. In Act III the women wore tight-bodiced, but full-skirted dresses and flowers in their hair while the men wore snug sailor pants and nothing on their chests but a sash. The numerous saints all wore relatively similar costumes. As the reporter from *Women's Wear Daily* described them, these costumes consisted of "simple, unshaped robes, with wide sleeves and cowl hoods, varied by lace bordered tunics like ecclesiastical surplices."[36]

Though the saints' costumes might seem like the least chic and elegant of the lot, these were the ones that garnered the deepest reaction. Evidence of this reaction comes not from the critics, but from a Bergdorf Goodman Department Store advertisement. The advertisement, which ran in *Vogue*,

Vanity Fair, House and Garden, and the *New York Times,* sought to promote the sale of a tea gown inspired by Stettheimer's costumes. Underneath the sketch of a tall, elegant-looking female figure with a patrician profile and one hand at her waist and the other behind her head in a pin-up pose wearing a spare, wide-sleeved, belted, full-length column ran the following copy:

> "Saint" in five colors.
>
> We call this seductive tea gown saints-robe because it looks like one of the thrilling costumes in the much-talked-of Four-Saints opera. The dramatic sleeves make the figure look sylph-like by contrast. The girdle a Franciscan twist of gold. In celestial blue, white, chartreuse, titian and black, $45.
>
> Negligees—Fourth Floor

The advertisement suggests that women who could afford a $45 nightgown during the midst of the Depression might want to imagine themselves as part of the cast of *Four Saints in Three Acts.* This intimates that the costumes, and I think by extension the people who wore them, were the absolute height of chic sensuality. In their boudoirs, rich, sophisticated women wanted to cast themselves as one of the opera's saints.

Maurice Grosser's scenario also contained elements that would have allowed audience members to reference various portions of the cultural constructions of African Americans. After both the libretto and the score were written, it was Grosser's task to set the work of Stein and Thomson in an identifiable context. He chose to imagine the opera as "a pageant, or Sunday school entertainment, on the steps of the cathedral." This choice certainly would have allowed audience members to improvise on the construction of African Americans as possessing a particularly childlike spirituality.

In the first act of Grosser's Sunday school pageant, "St. Therese enacts for the instruction of the saints and visitors scenes from her own saintly life. There begins the presentation of seven pictures, or tableaux, posed in the cathedral portal, chiefly by St. Therese II." Throughout the entire show, Grosser constructed very static images or tableaux. Rejecting narrative strategies, he instead placed the emphasis on spectacle. Even the most narrative section, the scenes from St. Therese's life in Act I were disconnected images: St. Therese painting Easter eggs, having her picture taken, and rocking an invisible child. The other acts contained "a dance of angels," the observation of a heavenly mansion through a telescope, a variety of "games," a funeral cortege, to name just a few of the images provided for viewers. The assembly of the images did not add up to a particular or coherent story. Instead, these static, nonnarrative images may have suggested that African American saints were unchanging and static and untroubled by personality or individual psychology—notions derived from the homogenizing force of primitivism.

This was not, however, the only way to read the static images of the scenario. *The New York Sun* art critic described the first minutes of the opera as follows:

> When the bright red curtain went up, or rather was pulled apart, there was a gasp of astonishment and delight. This audience all knew something about pictures and could see at once that the Saint kneeling in front and clad in voluminous purple silk was quite as ecstatic as anything El Greco had ever devised in that line, and that the costumes of the two Saint Teresas [*sic*] as well as the effect produced by the cellophane background and the remarkable lighting were all addressed to the painter's eye.[37]

This reviewer sees the image as having been constructed for the enjoyment of a highly knowledgeable and sophisticated spectator. He sees nothing simple or naive at all in the image, and one might assume that an African American performer at the center of such a refined image would not be considered inherently simple or naive, but rather an icon of sophistication.

One aspect of the scenario, or perhaps more specifically the blocking, seems to me likely to have encouraged contradictory readings of the African American women in the cast simultaneously. In at least three of the tableaux, either Saint Therese 1 or Saint Therese 2, clad in prim, long-sleeved and long full-skirted habits and wide-brimmed hats over scarves, are flanked in their poses by the scantily dressed female dancers, reminiscent of the costume worn by Josephine Baker in *La Folie du Jour* or *La Danse Sauvage*. In one photograph, Saint Therese sits within the arch of the cathedral posed with a stuffed dove that is supposed, according to the scenario, to represent the Holy Ghost. Saint Settlement, standing behind an old-fashioned tripod camera, prepares to take the picture as the chorus of saints, seated in pyramid formation on one of the sets of risers (see photo 2.3). Saint Therese, is not however, the only one posed as though prepared to have her picture taken. Two of the dancers, wearing very short lace skirts and halter tops that sling across one shoulder while baring the midriff, are also frozen in an elegant standing embrace as though they will be photographed simultaneously. Similar stage pictures occur both when Saint Therese is supposed to be having a conversation with herself and when one of the Saint Thereses is painting a giant Easter egg under the cathedral arch: Saint Therese is posed in the midst of some saintly pursuit while the dancers are frozen, bare legs extended from the hips, arms wrapped around their own bodies or the bodies of one of the other dancers, and heads cocked dreamily to the

Photo 2.3 *Four Saints in Three Acts* in 1934 (Yale Collection of American Literature, Beinecke Rare Book and Manuscript Library)

side. In these moments, the Saint Thereses seem to be linked to the dancers. In the process, so too are saintliness and sexuality.

In his praise of the 1934 production, Joseph Wood Krutch wrote, " '*Four Saints in Three Acts*' is a success because all its elements—the dialogue, the music, the pantomime, and the sparkling cellophane decor—go so well together while remaining totally irrelevant to life, logic, or common sense."[38] I believe my analysis has proven the first half of Krutch's statement largely accurate, while refining the second half. The various aspects of the performance text did go together well, but in a variety of ways, to reinforce a myriad of cultural stereotypes of African Americans. The racial perceptions invoked by the libretto, score, choreography, scenario, set, and costumes that fostered a sense of cohesion were often bereft of logic or common sense, but did paint a vivid portrait of an important segment of cultural life in 1934.

FOUR SAINTS IN THREE ACTS IN 1952

In 1934, Stark Young wrote, "It is horrible to think, if *Four Saints in Three Acts* turns out to be the success, or the vogue, more or less promised by the first night's reception from both the audience and the press in New York, what imitations of it will follow." Oddly enough it was only Virgil Thomson himself, eighteen years later, who failed to heed Young's warning not to attempt to replicate his earlier success.

In 1952 the American National Theatre and Academy, the sole nationally chartered theatre, decided with the private patronage of Ethel Linder Reiner, to stage *Four Saints in Three Acts* as part of its five-play season in New York City. Despite the production's auspicious beginning it failed to inspire the excitement aroused by the original production. There is nothing inherent in the process of mounting a revival that destines it for mediocrity. Revivals can be huge box-office attractions because of the familiarity of the material as well as critical triumphs, but most successful revivals do not seek to clone the first productions. Anthony Tomassini explains Thomson's self-imitative plan of attack as he prepared to mount *Four Saints in Three Acts*:

> Thomson was given complete artistic control. He decided, unwisely, it turned out, to try to reproduce as closely as possible the production from 1934. Since cellophane, even if it had been affordable, was prohibited by the fire department for use in a theater, it was decided to copy from sketches and pictures Stettheimer's cellophane sets by using woven plastic material that Thomson found "droopy, greasy, its blue-green color dismal." Stettheimer's costume designs were also copied by the designer Paul Morrison, but the colors were flatter, the textures less rich. Relying on the original promptbooks and Maurice Grosser's memory, the new choreographer, William Dollar, tried to replicate Ashton's movements with some success.[39]

Just as Thomson and his team of designers had difficulty in reproducing the set and costumes of the 1934 production, it would also prove impossible to replicate the effect that the all–African American cast produced in 1934. More significant than the changed fire codes that banned cellophane set pieces were the changes in cultural perceptions of race in the eighteen years between the productions.

The 1950s can, I think, be regarded as a liminal phase in perceptions of race. In 1952, as in 1934, there were surely multiple cultural messages generated by African American bodies on stage, but the messages most widely in circulation and the perceptions of the social import of those messages had changed. The Harlem Renaissance and the cultural intelligibility of primitivism that had accompanied it were no longer fresh in the popular white consciousness and thus not likely to serve as a kind of glue for the disparate elements of the production and a legend to the confusing map of Stein's libretto. Remnants of the notions that African Americans were simple, spiritual, and naturally gifted physically had survived, but now these stereotypes began to collide with ideas generated by the burgeoning civil rights movement.

The cultural tug-of-war over racial imagery appears vividly in the anticipation of and reaction to a television series modeled on the long-running *Amos 'n' Andy* radio show. After enjoying enormous success on the radio, the creators of the show, Freeman Gosden and Charles Correll, were eager to take advantage of the new opportunities offered by television. After conducting a two-year talent search, television's most exhaustive to date according to *Newsweek*, the partners eventually found African American actors, with voices "reminiscent" of their own but with "different faces" (Gosden and Correll were white) to play the roles they had originated. Meanwhile CBS bought out Gosden and Correll for $2,500,000 and Blatz beer spent $250,000 in promotion and advertising as the show's sponsor, clearly attesting to the anticipated success of the show.

Despite the success of their radio formula, Gosden and Correll felt that some changes had to be made to the show in order for it to succeed on television. *Newsweek* reports:

> In keeping with the show's attempts not to belittle the Negro, Andy's famous derby is no longer dented. Nor is Amos's taxi cap (worn by Alvin Childress) ragged and bent. Gosden says, "On TV we've eliminated jokes entirely. We do it now with action, not with words." There is little room for Amos, a human being of such dignity and goodness that he does not lend himself to the "amusing" incident.[40]

Though Gosden and Correll (and *Newsweek* as well) seemed to believe they had removed potentially offensive material from the show when they renovated some of the costumes and exchanged physical humor for verbal humor, one of their additions to the show was clearly demeaning. Since Amos, due to his "dignity and goodness," was so likely to find himself in "amusing" situations deemed improper for television, the producers decided to shift the focus to George Stevens, Kingfish of the Mystic Knights of the Sea. He is described as a man "beseiged by a nagging wife, and has yet to do an honest day's labor."[41]

Though Gosden, Correll, and CBS may not have realized that they were perpetuating harmful stereotypes about the laziness of African Americans, the NAACP certainly did. The NAACP attempted to sue the network to prevent the broadcast of the premiere. When that effort failed, *Newsweek* reports:

> *Amos 'n' Andy* raised the ire of the National Association for the Advancement of Colored People. The day after the show's premiere, the NAACP

convention in Atlanta, Ga., unanimously denounced both the *Amos 'n' Andy* and the Beulah radio and TV shows. Last week, the NAACP asked the makers of Blatz Beer, sponsors of *Amos 'n' Andy* on TV, to cancel the show.[42]

The fanfare and outrage surrounding the *Amos 'n' Andy* show reveal important evidence about attitudes toward the performance of race in the early 1950s. While the entertainment industry and its corporate sponsorship were clearly eager to profit from the popularity of *Amos 'n' Andy*, advocacy groups like the NAACP were fighting to challenge the circulation of harmful racial imagery. Images that had once seemed innocuous to many white Americans, were now marked with deeper social import.

The battle over the depiction of African Americans was also staged in reviewers' reactions to the 1952 *Four Saints in Three Acts*. Some reviewers, such as *New York Post*'s Richard Watts, praised the cast's simplicity:

> One of the major causes of the opera's rare charm is the presence of its fine Negro cast. As much as I like "Four Saints," I must grant that it might seem a little pretentious in its prankishness if the singers didn't bring to it, in addition to their splendid voices, such personal dignity, simplicity, and ease.[43]

The advertising copy for the opera that ran in *The New York Times* supported Watts's view, which was shared by *School and Society* reviewer William H. Beyer, who also lauded the cast's "shy innocence."[44] In addition to a lace border and palm tree evoking Stettheimer's well-known set design (that the words below promised would be reproduced by designer Paul Morrison) and some crudely drawn pigeons, undoubtedly seeking some grass (alas) on which to rest in order to capitalize on the most well-known line in the opera, the ad featured two fat cherubs perched above the words "Four Saints."

This attitude did not thoroughly imbue all critical reaction. Evidence that the softened version of primitivism, which emphasized simplicity and natural dignity in African Americans, did not succeed in unifying all elements of the performance text or in giving it a coherent message can be heard from the many reviewers who were singularly unimpressed with Stein's libretto, finding that it lacked any meaningful content. As Brooks Atkinson wrote in *The New York Times*,

> There is no use in pretending that Miss Stein's libretto, written in a form of sensuous gibberish, is equal to the music and the occasion. And the fact that *Four Saints in Three Acts* has no articulate theme leaves the whole work without a literary structure and a feeling of aimlessness. Although the music is full of grand harmonies that communicate a sense of religious experience and the

stage pictures are constantly changing, the emotional values of the work are repetitious and desultory. There is no life at the core; nothing is fulfilled in this panorama of talent, beauty, and skill. It is the apotheosis of sophistication—style and manner without content.[45]

This sentiment was reflected in slightly altered form in other reviews (in *The Daily Mirror*, *The New York Journal American*, *The New York Herald-Tribune*, *The New York Daily News*, *Newsweek*, and *Time*)[46] with an injunction not to attempt to take Stein seriously because there was no real meaning to be had.

The association between African Americans and native qualities unspoiled by the pernicious effects of civilization that had given one set of meanings to Stein's words in 1934 might have been problematized by the various legal issues of the day. Though the Supreme Court did not make the landmark ruling in *Brown v. Topeka Board of Education* until 1954, oral arguments were heard by the court in late 1952 and the issues that fueled this furor had begun to smolder in the lower courts far earlier. Further, *Brown* was not the first case challenging the inequality of *Plessy v. Fergusson's* "separate but equal" doctrine. Beginning in the late 1930s and extending into the early 1950s, a series of several cases, *Murray v. Maryland*, *Missouri ex rel. Gaines v. Canada*, *Sweatt v. Painter*, and *McLaurin v. Oklahoma State Regents for Higher Education* staked out the claim for African Americans' rights to higher education in these particular cases. (The *Brown* decision was considered a landmark because the court's ruling provided for educational rights not just in a particular or local situation, but across the board for all students attending public schools.) In addition to the cases dealing with educational equality, President Truman's order to desegregate the military in 1948 was a significant step along the road to an integrated society.[47] In short, the wrangling over the legality, if not the justice, of a segregated society was well under way when the curtain lifted on the African American cast of *Four Saints in Three Acts* in 1952. A set of intertextual messages that seemed inoffensively meaning-rich to the mainstream viewer in 1934 no longer read that way to his or her counterpart in 1952.

One of ANTA photographer Victor Shifreen's beautiful production stills of the first act of the 1952 production speaks to the problems with the production that I have described. It seems obvious from the photograph that Thomson and his colleagues tried to reproduce the details of the 1934 production, yet something feels very strange about it (see photo 2.4). St. Therese I is seated slightly off center. She is framed by the double cathedral arches, but they seem higher and narrower and the crystal beads look oddly less regal and more plainly geometrical than the arches of the 1934

Photo 2.4   Inez Matthews as St. Therese I seated "half indoors and half out of doors" in a scene from Act I of the ANTA production of *Four Saints in Three Acts* (photograph by Victor Shifreen)

production. The palm trees flanking the arches do seem to be drooping as Thomson had described them. Once again the surpliced chorus of saints sits on banks of pyramidial risers on both sides of the stage. The Commere and St. Ignatius stand downstage right while the scantily clad dancers and their gracefully posed limbs provide visual interest nearby. But the thing that seems to alter the stage picture most profoundly is the empty space around the principal performer center stage. The elements of the stage picture seem more loosely and tenuously connected in this image than they do in similar images from 1934. This sense of unfilled space, in contrast to the visual exuberance and profusion of the original production, is also very much apparent in Shifreen's photograph of Act II with both Saint Thereses and as well as Saints Plan, Settlement, Ignatius, and Chavez. The figures in the image are beautifully costumed and arranged in space, but a sense of emptiness remains, unsettling the viewer (see photo 2.5).

This literal, visual change had, as I have argued, a metaphorical counterpart. The primitivist stereotypes about African Americans that were available for import into the performance text in 1934, filling the space within and between the libretto, score, and choreography had either become less immediately accessible, in the case of Negro chic, or had become problematized, complicated, and less stable in their cultural meanings, as had the set of assumptions conflating African Americans with the noble savage. As a result, Thomson's 1952 staging was simply unable to replicate the effect of the 1934 production.

Photo 2.5   Calvin Dash as St. Plan, Martha Flowers as St. Settlement, Betty Lou Allen as St. Therese II, Inez Matthews as St. Therese I, Edward Matthews as St. Ignatius, Rawn Spearman as St. Chavez and members of the Chorus of Saints in Act II of the ANTA production of *Four Saints in Three Acts* (photograph by Victor Shifreen)

FRANK GALATI'S *EACH ONE AS SHE MAY*

In 1995 Frank Galati directed his adaptation of Gertrude Stein's story from *Three Lives*, "Melanctha" called *Gertrude Stein: Each One as She May* in the Studio Theatre of Chicago's Goodman Theatre. Though the story and the stage piece adapted from it are far more approachable than many of Stein's actual plays because they explore the romantic and intellectual conflict between the psychologically motivated characters named Melanctha Herbert and Jefferson Campbell, Stein's trademark repetitive and allusive verbal style guarantees a challenging evening of theatre. Galati made Stein's work even more accessible to the audience by creating a musical intertext: ragtime and the associations it carries with it filled the spaces in Stein's story and commented on her literary style. Furthermore, the dialogue Galati crafted between Stein's text and ragtime created a space in which the African American performers in its midst could reinscribe the codes of primitivism that animated both forms. As David Krasner explains in *Resistance, Parody,* and *Double Consciousness in African American Theatre, 1895–1910,* "Reinscription in African American theatre defined a performative act requiring black actors first to imitate, and second to refashion, the bodily gestures of white minstrel performers."[48] Though the performers in *Each One As She May* were not directly imitating the behavior of minstrel performers, they were, nevertheless, refashioning material recycled from several varieties of blackface performance. Gertrude Stein, her text, and her ideas, were restaged in a way that reproduced aspects of primitivist discourse, but at the same time, this repetition made redefinition possible as well, allowing Stein and "Melanctha" to be put to a new and more racially progressive use.

The inaugural staging of Stein's *Four Saints in Three Acts* in 1934, as I explained earlier, relied on primitivist assumptions to fill the spaces in the text and make it more accessible to audiences who would have otherwise been overwhelmed by Stein's dramatic innovations. It is likely that Galati encountered the tenacious residue of these same stereotypes when he mounted his own staging of *Four Saints in Three Acts* involving an all-black cast at the Chicago Opera Theatre in 1993.

Galati reengaged with Stein and African American performers in *Each One As She May* in 1995. Tom Valeo, reviewer for the *Daily-Herald* praised Galati's scripting:

> He has edited the story brilliantly, focusing on the prolonged verbal duel that forms the heart of Melanctha. In addition Galati has employed his exquisite sense of theatricality to give this amorphous narrative a vivid and well-defined shape. Without distorting Stein's prose, he has infused it with vitality, making it less an experiment in writing and more an account of two living, breathing human beings.[49]

Connie Lauerman echoed Valeo's evaluation of Galati's emphasis in her article on the production for the *Chicago Tribune* writing, "Galati's adaptation of the story focuses on the principal romantic relationship of Melanctha's life."[50] Both writers surely felt their opinions were safe since the Goodman's own press release referred to "Melanctha" as "Stein's African American love story" and made no mention of Stein's stylistic experimentation, but Michael North's interpretation of Stein in *The Dialect of Modernism* troubles these facile readings.

In *The Autobiography of Alice B. Toklas,* Stein said of "Melanctha" that it was "the first definite step away from the nineteenth century and into the twentieth century in literature."[51] North suggests that Stein's transgressive move into the twentieth century and modernism more precisely was made behind the mask of her African American characters in "Melanctha."

In *The Dialect of Modernism*, he unveils the fundamental relationship between literary versions of African American dialect and the development of modernism. From the 1880s through the 1920s, he reports, there was a movement to standardize and codify the English language. Against this movement, and in some sense within this movement as standard English was frequently defined by what it was not rather than what it was, stood a cadre of modernist writers. North argues that

> Dialect preserved an escape from all the social pressures implied by the standard language movement: "black" dialect was white dialect in hiding. This is not to say there was no actual black speech with its own order and rules, only that the acted, sung, and published versions of this language were almost always white products, no matter how much they may have resembled their black prototypes.[52]

The fabricated versions of black dialect appearing in many pieces of modernist literature were a series of blackface impersonations: white authors performed behind black linguistic masks that in some cases bore little resemblance to their human referents. Black voices and black bodies did not have the power to control their reproduction. While these masked performances offered white writers the chance to break away from artistic tradition and blaze new literary trails, they reified the primitivist stereotypes that ensnared black people socially and culturally.

"Melanctha" is a particularly interesting example of this phenomenon. Critics generally agree that "Melanctha" is a re-crafting of Stein's early autobiographical work, *Q.E.D.* In her first novel (though it was published posthumously), Stein explored the painful feelings that emerged from the dissolution of her relationship with May Bookstaver. In *Q.E.D.*, the character Adele represents Stein while the character Helen stands in for Bookstaver. When Stein revisits this difficult material in "Melanctha," she transforms Stein/Adele into Jefferson Campbell and Bookstaver/Helen into Melanctha.[53] Not only does Stein change the gender of one lover in her second version of the story, she changes the race of both lovers. On one level this masking allows Stein to retread literary and emotional ground with which she was not finished in the presence of her reading public, but on another more complex plane, as North argues, placing an African American mask over her own image—a move analogous to Picasso's famous transformation of her face in his portrait—facilitates "the step away from conventional verisimilitude into abstraction."[54]

Stein's move from the verisimilar representational strategies of the nineteenth century into the abstract representational strategies of the twentieth was propelled most forcefully by the form of African American dialect she used in her story. At the time of the story's composition, many readers thought the dialect spoken by the characters was quite realistic. The Goodman's program quotes Richard Wright's review of "Melanctha":

> As I read it my ears were open for the first time to the magic of the spoken word. I began to hear the speech of my grandmother who spoke a deep, pure Negro dialect and with whom I had lived for many years. All of my life I had been only half hearing, but Miss Stein's struggling words made the speech of the people around me vivid."[55]

When one looks at the story from a contemporary vantage point, however, the speech of the characters, which actually amounts to only a small percentage of the entire story, seems far less authentic. In fact, as North observes, "What Stein does instead [of reproducing actual patterns of contemporary African American speech] is to create a dialect in which conventions of verbal verisimilitude are played against themselves so that the speech seems simultaneously concrete and highly artificial."[56] The African American mask Stein wears in "Melanctha" only very loosely resembles any of the people of her day, yet because it was a much publicized example of the dialect movement in modernist literature, it became a device that constructed African Americans for white readers all the same.

Galati's adaptation retained large portions of Stein's dialogue and the narration of the characters' activities and inner thoughts verbatim as well as the central romantic story. As Adam Langer observed in his less than glowing review of the production entitled "Beautiful Bore" for the *Chicago Reader*, "Galati revels in the maddening repetition of Stein's dialogue, allowing pages of conversation to go on uninterrupted where a judicious editor might have got out some scissors."[57] Since Galati so faithfully maintained Stein's wording, he also reproduced her stylistic innovation—despite the racial implications that inevitably accompanies it.

Accompanying the text with ragtime music was an ingenious way to amplify the dialect emitted from Stein's highly artificial mask in "Melanctha." Rather than apologizing for what now surely strikes many readers as an offensive part of the story, Galati called attention to the dialect quite forcefully through the musical intertext that both repeated and revised aspects of the dialect's textual and social operations. In addition, ragtime brought with it considerable cultural baggage, which, when put into dialogue with Stein's text, filled the text's gaps and spaces in several possible ways. First, ragtime became popular at the turn of the twentieth century and in the first years thereafter. Ragtime thus grounds the production in a specific period.

Any historical knowledge the audience member might have about the era might then be imported into the text.

Second, ragtime has a nostalgic subtext. If audience members had read E. L. Doctorow's novel, *Ragtime*, or seen the film based on it (the stage musical adaptation directed by Galati would premiere in Toronto in 1996), the sentimental images of three intertwined American families might play in concert with the images of Stein's main characters. Of particular relevance to Stein's text is the love story of a young African American mother named Sarah and a ragtime musician called Coalhouse Walker.

Third, ragtime's style, its repetitions, or "ragging" of older forms and established classics, might remind the audience of elements of Stein's style—the way she revisits familiar words, sounds, and snippets of popular phrases, in order to force her audience to hear and experience these forms anew. Ragtime, could, therefore, make Stein's style seem less hermetic. Galati pointed to this aspect of ragtime in his interview with the *Tribune*'s Connie Lauerman before the production opened. He said, "Oddly enough, ragtime has the same kind of circular, repetitive, spiraling structural elements that Stein's prose has."[58] The *Tribune*'s reviewer Richard Christensen concurred with Galati's evaluation. After seeing the production he found that the musicians "provide lovely background music that is perfectly linked to the flow of the dialogue."[59]

Fourth, and perhaps most significantly, ragtime has a substantial racial subtext. Ragtime derived from musical forms associated with African Americans. Sophisticated listeners might recognize West African rhythms while those less attuned to these patterns might see ragtime's debt to the minstrel cake walk and the "coon song," two forms that invigorated primitivist stereotypes. Ragtime developed into a recognizable form by the 1890s in the United States, and its first manifestation was the "coon song," which Edward Berlin defines as follows:

> Coon song . . . has been retained by present-day historians for reference to the Negro dialect songs of the minstrel, vaudeville, and other musical stages that usually depicted blacks in a flagrantly disparaging (and supposedly humorous) manner. In the lyrics the words "coon" and "nigger" (or niggah) are common; black men are portrayed as ignorant, gluttonous, thieving (stealing chickens, watermelons, and pork pies), gambling, cowardly, shiftless, and violent (most often wielding a razor); the women are sexually promiscuous and mercenary, often leaving one "honey" (which rhymes with "money") for another of greater generosity, thus precipitating an altercation between the men.[60]

Another musical form associated with the beginning of ragtime is the cakewalk. Like the coon song, the cakewalk may have reinforced racial stereotypes in the minds of ragtime's first generation of listeners. The cakewalk was, as Berlin explains, "a grand promenade type of dance of plantation origins in which the slave couple performing the most attractive steps and motions would 'take the cake.' "[61] The cakewalk then moved from the plantation to the minstrel stage. White men in blackface performed a dance for a white largely working-class audience in which they imitated slaves imitating their masters' dancing style. Eventually a two-step dance that was a variation on the cakewalk became very popular as ragtime was emerging. For a time thereafter, the terms cakewalk and ragtime were used interchangeably. David A. Jansen and Trebor Jay Tichenor report in *Rags and Ragtime: A Musical History* that the cakewalk evolved into a high-society pastime thanks to its popularization of Broadway and Vaudeville stages while many African Americans came to regard the form as unrespectable.[62]

The coon song and the cakewalk are two forms whose portrayals of African Americans were, according to David Krasner, transformed by African American performers. It is this transformation by way of the presence of the "authentic" black body (as opposed to the white minstrel body) that begins to reveal a crucial difference from Stein's use of dialect. When Krasner discusses the process of reinscription—the method by which African American performers reproduced stereotypes so that they could rewrite them—he analyzes the performances of George Walker and Bert Williams in such productions as *A Lucky Coon*. Krasner finds that though Walker and Williams once billed themselves as "Real Coons" to capitalize on their difference as black performers from whites wearing burnt cork, and they maintained the use of the offensive word "coon" in their title, they successfully dismantled the coon's primitivist image by reconstructing their stage personae in accordance with the prototype of the more elegant and sophisticated "New Negro."[63] Krasner also discusses the hybridity of the cakewalk, particularly as it was choreographed by Aida Overton Walker. Walker, Krasner argues,

> Devised a choreography that was protean, flexible, and cognizant of the mechanisms of cultural expression. Armed with an understanding of call-and-response patterns, Walker was able to gauge the reception of her cakewalking. Her familiarity with contemporary dance techniques and styles as well as her readings of audience receptivity worked to her advantage. As a result, Walker articulated an embodied discourse as an instrument of her self-representation.[64]

The juxtaposition of Stein's dialect—which was largely uninformed by the actual patterns of speech by the African Americans of her day—with ragtime, a kind of expression that derived from forms that were refashioned by African American performers, begins to reveal to the revolutionary potential of this production. While Stein's text may be free of the influence of authentic African American voices as it exists on the printed page, when African American actors have the opportunity to speak the words and embody the characters, the stereotypes girding the dialogue are brought into confrontation with the descendants of the people who never spoke them. The actor's body and voice challenge the text, exposing Stein's masquerade and subduing the stereotypes on which it relied.

Adam Langer's review of the production in *The Chicago Reader* lends support to this point. He wrote:

> The actors are terrific, especially the charismatic Johnny Lee Davenport, playing against type as the prudish Campbell, and as Melanctha the uncommonly powerful and haunting Jacqueline Williams, who can rivet attention with a subtly drawn mischievous smile. But when you're paying more attention to a well-crafted smile or the way a suit hangs than to the words, there's a problem. Midway through Galati's adaptation, Stein's incessantly repeated words begin to lose their meaning, and one's eyes are ensnared by everything but the play. Rather than make himself invisible, as every great director does when a scene erupts, Galati can be seen at every turn. You see the way he's directed an actor to place a hand upon a knee, to move upstage, to give focus, and Stein's dialogue becomes a mere irritant.[65]

Langer applauds the actors, finding their work one of the most compelling parts of the production. It is worth noting that when he criticizes Galati's direction, he complains that the actors' physical work is too plainly visible. Instead of reading this as a flaw in Galati's procedure or conception of the piece, it might suggest that the actors' bodily presence overpowers the words, wresting control away from them. The African American bodies on stage rewrite Stein's text as artificial and inadequate.

One way that Galati's performance text achieved this effect was through his division of Stein's text into parts for the actors. The lines in Stein's text that were already written as dialogue between Melanctha and Jefferson went to Jacqueline Williams and Johnny Lee Davenport respectively. Though a great deal of Stein's text is not in the form of dialogue, these portions were also spoken by actors: Cheryl Lynn Bruce played the Female Narrator and Rick Worthy played the male narrator (see photo 2.6). Both narrators commented on the action in various ways. For example, when Melanctha and Jefferson's relationship was in full bloom, the Female Narrator said, "One day there had been much joy between them, more than they ever yet had had with their new feeling. All the day they had lost themselves in warm

Photo 2.6 The Narrators (Rick Worthy and Cheryl Lynn Bruce) look on as Melanctha and Jeff (Jacqueline Williams and Johnny Lee Davenport) "lost themselves in warm wandering" in this scene from the Goodman Theatre's *Gertrude Stein: Each One as She May* (photograph © Liz Lauren)

wandering."[66] But in addition to these sorts of lines both narrators told the audience about Melanctha's, and more frequently Jefferson's, internal feelings. These lines of the Female Narrator are typical of this kind of passage: "Jeff always loved now to be with Melanctha and yet he always hated to go to her. Somehow he was always afraid when he was to go to her, and yet he had made himself very certain that he would not be a coward."[67] Though the narrators occasionally exited the stage, they spent a large portion of the performance watching Jefferson and Melanctha from its periphery.

Galati's division of the text led to casting choices and blocking that both illustrated and commented on Stein's writing: he split Stein's characters into multiple bodies. The inner life of the character was made material and distinct from the outer form of the character through the physical presence of the narrators. This fracturing led to a denaturalization of character, a fitting analogue to Stein's break from nineteenth-century verisimilitude. Spectators could not retreat into the illusion that the people on stage were really Melanctha and Jefferson since multiple bodies represented the characters on stage. Instead attention was called to the construction of the performance and the performers' skill: the mellifluousness of their voices, the grace of their gestures, or the beauty of their physical forms in space. Meanwhile the physical positioning of the actors playing the narrators reminded the audience of its voyeuristic presence outside the action through the watching of the narrators. But beyond the abstract presentation of character, the narrators de-authenticate Stein's presence in the work as they re-embody her authorial position and divide it between them. The African American performers who play the narrators seem to write the abstract stage action by setting the scene, telling the audience what has happened or will happen, and revealing the characters' internal states. Though the words they speak are almost exclusively Stein's as Galati's interventions into the text are infrequent, their physical presence creates the illusion that they have taken control of the construction of the narrative. Like George Walker, Bert Williams, and Aida Overton Walker, they reinhabit an old blackface form and refashion it by marking Stein's presence as inauthentic through juxtaposition with their own powerful physical presence.

The visual aspects of the performance text were kept very minimal. This served to highlight the presence of the actors and cement the reinscription of the primitivist ideas animating Stein's story. The set was extremely spare and pristine, consisting of a raked floor of pale wood planks, a large set of stairs in the center of the stage and a small, railed balcony. A scrim enveloped the set, occasionally interrupting the placid aura of the environment with a surge of intense color as Melanctha's passion threatened the tranquil harmony of Jefferson's world and worldview. The costumes, reminiscent of the first years of the twentieth century, were in a palette limited to black and white. The actors' movements in this beautiful yet subdued stage environment were very precise. Most scenes were nearly static; the actors occasionally moved slowly up and down the stairs or across the stage, but they were most often seated on the staircase or on the floor beside it. In their seated positions, the actors' bodies were often torqued in multiple directions: the torso would be angled in one direction while the legs pointed to another and the arms and legs were often sharply bent. The effect of this blocking as it emerged from the staid background, in keeping with Eugenio Barba's principles of extra-daily behavior and luxury balance, was one of highly charged but expertly controlled physicality.

The sensual precision of stage picture provided more than aesthetic pleasure: it offered a sharp rebuke to the primitivist ideas about African American sexuality that Stein had laced through her story. In "Melanctha" Stein stages a fierce confrontation between the version of sexuality and morality espoused by the adventurous Melanctha Herbert and the views held by the conservative Jefferson Campbell. The female narrator uses Melanctha's love of the railroad yard as metaphor for her passionate and sensation-seeking nature when she introduces her to the audience:

> Melanctha liked to wander, and to stand by the railroad yard, and watch the men and the engines and the switches and everything that was busy there, working. . . . It is very nice to get the swelling in the throat, and the fullness, and the heart beats, and all the flutter of excitement that comes as one watches the people come and go, and hears the engine pound and give a long drawn whistle. . . . For Melanctha the yard was full of the excitement of many men, and perhaps a whirling future.[68]

At the opposite end of the spectrum from Melanctha's voluptuous embrace of passion is Jefferson's definition of the appropriate lifestyle. He says:

> I ain't got any use for all the time being in excitements and wanting to have all kinds of experience all the time . . . I don't believe much in this running around business and I don't want to see the colored people do it, I am a colored man and I ain't sorry, and I want to see the colored people like what is good and what I want them to have, and that's to live regular and work hard and understand things, and that's enough to keep any decent man excited.[69]

The tensions that persisted during the course of the story between Melanctha and Jefferson's worldviews embodied two stereotypes of black sexuality, both of which have their roots in primitivism. In *Race Matters*, Cornel West argues, "Americans are obsessed with sex and fearful of black sexuality . . . . The dominant myths draw black men either as threatening creatures who have the potential for sexual power over whites, or as harmless, desexed underlings of a white culture."[70] Stein's text incarnates the pernicious polar myths about black sexuality that West describes in the characters of Melanctha and Jefferson. Galati's performance text, with its marriage of sensuality and precise physical control, revises these harmful images. Stein's words again register as inauthentic and inadequate when coupled with the actors' performance against the appearance of the stage.

When Krasner outlines the "analytical merits" of using the concept of reinscription to investigate the history of African American performance, he argues:

> Looking at how subordinate groups reinscribe the practices of the dominant society enables us to see how cultural [re]appropriation, as [Edward] Said notes, implies a tragic dilemma. Said points out that the tragedy of cultural resistance is that "it must to a certain degree work to recover forms already established or at least influenced or infiltrated by the culture of empire" (210). Black performers work to recover their stage representation already entrenched in white caricatures.[71]

In the particular case of Frank Galati's production of *Gertrude Stein: Each One as She May*, the performers did have to undergo the tragedy of recovering the caricatures of African Americans contained in Stein's story and conveyed by her dialogue. But through the use of ragtime music, and the model of reinscription it provided, the performers were able to restage Stein's harmful primitivist images and take physical control of their representation. Gertrude Stein, her story, and her writing style, were radically reconfigured as vehicles for African American empowerment.

In chapter 3, I continue to explore the ways that contemporary culture both shapes perceptions of Stein and infiltrates the spaces in her texts, reshaping them in ways unimaginable when the texts are encountered outside the realm of live theatrical performance. Just as primitivism formed Stein's image both literally and metaphorically, ideas about abstraction and Stein's relationship to mass culture reshaped her persona once again as well as the range of available meanings of the Living Theatre's inaugural production, *Doctor Faustus Lights the Lights*, and the Judson Poets Theatre's production of *In Circles*.

3. Exile from Mass Culture: Charting the Open Spaces of Perceptual Freedom in the Living Theatre's *Doctor Faustus Lights the Lights* and the Judson Poets Theatre's *In Circles* ✎

Gertrude Stein sat at the helm of early-twentieth-century revolutions in art and rebelled against some types of social conformity, but she also held a deep and abiding affection for several icons of mass culture and spent much of her life hungering for wide public acclaim. Stein loved the automobile and the motion picture, pulp detective fiction and the American soldier, just as much as she loved paintings and operas, poetry and the avant-garde artist. And while she had the daily pleasure of seeing her face on a painted canvas,[1] she longed to see her image flash across the silver screen.[2] Though Stein's demanding writing style taught her readers and audiences to see the world anew and to perceive differently, she did not reject the products and preoccupations of mass culture as tools for reaching this goal. Thus it is only appropriate that when trail-blazing theatre artists like the Living Theatre and the Judson Poets Theatre revisited Stein and her aesthetic in hopes of re-embodying her revolutionary potential, the concerns and images characteristic of the early 1950s and late 1960s crept back into the mix despite the artists' efforts to the contrary.

Though the Living Theatre and the Judson Poets Theatre were valiant in their attempts to preserve Stein's textual spaces through their bold forays into abstraction, contemporary culture still exerted a tremendous force on these productions. In order to understand her mid-twentieth-century stagings, and the consequences of the artists' abstract production choices, one must first make acquaintance with the mass culture–loving aspects of Gertrude Stein.

IDOLS OF MASS CULTURE: MEETING DASHIELL HAMMETT AND CHARLIE CHAPLIN

Stein's American tour moved the starry-eyed side of her persona upstage center. When she visited California in 1935, Carl Van Vechten asked Stein to dine with his friend, Lillian May Ehrman. Mrs. Ehrman, no doubt wanting her dinner party to be a success, asked Stein whom she'd hoped to meet in Hollywood. Stein expressed her preference for Dashiell Hammett and Charlie Chaplin. Stein's interest in these mass culture icons, who like Stein herself were far more complex than they might appear at first glance, reveals an important, if often overlooked aspect of her place in the cultural landscape. Stein, Hammett, and Chaplin all had a hunger for the spotlight and a desire for success in the arena of mass culture, but at the same time, they were all busy subverting the conventions of their respective media in surprisingly analogous ways. Stein's relationship to Hammett and Chaplin demonstrates that mass culture and alternatives to it have merged at some surprising points rather than being separated by a great divide. Had the artists who produced Stein celebrated these aspects of her work instead of sublimating them, they might have seen further possibilities for staging her work.

Stein's meeting with Hammett was so important to her that the fourth paragraph of the introduction to *Everybody's Autobiography*, reads, "That is the way any autobiography has to be written which reminds me of Dashiell Hammett."[3] Her interest in Hammett, she explained, was due to her taste for detective stories. She wrote, "I do like detective stories. I never try to guess who has done the crime and if I did I would be sure to guess wrong but I like somebody being dead and how it moves along and Dashiell Hammett was all that and more."[4] Despite Stein's interest in Hammett, his presence at the dinner was far more difficult to arrange than Chaplin's. Mrs. Ehrman did not know Hammett, but she sought him out anyway because of Stein's request. Further, Hammett already had plans that evening and wouldn't come unless "his hostess" for the evening—Lillian Hellman— could come too.[5] Ehrman gave her consent, despite Stein's demand than the number at the table be limited. When Hammett arrived, Toklas reports in *What is Remembered*, his presence was in even more danger than suspected. Toklas writes, "When we got there and Dashiell Hammett appeared, he said to Gertrude Stein, It's the first of April and when I received the invitation

I said, 'It's an April Fool's joke.' Well, said Gertrude Stein, you see it isn't!"[6] What also isn't a joke is Stein's interest in and relationship to Hammett as he is very revealing of her connections to mass culture and the correspondence between avant-garde and popular culture strategies of the time.

When Stein met Hammett in 1935, the period of his literary output was largely over, though neither of them would have known that at the time. Between 1922, when his story, "Immortality," was published in *10 Short Story*, and 1934 when his novel *The Thin Man* was released, Hammett wrote more than sixty short stories and five novels. After 1934, Hammett was one of Hollywood's most popular writers as adaptations of his work filled the silver screen, the television screen, and the radio waves, but he stopped composing new work. In 1961, fifty pages of his uncompleted novel, *Tulip*, were published posthumously.

So by the time of their dinner, Hammett had already succeeded in both popularizing and subverting the main features of the hard-boiled detective fiction Stein loved. As Sinda Gregory explains in *Private Investigations: The Novels of Dashiell Hammett*, hard-boiled form was emblematic of the changes in modern life:

> As changing values disrupted intellectual, artistic, and social life in the 1920s and produced a new kind of serious American literature, the hard-boiled school of detective fiction merged as an alternative to the classical style. The tidy puzzle, the carefully drawn lines between good and evil, and the finality of both the mystery and the solution seemed no more appropriate to many detective story writers than did drawing room drama to Sinclair Lewis and Sherwood Anderson.[7]

Hammett's particular contribution to this form, in addition to providing the archetype of the cynical private eye, was questioning the primacy, or perhaps even possibility, of human reason as a tool for coping with modern dilemmas. As Cynthia Hamilton argues in *Western and Hard-Boiled Detective Fiction in America: From High Noon to Midnight*, in Hammett's work:

> Attention is continually engaged by the immediate foreground. The focus is so precise that one sees everything in sharp detail, but lacks the distance necessary to permit judgment of the phenomenon. The frustrations involved in this narrowed viewpoint reflect Hammett's vision. He sets the reader's need to order and interpret against a narrative designed to confound interpretation.[8]

Herein lies the similarity to Stein's work, despite what are usually perceived as the differences between pulp fiction and avant-garde dramatic expression.

Just as Hammett's tight focus foregrounds detail, Stein's play with language—
with words that lose all conventional and grammatical sense, thus becoming
bits of nondiscursive aural detail—shifts the reader's or viewer's perception
in ways that disorient her and make the usual modes of rational interpretation difficult if not impossible as she perceives the dramatic landscape.
Both Hammett and Stein created work that radically altered the reader or
viewer's relationship to the work of art, whether that art was mainstream or
avant-garde.

When Stein returned home to France after her tour, and sought to give
her final definition of what constituted her unique brand of dramatic creation in *The Geographical History of America*, she repeatedly used detective
stories as a theoretical tool and point of comparison, as she does in this representative passage: "And a description of how the earth looks as you look
at it which is perhaps a play if it can be done in a day and is perhaps a detective story if it can be found out. Anything is a detective story if it can be
found out and can anything be found out. Yes."[9] Clearly reading Hammett
and her dinner with him fed Stein's imagination and helped propel her into
a new phase of her work.

Stein's connection to Charlie Chaplin is just as illuminating as her
relationship with Dashiell Hammett. In *What is Remembered*, Alice writes
of the dinner, "When Mr. Chaplin arrived I said to him, the only films we
have seen are yours, which flattered him but which was not exactly exact."[10]
Regardless of what else they had seen, it is likely, since they were Chaplin
fans, that they might have seen the great films of the 1920s and early 1930s
like *The Kid, Gold Rush, The Circus,* and *City Lights.* At the time of the dinner in 1935, Chaplin was still wrestling with the introduction of sound that
occurred with such films as *Don Juan* (1926) and *The Jazz Singer* (1927).
Stein writes of their conversation,

> Anyway we naturally talked about the cinema, and he explained something.
> He said naturally it was disappointing, he had known the silent films and in
> that they could do something that the theatre had not done they could
> change the rhythm but if you had a voice accompanying naturally after that
> you could never change the rhythm you were always held by the rhythm that
> the voice gave them.[11]

Though Stein often balked at comparisons made between herself and other
contemporary literary figures, she seemed to have no trepidation about
likening her own work to Chaplin's filmic style, which was struggling to
keep pace with the latest technical innovations. She writes, "He wanted the
sentiment of movement invented by himself and I wanted the sentiment of

doing nothing invented by myself, anyway we both liked talking but each one had to stop to be polite and let the other one say something."[12]

Michael North's reading of Chaplin's relationship to modernism helps to explain what Stein meant by Chaplin's "sentiment of movement." According to North, Chaplin

> defeats what would seem the primary power of film, the illusion of presence, of immediacy, that it is able to give. In bringing a rhythm back into realism, he stalls or syncopates or reverses the seemingly natural order of things, disrupting that powerful sense of the given that always attaches to the purely visual. In particular, the repetitiousness of his movements, or certain props like the wayward lift [in *Pay Day*], makes the whole process of copying, without which the movies are unimaginable, visible, and in so doing it highlights the inherent instability of every object and every person in a film.[13]

In her Lecture "Plays," Stein talked about her desire to alleviate the syncopation in the audience member's emotion between things heard and seen on stage by making the theatre like scenery, or what she calls above, the "sentiment of doing nothing." Though the creation and erasure of syncopation might seem to be opposite strategies, they both "disrupt the powerful sense of the given" and make the process of artistic production, and I would add perception, visible. Thus we see that though Chaplin was an icon of Hollywood and Stein an icon of the Left Bank, both worked to subvert the expectations of their audiences and the limits of the forms in which they worked.

Though Stein doesn't continue to draw parallels with Chaplin's work in *Everybody's Autobiography*, there are others she could make with his pre–*Modern Times* (1936) films.[14] Most notably, both figures had a double persona that both gave them popular appeal and frustrated them by limiting their avenues for serious expression. Beginning with *The Kid*, Chaplin had included autobiographical material in his work, drawing primarily from his childhood memories. Throughout his time at United Artists, Chaplin reworked his experiences, often molding the characters in his films after different sides of his personality.[15] The kind of character to which audiences were most drawn, however, was the sentimental hobo figure of Charlie. Though Charlie expressed a part of Chaplin, Chaplin also wanted to be taken seriously as an artist and thinker.

Critics frequently analyze the "doubleness" of Chaplin: Charles the artist was in conflict with Charlie the character. North writes,

> The conflict between Charles and Charlie incarnated the relationship between popular culture and young intellectuals. Whether Charles might ever express

his deeper intellectual yearnings as Charlie, without losing any of his popular appeal, is a question that seemed very much in the balance in 1922, and it was a question full of implications for American popular culture, the young intellectuals, and the relationship between them.[16]

Likewise for stagings of Stein, new generations of intellectuals and artists have had to contend with her dual persona. While the avant-garde icono-clast holds perennial fascination, the mass culture enthusiast is frequently neglected or intentionally subdued. A negotiation between the ideal and the entire Stein certainly seems to have taken place as the Living Theatre mounted *Doctor Faustus Lights the Lights* in 1951 and as the Judson Poets Theatre staged *In Circles* in 1967–8. Though both companies privileged Stein's nonconformist qualities and sought abstract or indeterminate visual and aural devices to mirror them, the concerns of mass culture, consistent with her interests, could not be fully suppressed in the production of her work, despite the directors' and designers' most strenuous efforts. Before exiling the artists and audiences from mass culture, Stein's textual absences brought them into more intimate and local contact with it by creating the space for fierce cultural debate.

THE LIVING THEATRE'S *DOCTOR FAUSTUS LIGHTS THE LIGHTS*

Before Beck and Malina attained their iconic status in the 1960s,[17] they began to envision a new kind of theatre in the late 1940s and early 1950s. As Beck and Malina were struggling to define the aesthetic of their nascent company, they were inspired by their image of Gertrude Stein. In her May 29, 1951 diary entry, Malina wrote

> Plays should be short enough to be easily rehearsed so that they do not deaden in the process. The plots simple. The style pure, direct; not too much scenery; music, but not too much, poetry, but not too many words; perfect tempo. Attain the perfection of production through the perfection of imme-diacy. The Noh is a perfect medium, but the Noh is too rigid. Better than the Noh's strictness is the short enacted poem, the active, living poem. Gertrude Stein has clues. Work on this![18]

And work on Stein they did. The Living Theatre's official inaugural production was of her libretto, *Doctor Faustus Lights the Lights*, staged in December of 1951.[19] In this production, Beck and Malina emphasized the qualities that drew them to Stein—pure, direct style, music and poetry—through abstract and indeterminate production elements. Beck and Malina used this tactic—one very different from the choices they made in their better-known and blatantly politically confrontational work of the 1960s and beyond—in an effort both to celebrate Stein's unique aesthetic that granted the viewer enormous perceptual freedom and to avoid producing propaganda that they believed would affirm the dominant Cold War ideology. What they failed to realize, I demonstrate as I analyze their choices for audience interaction, set, lighting, costumes, blocking, and music, is that abstract construction is neither artistically nor politically neutral. Abstraction's political and social implications in this particular cultural moment spilled into the spaces in Stein's textual landscape, transfiguring it just as profoundly as if they drew some of the parallels with contemporary culture that *Doctor Faustus Lights the Lights* seemed to beg them to make. Mass culture, its images, and concerns haunted the spaces of their abstract performance text precisely because of the Living Theatre's attempts to escape from it.

Doctor Faustus Lights the Lights is Stein's reworking of the Faust myth. In her version, Doctor Faustus sells his soul to the devil in exchange for the power to claim the invention of electric light. Several elements of this tale could be shaped to reflect the political situation in 1951. First, on June 23, 1951, the Russian ambassador to the United Nations, Jacob Malik, proposed that the two sides engaged in the Korean War discuss a ceasefire agreement. By the time of the production in December, the talks were still going on, after several breakdowns. Throughout the six months of talks, new reports emphasized a distrust of any terms the Russians might offer. Though American soldiers were not fighting Russian soldiers, Marty Jezer explains in *The Dark Ages: Life in the United States 1945–1960* that "American policy makers assumed that the North Koreans were acting under orders from the Kremlin."[20] Further testimony that public opinion positioned the Russians as the "true enemy" in Korea comes from a *Newsweek* piece entitled "Peace, but with our guard up:" "No responsible authority in the free world was so optimistic as to believe the Russians, in proposing a cease-fire in Korea, had abandoned hope of conquering the world for Stalin in memory of Marx."[21] The idea circulating through this piece is that in signing a deal with the Russians, the agents of Stalin and Marx, the Americans might as well be signing a deal with the devil since it risked the demise of the free world.

The libretto's concern with the dangers of technology surely struck an equally sensitive cultural nerve in 1951. In *Doctor Faustus Lights the Lights*, it is Faustus's hunger for technological knowledge, specifically the seemingly innocuous development of electric light, which leads him down the path to hell. In 1951 the dangers of technology were shockingly apparent.

In October, two months before the production opened, and only weeks before rehearsal began, the Soviets conducted their second nuclear test, leading to speculation about the possible use of atomic weapons in Korean War and the end of the illusion that the nuclear arsenal of the United States could serve as a permanent, effective deterrent to large-scale nuclear conflict. While the first Soviet test in 1949 let the world know that they had developed nuclear capabilities, the second test was read as a sign that the Soviets were quickly developing a sizable arsenal that could soon be employed in military conflicts.

A final aspect of contemporary culture that could have been viewed through the lens of Stein's text was the appropriate exercise of female sexual identity. In Stein's libretto, Marguerite Ida and Helena Annabel, the multiply named yet singular heroine, undergoes a series of identity crises as a result of the sexually charged "viper bite" she receives and her incendiary interactions with Faustus, during which she manages to appropriate Faustus's hard-won technological power. As Elaine Tyler May noted in "Explosive Issues: Sex, Women, and the Bomb," containment of female sexual energy—associated with the same potentially deleterious effects as atomic bombs—was a prime cultural operation in the postwar years.[22] A diverse array of cultural objects and practices—from the girdle to *I Love Lucy*—were enlisted for this task. Marguerite Ida and Helena Annabel's assertion of sexual autonomy stands in sharp contrast to the female sexual ideal of the early 1950s and could easily have been offered audience members as a model of resistance to the images circulating in mainstream culture.

That Malina and Beck did not try to import any of these elements directly into their performance text, in order to fill the spaces in Stein's libretto and to call their audiences to action, seems quite surprising at first glance given their much heralded theatrical responses to the Vietnam war in the next decade. But in a recent interview, Malina explained the motivating force behind these choices:

> We were pacifists and we were anarchists and we did not feel at that time that one could create a political theatre . . . . During that whole period [the early 1950s] there was really no question about our commitment and that our commitment was political. But we believed with the times, perhaps we were right, that, at that time, political theatre meant something which could be oversimplified as cheap propaganda. It was the sort of thing the Russians were doing; it was the sort of thing that had no subtlety that tried to tell you what to think.[23]

Malina's perceptions of the possibilities or absence of possibilities for politically engaged theatre in the early 1950s provide what Clifford Geertz has called an "ethnographic miniature." He explains that "social actions are comments on more than themselves; that where an interpretation comes from does not determine where it can be impelled to go. Small facts speak to large issues."[24] In the small choices of the Living Theatre's performance text, in their various strategies for disengaging from Cold War propaganda, a portrait of one larger feature of Cold War culture begins to emerge.

In *The Culture of the Cold War*, Stephen J. Whitfield describes Arthur Miller's stint before HUAC:

> Citizens were expected to enlist in the Cold War. Neutrality was suspect, and so was a lack of enthusiasm for defining American society as beleaguered. Near the end of Arthur Miller's testimony before HUAC a congressman [Clyde Doyle of California] asked him to help make literature engagé. "Why do you not direct some of that magnificent ability you have to fighting against well-known Communist subversive conspiracies in our country and in the world?"[25]

Miller's experience demonstrates that refusing to create hyper-patriotic and avowedly anticommunist art in the early 1950s was tantamount to embracing political perversion. In this context, art that refused to assert any clear political ideology ended up making a blatant political statement through its attempted disengagement.

In *The Culture of Spontaneity: Improvisation and the Arts in Postwar America*, Daniel Belgrad links the work of several groups of artists—the abstract expressionists, the beat poets, and bebop musicians—who did this very thing through various improvisatory forms. He writes:

> Spontaneity's challenge to the existing social order was founded on a belief in the value of the unconscious mind as the locus of possibilities denied legitimacy within the prevailing ideology. Writers, artists, and musicians, hoped the spontaneous work of art might serve as a communication from the "open" realm of the unconscious to the ideologically restricted world of consciousness.[26]

Though Belgrad excludes the theatre world from his study, the Living Theatre's work in this period is entirely in step with the movement he describes.[27] Malina's explanation of what had attracted her to *Doctor Faustus Lights the Lights* mirrors Belgrad's tenets of spontaneity:

> The Living Theatre's model at the beginning . . . was the energy that came out of the Parisian and European post-war poetry and theatre. That still had the energy of being a resistance Theatre, like Picasso's *Desire Caught by the*

Tail, which really embodies the spirit of the artists living in Paris in dire straights under the occupation, with an artistic resistance that hardly ever speaks of politics, though it touches it here and there, but hardly ever uses a political word.[28]

Malina's emphasis on a kind of unharnessed energy that manages not to fall prey to propagandistic depictions of politics while still engaging with political impulses perfectly harmonizes with Belgrad's description of the alternative aesthetic culture of the 1950s.

Most of Stein's work, including the 1938 *Doctor Faustus Lights the Lights,* predates the official beginning of World War II. Furthermore, Stein did not spend World War II in Paris participating in the Resistance or Resistance theatre; she was hiding out in the French countryside, likely protected by a high-ranking member of the Vichy government.[29] Nevertheless, the aesthetic described by Malina and Belgrad is also congruent with Stein's artistic principles that privileged the present-tense interaction of sight and sound over narrative. Central to Stein's dramatic theory is the possibility for the spectator to reacquire perceptual skills (in the avant-garde echoing of Hammett that I discussed earlier). In the context of the early 1950s, this process had much political potential as it offered the spectator the opportunity to see dominant social messages anew and to imagine alternative constructs both personally and politically.

The Living Theatre's staging of *Doctor Faustus Lights the Lights* attempted to realize the potential of these theoretical principles. An examination of several key elements of the performance text—the desire for actor/audience interaction, set and costume elements designed to evoke a poeticized and otherworldly feel, and the ambient music—reveals that Malina and Beck's use of abstraction and their attempt to preserve the open spaces in Stein's text was culturally and politically subversive in the context of the early 1950s as it sought to create a community of persons with full access to perceptual freedoms.

One of the Living Theatre's tactics for freeing the audience members' perceptions was by realigning his/her relationship to other audience members and to the actors on stage. This sentiment was reflected in an essay printed on the first page of the program. In "Vanguard and Theatre," Paul Goodman wrote:

> The life of art is in general a lonely one; one writes it as he must, makes his own rules, goes his own way. And of course the creation of art in our times is lonelier and more eccentric still; we are what they call "alienated." But what are we trying to prove, we "aliens"? We are trying to prove that our way of looking at it, doing it, is precisely yours, only you don't recognize it; that our

language is the more elementary language; our feelings the simpler (even childlike) feelings. We stubbornly belong to your community tho [*sic*] you often seem not to like that. But now, in the theatre, we suddenly find that we have a community indeed . . . . And in our days, when people seem so very alienated from one another, so lacking in community (tho [*sic*] there is the devil's plenty of uniformity), my chief aim an artist is—that we suddenly meet—in this theatre—to our mutual surprise.[30]

As described by Goodman, the vanguard, which he implies the Living Theatre is leading, had the goal of forging a community of people committed to seeing the world differently and then sharing these insights with each other.

The desire of the Living Theatre to forge a sense of community was aided by the physical layout of the Cherry Lane Theatre in 1951. Ground plans of the theatre in the Living Theatre's papers show an intimate space. The seating capacity was limited to 220 people. The audience sat in two banks of fourteen rows, divided by a four-foot center aisle. They all faced the equally intimate 18′ by 12′ playing space.[31]

It is likely that some of the people present for the Living Theatre's inaugural production already had communal bonds. This event was open to the public, unlike their unofficial first production held in Malina and Beck's apartment for which Beck hand-designed each invitation,[32] but as John Tytell writes, "the play was produced for the coterie of underground artists who would appreciate it despite its murky labyrinthine mood."[33] Malina and Beck were part of a community of New York alternative artists—including Larry Rivers, Merce Cunningham, John Cage, and William Carlos Williams. Though there are no extant records of who did attend the full run of the show, it is certain that at least Williams was there because he wrote a letter published in the *New York Times* expressing his admiration for the Living Theatre's project. There are also records of who had tickets for opening night. Among those illustrious guests were Carl Van Vechten, Lincoln Kirstein, Vernon Rice, Harold Clurman, Eric Bentley, Alfred Kreymborg, Uta Hagen, Hume Cronyn, Virgil Thomson, John Cage, Merce Cunningham, Aimee Scheff, and Audrey Hepburn.[34]

Malina tried to import the para-aesthetic sense of community the audience likely felt into the aesthetic realm in order to turn it back out once again. In his unpublished dissertation, *The Living Theatre: Alive and Committed*, Jack Wright observes, "In each of the five productions [of the 1951–52 season] an attempt was made to involve the audience in the action of the play and to seek greater participation. Actors approached audience members . . . in an effort to force members into some kind of activity."[35]

When the audience member is participating in "some kind of activity" rather than sitting passively, accepting the images presented by the artist without discernible signs of struggle, she or he refuses to allow the culture machine to control her or his thoughts and perceptions. The individual audience member is encouraged to participate actively, presumably in the construction of the performance environment and in the production of meaning. While the audience member performs these tasks however, she or he is not simply affecting her or his own perception of the production, but that of other audience members and the actors as well. The audience member's individual participation has a communal effect and works toward building a kind of artistic community. Equally important was the fact that active participation in the service of community building meant that audience members did not just passively accept the theatrical process the artists were pedalling. In short, the textual space became communal space for active audience interaction. This sort of active communal space was in direct opposition to the spatial division that would characterize 1950s suburban life: the ranch-style house, with its garage, basement, and fenced off backyard built on a cul-de-sac forced isolation from urban threats and from other suburban dwellers.[36] The Living Theatre's method offered a powerful, if small-scale, alternative to the geography of mass culture.

It is worth noting that while Malina and Beck were imagining new kinds of audience activity and participation, they had not yet conceived of nor implemented a new structure for the actor's process. Among the Living Theatre's papers in the Billie Rose Theatre Collection is a rehearsal and production schedule. These documents show that Beck completed his plans for the setting on September 5 and executed this design on November 16. He completed his costume designs on September 28. Meanwhile Malina had finished her directing book by September 29. Rehearsals began in late October with five nights of table work prior to a read through on stage on November 5. After that the company began a series of blocking rehearsals, before run-throughs and "perfects." Eventually music was added on November 17 and closed dress rehearsals preceded previews on November 30 and December 1. The show opened December 2. Clearly this was a textbook production process without the kinds of innovation or possibilities for actor participation for which the group would be famous later in their history.

Several components of Malina's performance text demanded active audience participation in the sense that much cognitive input was required to make sense and meaning out of them. As the Living Theatre put it in one of their publicity letters describing their aesthetic practice in general and the production of *Doctor Faustus Lights the Lights* in particular, "The staging of the play naturally tends toward the abstract."[37] Abstract visual elements of the production included the set, lighting design, costumes, and movement of the actors. The aural portions of the performance text were also abstract. In addition to Stein's poetic language, the live music playing constantly throughout the performance also forced audience members into active communion with the performance text if they wanted to generate meaning. Within the spaces of the performance text, Malina and Beck offered audience members the opportunity to rehearse strategies of active and imaginative engagement that could be taken with them outside the theatre in order to resist the temptation to consume passively propagandistic and ideological messages.

The set Julian Beck designed also required active and imaginative audience engagement. Its most dramatic element was a towering wall broken into a conglomeration of long, thin, rectangular panels framed by untreated wood. Some of the frames contained empty spaces into which actors could step and pose high above the stage floor. Other panels were curtained; in the spaces of others, thick ropes drooped. Still others were slathered with thick strokes of paint and plaster reminiscent of another artist of spontaneity, Jackson Pollock. In front of the paneled set piece stood a small, four-tiered riser. Other than that, the set provided unobstructed space in which the actors could move. Though Beck's set provided a variety of playing areas at a variety of physical levels, it offered no indication of a specific locale, thus leaving this aspect of the performance open to the individual audience member's imaginative contribution. Faustus's study and the wild wood in which the viper bites Marguerite Ida and Helena Annabel had to be constructed by the individual viewer if she or he wished to experience them.

In one of the company's several publicity letters for the production, Beck's set and its relationship to the production was clarified:

> Every aspect of the production has been worked out to complement the presentation of the play as a picture of man's mind and thoughts. This has been the element most emphasized in the direction and the designs. The setting consists of a structure composed of raw materials . . . .Its object is to imply a mechanical structure akin to a brain (without mimicking a brain) and to underline the solid and basic language that Miss Stein used as a medium. The glass, wood, etc. represent the materials composing the cells of a mind and the flashing lights represent the rhythms of thoughts.[38]

The lighting design, heavily reliant on strobes, generated a sense of disorientation when viewed in concert with the abstract set. The Living Theatre's publicity letters for the production also described the relationship among the text, set and lights as follows:

> The text of the play calls of intricate interpretation and Miss Stein gives free rein to her directors and designers by omitting most stage directions and all scenic description. This is at once a challenge and a pleasure. *Doctor Faustus Lights the Lights* calls for novel and complex effects in lighting and integration of motion picture projection with the dramatic action. There will be a ballet of lights which will be executed in part by an abstract film in color.[39]

As the reviewer for the *New York Times* put it, "The set, consisting largely of flashing lights, suggests a gigantic angry pin ball machine (tilted)."[40] Another reviewer, Aimee Scheff of *Theatre Arts*, thought the set "was designed to express the structure of Faustus's brain." These critics' comments affirm that the lighting and set of the production in no way suggested a realistic or historically identifiable location. Instead the set, and the lighting that further distorted it, seemed more akin to Faust's brain or Stein's fissured text than any conventional place.

Black-and-white photographs of the actors taken by Carl Van Vechten document Julian Beck's costume design in concert with Beck's own rough pencil sketches of the costumes, which indicate basic color choices. The photographs of Doctor Faustus and Mr. Viper are representative of the others and clearly indicated that Beck aimed at poetic abstraction as directly with his costume design as he did with his set design. Doctor Faustus, played by Donald Marye, was dressed in a short, dark grey velvet tunic, belted at the waist with a white sash. Over the tunic he wore a long, loose grey velvet robe. The left sleeve was cuffed with a band of white. Some photographs also show Faustus with big, asymmetrical patches of white sewn onto the skirt of the tunic. His tights are also grey. In some of the photos, simple, dark grey Chinese slippers complete the costume. In other he wears more elaborate slippers with long, curling toes.

Mr. Viper, played by Remy Charlip, who also choreographed the show, had two main costume pieces: a black, short-sleeved, boat-necked shirt, and black pants. The shirt had an asymmetrical hem that came to a point in the back and was adorned with snake-like coils of pale rope on the left sleeve and back as well as big triangular patches of a dark emerald, satiny material that suggested fangs. The pants were also decorated and asymmetrical. The right leg was torn in a triangular shape at mid-calf, while the left side was tucked into a black stocking. The right leg was decorated with more triangular patches, while the left side featured a piece of rope that wrapped down and around the entire length of Charlip's leg before slithering back up again.

Conventionally, costumes provide narrative details about the characters who wear them such as the historical period in which they live and their economic and social status. Beck elected to provide none of this information through his design. Instead the luxurious textures and shapes of the costumes served largely to enhance the poetic impact of the tableaux struck by the actors. A production still used in the publicity materials to promote the show (and published in *Theatre Arts Magazine*) reveals this imagistic use of the actors' costumed bodies. In this image, Doctor Faustus stands on the bottom step of the riser. His head and torso are held in profile as he stares off into the distance. His left hand rests on top of the riser with his wrist cocked at a severe angle that forces his shoulder out of square alignment. His left foot extends behind him, bent at a ninety-degree angle at the knee, while his right foot shoots diagonally off the riser. This nonnaturalistic pose gives little narrative suggestion. The viewer does not, for example, have the impression that Faustus is engaged in any kind of particular activity like pouring over his books looking for either the secret to inventing electric light or instructions for summonsing the devil. Since narrative is unavailable for making sense of the image, the viewer has to use her imagination to cull meaning from the geometrical accumulation of cues. Through the distorted planes of the actor's body, something like a fragmented and tortured self pulled in multiple directions begins to emerge. Meanwhile, King Moody's Mephisto insinuates his body into one of the open frames in the set, leering down on Faustus. His right hip, leg, and forearm (bent and held at shoulder height) touch the interior of the frame's right edge while his left foot is turned out at the ankle and his left hand reaches out of the frame. Like Faustus, Mephisto does not seem to be *doing* anything. Nevertheless, the off-kilter pose suggests a brazenness and a refusal to be contained within the confines of the dimension Mephisto is supposed to inhabit, while the height from which he looks down at Faustus clearly conveys his superior power.

The musical elements of the production were equally unconventional. Though *Doctor Faustus Lights the Lights* is generally called a libretto, no music was written for it in 1951. Lord Gerald Berners, who had written the score for Stein's play, *A Wedding Bouquet. Their Wills*, which became the ballet, *A Wedding Bouquet*, had agreed to write the music for *Doctor Faustus Lights the Lights*. In 1939, however, Berners found himself overwhelmed by a case of writer's block that he blamed on the war. Though the war eventually ended, his motivation to work on the Stein piece never returned. Since there was no score, Malina initially believed she would have total control over the production's aural environment. She reports in her diaries that she was very anxious to have John Cage—one of Belgrad's exemplary spontaneous artists—work on her music, but Carl Van Vechten, who held the production rights to Stein's work, refused to approve of Cage and forced her to use little-known composer Richard Banks instead. Malina quotes Van Vechten in her diary saying disdainfully of Cage, "He'd probably score it all with drums."[41] What she ended up with instead were two oboes (played by Gloria Glass and Terry Feldman) and a piano (played by Alicia Khan) that produced atonal music constantly through the performance while the actors spoke, rather than sang, their lines.

Though the aural elements of *Doctor Faustus Lights the Lights* might not have been as spontaneous as they would have been had Cage been in charge, they were hardly what one usually expects of opera. They bore very little resemblance, for example, to what New York audiences would hear just four months later in the revival of Stein's more famous opera, *Four Saints in Three Acts*, under the guidance of that opera's composer Virgil Thomson. Like the set and costumes, the music added neither references to contemporary culture nor narrative information to help close the gaps in Stein's libretto.

The sum of the various abstract elements composing the performance text did not add up to a unified artwork. Instead they remained isolated and abstract poetic fragments that required active reassembly on the part of the viewer. As such, Malina seemed to refuse a portion of conventional directorial authority. Pieces of the performance text were left unsynthesized in order to allow the spectator to participate in the creation of theatrical meaning. This dispersal of creative authority and responsibility gave the audience a new sense of control over the forging of ideas. Once they tasted this power inside the theatre, perhaps they also began to hunger for it more intensely outside the theatre, refusing to follow blindly the demands of dominant Cold War ideology.

While Malina and Beck tried to avoid the obvious cultural connections between *Doctor Faustus Lights the Lights* and contemporary political and popular culture, they nevertheless staged, within the jimmied-open spaces of the libretto, another often-overlooked aspect of early 1950s culture through their emulation of Stein's theatrical aesthetic. Implicit in their production choices were the shared tenets of a subculture of spontaneity held by avant-garde artists from a variety of disciplines. The ideas given visual and aural form in *Doctor Faustus Lights the Lights* were characteristic of an alternative code of American conduct for those seeking exile from mainstream American Cold War culture. In this context, the open textual spaces of the performance text do not seem neutral or empty. Instead they seem forcefully crafted by a particular subculture embroiled in conflict with the mass culture of the day.

THE JUDSON POETS' *IN CIRCLES*

Like Judith Malina, Lawrence Kornfeld and Al Carmines chose not to fill the gaps in *In Circles* with overt references to contemporary culture in their 1967–8 Judson Poets Theatre production. Though *A Circular Play, A Play in Circles*, written in 1922, is one the most hermetic of Stein's plays to make it to the stage, they did not try to coddle the audience by letting the production devolve into a straightforward meditation on the escalation of the Vietnam war, the contentious presidential election, a widening generation gap, or the continuing struggle for civil rights, even though it would not have been especially difficult to do so given the exceptionally open structure of the play and the exceptional upheaval in the political and social realms at the time. Nevertheless, the Judson Poets clearly captured the imagination of, and as the reviews of the production indicate, spoke to, the cultural concerns of audiences of the day. The history of the show's run and its critical acclaim tell part of the story: *In Circles* played first off-off Broadway at the Judson Church, off-Broadway at the Cherry Lane (the first home of the Living Theatre), and at a larger off-Broadway venue, the Gramercy Arts Theatre. The production ran for 222 performances, the longest run of any work by Gertrude Stein staged in the twentieth century. Finally, *In Circles* won the Obie for best musical in 1968. The other part of the story is told by various elements of the performance text. As I analyze the set, costumes, organization of the script, method of rehearsal, and the music, I argue that, like the Living Theatre, the Judson Poets' nondirectly referential production choices staged the desire for both the individual's freedom from the ideological constraints of mass culture and for the creation of a utopian community through shared artistic and perceptual freedom. These choices provide another set of ethnographic miniatures, this time of late 1960s alternative culture.

Before turning to the performance text, I first briefly describe *A Circular Play, A Play in Circles* as it appears on the page. The first thing that one notices is that there are no character designations or stage directions—none of the conventional script devices are present.

The written text is not without structure, however. Rather than breaking the text into scenes or acts, Stein groups pieces of text under titles centered on the page. There are forty-six of these titles such as "First in a Circle," "Circle Hats," "Encircle," "Not a Circular Saw, "Leave a Circle," and "Circular Dancing," to name a few of the titles. The pieces of text that follow the titles are not of any uniform length—sometimes only a single line follows, sometimes an entire page, but each piece is a meditation on the title that immediately precedes it, contemplating what a circle might entail in this particular instance. Sometimes the circles refer to shapes of objects—like eyeglasses, wheels, plates, hats, and apples. Other times circles are formed by the mouth as it forms the sounds of "tobacco," "Morocco," and "tomorrow." Elsewhere circles seem to represent groups of people like religious affiliations—she mentions Catholics and Jews; nations—she mentions Indians, Chinese, Americans, and Africans; or more private affiliations—the name Alice, possibly referring to Alice B. Toklas, frequently appears during the course of the play, as in the following passage:

> A circlet of kisses.
> Can you kiss to see.
> Some see.
> Can you kiss me.
> I see.
> Can you hear of kissing me.
> Yes I see where you can be.
> Do I sound like Alice.[42]

This particular circular meditation combines two of the types of circles. Certainly there seems to be a private, domestic circle of affection between the speaker and another person. The kiss that the speaker discusses also provides another kind of circle—the literal shape that the lips make as the kiss is offered and delivered.

The dramatic action of *A Circular Play, A Play in Circles* consists not in an unfolding narrative, but in the viewer/reader's refining of perceptual skills. Often one circular meditation revisits an image, word, or sound from another circle, thereby linking two or even a series of the circles together. As the viewer/reader makes these connections, as she learns how to see, hear, and think outside of the confines of conventional narrative, she stages her own fascinating, personal drama.

Clearly, when Kornfeld, Carmines, and their team of artists approached Stein's text, there were many spaces for them to fill. They had virtually complete freedom in terms of devising a set, constructing characters and their costumes, constructing a scenario and blocking, and composing music. But rather than placing debilitating restrictions on the audience's imagination and perceptual possibilities, they kept many of these choices abstract, sharing with the audience the freedom that the text allowed by trying to preserve many of the spaces Stein created.

The set, designed by Roland Turner and Johnnie Jones, placed the action in some sort of garden. Black-and-white production stills indicate that the major set piece was a painted backdrop of a balcony overlooking a formal garden. Several reviewers found it reminiscent of Versailles, but the Matisse-inspired lush, flatness of the painting style took it out of the realm of the directly referential as far as other critics were concerned. Harold Clurman's appraisal of the setting as "fragrantly floral in the manner of a display for sweets"[43] is an example of such a reading.

Both readings were made possible, at least in part because, the stage, like Stein's text, had a great deal of open space and many indeterminate elements. Directly in front of the painted drop was a two-tiered riser and a fairly large platform, which provided one of the main acting spaces. Three more steps led down from the top platform to another platform largely occupied by the grand piano at which Al Carmines sat to provide musical accompaniment. Downstage of the piano was another substantial acting space provided by a slightly raised platform. Adorning each level of steps were pots of paper flowers and atop the piano, one photograph showed a set of tea cups and saucers. Michael Smith of the *Village Voice* described the net effect of the set: "Roland Turner's setting, oversize, overdecorated, elaborately clumsy, creates a context of decayed, impossible gentility and outrageously naive, touching pretensions to elegance and grandeur, nostalgic and inspired."[44]

Smith's comments about the setting speak more directly of the costumes, in my opinion, than the rather open set, because the costumes seemed to me to reflect the characters' somewhat misguided attempts at dressing up for an elegant garden party. George McGrath wore a patterned vest over a dark turtleneck and slacks. Elaine Summers wore an India-print floral tank top and belted wide-legged pants that came to the middle of her calves. Arlene Rothlein wore an above-the-knee, a-line, tiered, sleeveless mini-dress of shimmering lame and long leather boots. David Vaughn and Theo Barnes wore blazers and slacks with dark ties. Nancy Zala wore a white-ruffled poet's shirt with a deep v-neck and a long skirt. Arthur Williams wore a plaid dress shirt and dark slacks. Lynn Colton wore a floral print baby doll dress with a gathered peasant neck line and large bow in her hair. Lee Crespi wore a dark, long sleeve, loose dress. Al Carmines wore a black turtleneck and slacks and a large silver cross. No costume designer was listed for the production, suggesting that the clothing may have belonged to the performers.

The character descriptions printed in the program were nonsensical snippets from Stein's text, some of which also contributed to a pretense of gentility described by Smith. Examples include Arthur Williams, the citizen, who was "an innocent abroad" and Nancy Zala who played Lucy Armitage, "a lady of culture and understanding." Lee Crespi's Mable stood between the nonsensical and the gentile, described as "she serves tea and circles."[45]

The countrified gentility of the costumes, set, and some of the character descriptions was never made to appear genuine; there seemed to be considerable space between this facade and something not quite nameable underneath. The forthright falsity of these images forces one to contemplate what might be lurking behind the bucolic bliss. Though an answer never seemed to be articulated plainly, one possibility is the opposite of the happy country lifestyle—the reality of modern urban life. In *The Twentieth-Century American City*, Jon C. Teaford refers to the period 1964–79 as the "Age of Urban Crisis." Teaford reports that in 1966 twenty-one major riots and civil disorders occurred, while in 1967 the number jumped to eighty-three.[46] He also points out that while the middle class was fleeing for the supposed safe haven of suburbia, "by the late 1960s America's greatest cities seemed on the verge of breaking apart."[47]

The Judson Poets used the set, costumes, and character descriptions to encourage their audience see their own physical and social environments anew, whether they contemplated urban strife directly or not. A likely thematic after-effect of this enterprise would be the desire to reimagine the possibilities for communal interaction. Though this interest in redefining community has no particular corollary in Stein's dramatic theory, it certainly does in the way she lived her life. Stein left the mores of early-twentieth-century Baltimore behind her, settling instead in Bohemian Paris. There she reimagined the possibilities of what family life might mean, calling herself Alice B. Toklas's husband, and surrounding herself with a family of her own choosing through the artists and writers she invited into her salon at 27 Rue de Fleurus.

Evidence supporting the idea that Carmines was interested in emulating Stein's personal as well as aesthetic characteristics can be found in his appearance at the time of the production. As I sat in the New York Public Library pouring over the production stills of *In Circles*,[48] I was immediately struck by the strange physical similarity that Carmines bore to Stein, but I shrugged it off, thinking I had clearly been sitting in the library thinking about Gertrude Stein far too long. When I returned to the library the next day, I was pleased to discover that I was not the only one who had seen this curious resemblance. In an article on Carmines in *Cue*, Marilyn Stassio wrote:

> To begin with, Al Carmines looks like Gertrude Stein; that is he looks like Gertrude Stein would have looked if she had been a thirty-one year old minister who combed his hair over his ears; affected, with the judicious application of mascara the goggly-eyed air of a schizophrenic; and donned a delicate silver chain over his discreetly basic-black Army/Navy store sweater.[49]

The *New Yorker* reviewer, echoing Stassio's sentiment, observed that Carmines "looks just enough like Picasso's famous portrait of Gertrude Stein to get everything off to a great start."[50] Though Carmines was not officially playing Stein in this production, his character name was listed as "Dole" in the program, he did go on to play Stein in a later production—in 1989 he composed the music, played the piano, and represented the voice of Gertrude Stein in *The Making of Americans* directed by Lawrence Kornfeld at the Center Stage in Baltimore—suggesting that he was aware of and perhaps even cultivated this resemblance for his stage persona. Given his appearance and later performance of Stein, it seems that Carmines was interested in imagining himself as sharing a very personal sort of community with Stein and as setting himself up as an effigy of her on stage.

The interest in the changing nature of community was one of the themes reviewers gleaned from the spaces of the Judson performance text. In his extremely positive review of the production, Robert Pasolli of *The Village Voice* wrote the following:

> The production says in brief, that a circle is people connected by whatever decent means, a non-circle being people alone or dead. According to Miss Stein each person has his own circle, or sometimes does, but in this production that merely means that each person has a potential for connecting with others. *In Circles* makes this statement because Carmines' songs so frequently make a group sing out of a line or lines originally delivered by a single character. There are solos and arias to be sure, but they tend to evolve into duets and trios, and ultimately to a musical apotheosis in group chorus . . . . The essence of this production is the movement back and forth from individuation to collectivism.[51]

Unlike Passoli, some reviewers, like Dan Sullivan of the *New York Times*, Jerry Talmers from the *New York Post*, and Leota Diesel from the *Greenwich Villager* focused on the lack of conventional sense generated by Stein's words.[52] One of the freedoms that Stein's text provided Kornfeld and Carmines was the ability to dissociate words from their conventional meanings. Instead of relying on rules of grammar and dictionary definitions, they were able to capitalize on the spaces in Stein's text, constructing an alternate kind of sense through nonverbal means. Sullivan wrote:

> Mr. Kornfeld's actors make it clear that although what they are talking may be nonsense to us it is perfectly—sometimes appallingly—clear to them . . . . It works. By imposing an ever-moving and ever-interesting pattern of feeling on Miss Stein's apparent nonsense, Mr. Kornfeld gives the play shape and even an unspoken moral: that the words we use in talking to each other are

almost ludicrously dependent on gesture and tone of voice for their emotional significance.[53]

Passoli's interpretation of the production is actually related to Sullivan's despite the fact that they reached different conclusions. Both reviewers used gesture, blocking, and in Passoli's case nonverbal vocal communication to arrive at their readings of *In Circles*. Stein's words, in the hands of the Judson cast, did not serve the function that words ordinarily do. The cast made the words appear to have meaning, yet they preserved a sense of the textual space by developing an alternative, nonnarrative system of communication. As such, audience members were also given the freedom to explore other methods of communication and interpretation, one route, as the Living Theatre's production of Stein suggested, to finding a new kind of community.

This drive to use Stein's textual spaces to find freedom from rules and socially sanctioned systems of behavior was also present in the rehearsal strategies used by Kornfeld and Carmines. In an interview with Allan Wallach, Carmines described the preparation for the show:

> We did *In Circles* much the same way [as we did *What Happened*] except it was ten pages this time of lines [instead of five]; no characters, no stage directions, no act divisions. . . . We asked ten people who we felt were creative, musical, and imaginative—not simply good actors and actresses, but people who we felt were very imaginative, creative people—and we worked for two weeks every night, sitting in the living room of my apartment simply going through the lines. I would occasionally say, "Aaah, that should be set to music." The actors picked out their lines themselves at that time and gradually we put the play together in that way.[54]

Carmines described a very collaborative rehearsal strategy. Rather than dictating all aspects of their performance to the actors, Carmines and Kornfeld seemed to be looking for people capable of making a significant contribution to the shape of the production. Most innovative in this regard, is the collaborative scripting of the piece and the actors' freedom to choose the lines they wanted to speak. Just as Stein chose not to dictate the structure of the performance to directors, these directors chose not to dictate the structure of the performance to their actors. Creative space was shared. This method of production, in addition to representing a break from typical rehearsal strategies and director–actor relationships, also circles back to the interest in developing new forms of community. The collaborative preproduction work seemed to engender a different, more egalitarian, kind of artistic community.

That the attention of artists was occupied in finding ways to express freedom from rules and canons is precisely what one would expect from the mid-1960s. As Dominick Cavallo observed in *A Fiction of the Past: The Sixties in American History*, the Vietnam war "prompted a legion of young people either to 'drop out' of society altogether and join the counterculture or display their alienation from mainstream America by selectively adopting elements of the hippie lifestyle."[55] The artists working on the Judson production transformed the larger cultural impulse of establishment questioning into an aesthetic one without having to refer directly to factors driving their desire for change. Gertrude Stein, and her texts that forced those who encountered them to reject conventional modes of understanding and seek instead to perceive and experience anew, were perfect vehicles for this project.

The music Carmines composed for *In Circles* emphasized the importance of the everyday, or non-extraordinary, and reveled in a kind of playfulness. Though these tendencies also did not reference specific cultural events, they nevertheless seem to be born of the period and its unrest. When the world seems to be in a state of extraordinary chaos, one response is to seek relief by turning to things more comforting and familiar. Carmines created a richly varied musical sampler, borrowing from diverse sources ranging from the popular to the classical, thereby giving virtually every listener something recognizable. Reviewers described the astonishing variety in his music: "Carmines's brilliant songs . . . leap nimbly from fugues to rounds to tangos to waltzes, do-si-dos, gypsy airs and chorales";[56] "The songs vary from popular numbers and blues to gospel songs and Moonlight Sonata-ish Beethoven";[57] "Influences of Verdi, Bizet, barbershop quartet, Weill, ragtime, spirituals and obviously all that jazz float around in his music with happy unconcern about being influential";[58] "Mr. Carmines's potluck score, a little this-a, a little that-a, [is] part Palace Theayter, part Old-Fashioned Revival Hour."[59]

Carmines's positioning of popular music alongside the music of high culture suggests a valorization of everyday sound and an interest in ordinary life as well as extraordinary, aestheticized life. The spirit in which he made these combinations and presented them to the audience—the *New York Post* reviewer describes him seated "with cigar . . . rippling out that marvelous music which he has cheerfully incorporated from everywhere"[60]—also suggests playfulness. This playfulness is yet another avenue of escape from society's most pressing concerns.

Carmines's composition can be read as a kind of open, multivalent musical equivalent to the Living Theatre's abstract, disjunctive performance text. The playful conglomeration of popular sounds and "high art" sounds—such as Beethoven, Verdi, and Liszt—were all stripped of their autonomy as they became small pieces of an altogether less sacred work and became dependent on the relationships they shared with other snippets of music. Even within the music, there was a new kind of community.

Carmines's playfulness and interest in the everyday are characteristics also found in Stein's writing. In his preface to *Geography and Plays*, Sherwood Anderson praised Stein's willingness to "go live among the little housekeeping words, the swaggering bullying streetcorner words the honest working, money saving words, and all the other forgotten and neglected citizens of the sacred and half forgotten city."[61] Stein puts these everyday, "little housekeeping words" together with gleeful abandon, unexpectedly juxtaposing disparate ideas and reveling in sound unfettered by grammar or conventional sense. Carmines's composition exploits these qualities, inviting the listener into a world at once familiar and also bursting with the promise of perceptual play. Such qualities were no doubt extremely appealing in the turbulent context of 1967–8.

CONCLUSION

In "Celebrity and the Semiotics of Acting," Michael Quinn argued that when a famous star is cast in a particular role, we inevitably see elements of his or her off-camera exploits and traits infiltrating and reshaping the scripted character.[62] Try as they might, film icons from Charlie Chaplin to Tom Cruise, will never fully disappear into the roles they play. Their reputations become a sign for the audience to read and interpret. The audience's image of "the real" Tom Cruise—so reliably gleaned from the tabloids, interviews, and previous film roles he has played—rewrites and reshoots the movies in which he stars, for better or for worse. In the case of Gertrude Stein's plays as they were produced at mid-century, it was not the renown of the actors playing the parts that augmented the written text, filling its spaces and absences, so much as it was the fame, selected tastes, and philosophy of Stein herself that affected what audiences saw produced on stage.

The Living Theatre and the Judson Poets both emulated and improvised on particular aspects of Stein's image and/or her aesthetic theory and techniques in order to steal perceptual, political, and artistic freedom from dominant mid-century American culture. The particular choices composing these performance texts thus provide the mementos for remembering an alternative culture, in a self-imposed exile from (and inevitable dialogue with) mass culture, and ironically enough, significant aspects of their culturally omnivorous role model as well.

In chapter 4, which explores two very different productions of *The Mother of Us All*, I continue to be interested in the ways that the elements of the performance text reflect a struggle to define American culture's terrain. The artistic strategies of the artists who staged Stein's libretto at The Santa Fe Opera and the Glimmerglass Opera were once again selective in the ways they remembered Stein, but they used a very different strategy than the artists at the Living Theatre and Judson Poets—they consciously sought to bring contemporary culture into the production, either to overwhelm aspects of Stein's text that did not serve their purpose or to put her text into dialogue with recent political and social events.

4. Pop Parades and Surreal Pageants: Staging National Identity and the Struggle for Women's Rights in *The Mother of Us All* ⌦

In the interlude between Acts I and II of *The Mother of Us All*, Susan B. sings to Anne, "When this you see remember me."[1] The Santa Fe Opera and the Glimmerglass Opera, in 1976 and 1998 respectively, were, like the Living Theatre and Judson Poets Theatre before them, quite discriminating when they remembered Gertrude Stein. When the Santa Fe Opera and the Glimmerglass Opera mounted Stein's libretto about Susan B. Anthony, they were highly selective as they pictured Stein's relationship to the themes of American patriotism and feminism that the opera invokes.

In 1976, Stein's self-casting as an American patriot still played uncontested, but from the perspective of the early twenty-first century, that image no longer remains unassailable. If the artists and audiences of the bicentennial *The Mother of Us All* at the Santa Fe Opera had read Stein's World War II writings in the way scholars do today, a Stein text might never have been chosen for a bicentennial celebration. The complexities of Stein's relationship to feminism, well outlined by summer 1998 when the Glimmerglass staged *The Mother of Us All*, are equally problematic. While Stein's writing in general, and *The Mother of Us All* in particular, can be read as having feminist concerns or employing feminist authorial strategies, it is difficult to say the same unequivocally of Stein's relationship with Alice B. Toklas. Knowingly or unknowingly, the producers of the 1976 and 1998 versions of *The Mother of Us All* were rather choosy about which aspects of Stein they elected to stage alongside her text.

AMERICAN CONTRADICTIONS: GERTRUDE STEIN'S PATRIOTISM AND FEMINISM

In the last years of her life, Stein was quite aggressive in using her writing to market an image of herself as patriotically American. Examples abound in *Paris, France* and *The Mother of Us All*, but *Wars I Have Seen* seems particularly designed to promote the Americanophile Stein. Near the end of the work, she writes of the changes she had observed between the American soldiers of World War I and those of World War II:

> When I was in America in '34 they asked me if I did not find Americans changed. I said no what could they change to, just to become more American. No I said I could have gone to school with any of them. But all the same yes that is what they have changed to they have become more American all American, and the G.I. Joes show it and know it. God bless them.[2]

Stein would be hard-pressed to create a more flag-waving self-portrait. Burnishing this image was the story of how *Wars I Have Seen* reached the American readership. The advertisement for the book in *Publisher's Weekly* proclaimed, "this entire book was written in longhand under the very noses of the Nazis. After they were driven out of France, Alice Toklas typed the manuscript and Frank Gervasi, who moved in with General Patch's Seventh U.S. Army, brought it back with him to America."[3] With the tale's aid, Stein's work figures as a boldly patriotic act.

Recent scholarly work has blurred this carefully constructed image. Most notably, Wanda Van Dusen's 1996 article, "Portrait of National Fetish: Gertrude Stein's 'Introduction to the Speeches of Marechal Petain' (1942)," suggested evidence for Stein's support of the Vichy government indelibly marks her unpublished introduction to Petain's speeches. Van Dusen reports that Bennett Cerf, the editor at Random House to whom Stein sent her introduction, wrote across the top of the manuscript, "For the records. This disgusting piece was mailed from Belley on Jan. 19, 1942."[4] So startling were Van Dusen's revelations that *The Chronicle of Higher Education* reported on them in "A Study Shows that Gertrude Stein Backed the Vichy Government During World War II." *The New Yorker* published a related exposé for their more mainstream audience in June 2003 by Janet Malcolm, titled "Gertrude Stein's War: The Years in Occupied France" in which Stein's relationship with Nazi collaborator Bernard Faÿ was chronicled.

The work of Van Dusen and Malcolm was not available to the producers of the 1976 *Mother of Us All*. Perhaps if it had been, a work by Stein would not have been selected for a bicentennial celebration. But the fact remains that the signs Van Dusen and Malcolm interpreted in their analyses did exist quite plainly in her writings and letters; it was only that Stein's marketing of herself as an American patriot had been so compelling, that no one had chosen to question it for fifty years. Stein's performance of herself, and the American public's willing acceptance of it, allowed the Santa Fe Opera production to proceed unhindered.

The central issue in comparing perceptions of Stein to the staging of the Glimmerglass *The Mother of Us All* is Stein's feminism. Over the years, many critics have analyzed the feminist aspects of Stein's work,[5] and it is fairly common to identify Stein as the "mother" of twentieth-century female experimental writing.[6] But labeling Stein the great feminist literary mother is somewhat awkward since Stein herself frequently shunned the feminine, preferring to characterize herself as masculine instead.

Perhaps one of the most volatile scenes for investigating this performance is Stein's relationship with Alice Toklas, in which she played the husband to Toklas's wife. An anecdote Stein records about her stay in America in 1934 sets the scene. In *Everybody's Autobiography*, she writes about a photographer who wanted to design a photographic layout consisting of four or five images of her "doing anything:"

> All right I said what do you want me to do. Why he said there is your airplane bag suppose you unpack it, oh I said Miss Toklas always does that oh no I could not do that, well he said there is the telephone suppose you telephone well I said yes but I never do Miss Toklas always does that, well he said what can you do, well I said I can put my hat on and take my hat off and I can put my coat on and I can take it off and I like water I can drink a glass of water all right he said do that so I did that and he photographed while I did that.[7]

Behind the humorous façade of the story lies a clear image of the division of labor in the Stein/Toklas household. It was Stein's job to take literature into the twentieth century; it was Toklas's job to make sure Stein's every need— cooking, cleaning, typing, unpacking, telephoning—was accommodated along the way. While Stein assumed the traditionally masculine prerogative of blazing a trail across the literary and cultural landscape, Toklas's role in the domestic landscape looked much like the one that women had played for their husbands for centuries. Even an acknowledgment of Toklas's power in the relationship—she was hardly a retiring figure or one without considerable influence over Stein privately—fails to rewrite another traditional model of female domestic behavior.[8]

As Lisa Walker observes in *Looking Like What You Are: Sexual Style, Race, and Lesbian Identity*, "As an experimental writer with a distinctly masculine persona, especially in her relationship with Alice B. Toklas, Stein produces conflict for some of her most dedicated and sophisticated readers. . . . Readers have both pathologized Stein's masculine persona and excused it as the anachronistic coping mechanism of a lesbian writer in the early twentieth century."[9] Walker notes that while Catherine Stimpson reads Stein's adoption of the masculine as a limit on her imagination and emblematic of some of her other unsavory views on subjects like race and class, Marianne DeKoven thinks this same strategy may have enabled her to assume the power of creation otherwise limited in the sexist society of the first decades of the twentieth century. Walker goes on to suggest that an understanding of butch/femme relationships as comprising specifically lesbian identities is crucial to avoiding these kinds of single-faceted readings.

It is, then, more discerning to read the Stein-as-husband, Toklas-as-wife scenario as Walker does: as a butch/femme performance, because this constellation of roles reflects a lesbian rather than a heterosexual orientation. The butch and the femme do not, Walker reminds her reader, have to restage heterosexual patterns uncritically, though ultimately she finds that Stein's "investment in occupying the dominant position of the masculine" seems to have disarmed her performance of its ironic and revolutionary potential.

In sum, Stein and her image demand to be read in their heterogeneity. While she was an iconoclastic writer, achieving what few female writers had before her, she also adopted a specifically masculine persona (seemingly free of ironic nudges and winks that might have challenged masculine imperatives) as she reached her revolutionary goals. In her life with Alice, she seems to have enjoyed the privileges that have traditionally gone along with masculinity. Her place on stage—quite literally as there is a character in the libretto named G. S.—next to Susan B. Anthony, particularly in a version of the opera seeking to celebrate feminist history alongside the sesquicentennial of the Seneca Falls Convention, is far more complicated than it might first appear.

STEIN'S VERSION OF *THE MOTHER OF US ALL*

The patriotic, image-constructing agenda of *The Mother of Us All* required that the text be more approachable than Stein's hermetic plays of the 1910s and 1920s. And while *The Mother of Us All* is a more accessible text than much of her earlier work, she was able to maintain many of her finest authorial techniques in somewhat modified form.

Stein began the process of writing *The Mother of Us All* in 1945 when she and composer Virgil Thomson received one of Columbia University's

Ditson Fund commissions to create a new opera at the University's theatre. Stein and Thomson agreed that the opera should have a nineteenth-century setting, and then it was left up to Stein to settle upon the precise subject, so long Thomson said, as she did not attempt to write an opera about Abraham Lincoln. Stein contemplated treating the impeachment trial of Andrew Johnson, as seen through the eyes of journalist Georges Clemenceau, before she decided to write an opera about Susan B. Anthony and her struggle to win the vote for women.

Anthony was not the only historical figure that Stein chose to write into her opera. As Anthony's nemesis, Stein selected Daniel Webster, a senator from Massachusetts who spoke out against women's rights and who also opposed the abolitionist cause. Other historical figures that Stein chose as characters were President Andrew Johnson; Anthony Comstock, a Christian moralist who attempted to censor literature; Thaddeus Stevens, an Abolitionist; President John Quincy Adams; President Ulysses S. Grant; actress Lillian Russell; and various friends of Stein's including Constance Fletcher, Donald Gallup, Joseph Barry (Jo the Loiterer in the libretto), and Virgil Thomson (V. T. in the libretto). There is also a character called G. S., but she is an invention of Thomson's, not Stein's. Stein died of cancer in 1946 before Thomson finished his score. The bereft Thomson took the liberty of adding the G. S. character as a companion for V. T. (whom Stein had at one time deleted when she had a disagreement with Thomson). In the completed version of the opera, G. S. and V. T. act as masters of ceremonies, in some sense paralleling the Commere and Compere of the earlier highly successful Stein/Thomson collaboration, *Four Saints in Three Acts*.

While a cast of characters with well-known historical counterparts is distinctly more conventional than Stein's early plays in which there are absolutely no characters designated at all, one must also note that these are hardly intimately rendered psychological portraits. Instead the characters are more like bright, vivid flashes of historical color. Further, the historical figures that these characters represent did not all live at the same time. For example, even though lifetimes of Webster and Anthony overlap, their years in the public sphere were parts of different generations. Stein takes quite generous liberties with chronology in bringing her diverse cast of characters together. In this sense, the characters function like the words in Stein's earlier plays: torn from grammatical contexts and conventional usage, they take on new and different meanings. In bringing all the characters into a singular dramatic time, Stein crumples the trajectory of linear chronological time in a manner akin to her Cubist counterparts in the visual arts. Pieces of history, seen from unfamiliar angles, are juxtaposed with other bits of historical color in order to call into question standard patriarchal notions of historical development. Such a strategy, in its clear parallels with collage, necessarily involves gaps and fissures rather than seamless linear organization. Stein leaves spaces in her text into which the reader can paste her own historical moment as points of further comparison.

The fact that these characters have lines directly assigned to them is also a departure from Stein's early work where there is no division of lines since there are no characters. Stein even took some of the lines that she assigns to her characters from the pages of history. Portions of Anthony's lines come directly from her address to The Daughters of Temperance, her first public speech, given in 1849, while others allude to a speech she made to the Washington Convention of the National American Suffrage Association, given in 1896.[10] Likewise, she takes portions of Webster's speeches directly from an 1830 debate with Senator Hayne from South Carolina.[11] Though line divisions are absent in her early compositions, Stein's appropriation of preexisting material is a strategy that she used in these more abstract works. In the early plays, Stein inserted snippets of nursery rhymes, bits of jingles, clichéd phrases or other familiar sayings into her punning abstractions in order to play with the reader's ear, making the familiar unfamiliar and vice versa. This linguistic play was a way of encouraging the reader to abandon familiar modes of perception, inadequate to Stein's peculiar dramatic situations, and seek more adventurous ones. In the context of *The Mother of Us All* this technique seems to have become directed toward a more specific goal. Stein uses Webster's actual political rhetoric to show the nonsense of his message. When the Webster character delivers a fragment of the historical Webster's actual speech lifted from the original context— "Mr. President I shall enter no encomium upon Massachusetts she need none. There she is behold and judge her yourselves"—his words seem only slightly more logical than the increasingly blind Constance Fletcher's musings—"I do and I do not declare that roses and wreaths, wreaths and roses around and around, blind as a bat, curled as a hat and a plume, be mine when I die."

Anthony's lines, some which also come directly from the words of the historical Anthony, seem to have a different purpose. In the crazy quilt that is the libretto, Anthony's words seem the most logical and are the center around which the themes of the work cohere. In a speech delivered in Act 2, Anthony says, "Ladies there is no neutral position for us to assume, If we say we love the cause and then sit down at our ease, surely does our action speak the lie."[12] The lines surrounding her speech are little more than a jumble of sounds, but Anthony's words make profound sense. By placing her speech and its attendant message in the midst of linguistic confusion, they stand out all the more strongly as the voice of reason.

The Mother of Us All also contains something verging on a plot: Anthony struggles and eventually fails to enfranchise women. After her death, the Anthony memorialized in statue form learns that women eventually attained her dream. The way Stein has Anthony get to know the obstacles in her path toward securing the vote for women is, however, much like the way she had her reader make acquaintance with one of the early plotless plays. The reader knows the text only in pieces, as verbal and aural images float before her. It is then the reader's task to sift through these pieces, arriving at her own perceptions, rather than aimlessly following the trail of an author's predetermined and flowing narrative. Likewise Anthony knows her predicament in flashes, as she watches what women sacrifice to marriage in the wedding of Indiana Elliot, as she sees John Adams doggedly court Constance Fletcher, as she observes the beautiful Lillian Russell parade around the stage, and as she talks to an African American man, for whose rights Anthony once campaigned, about why he is willing to deny his wife the right to vote, preferring to keep it only for himself.

Though the play has characters, lines drawn from the pages of history, and even a semblance of a plot, there are still many forms of provocative absence into which the reader must place her own experiences and perceptions if she wants to construct a coherent image of the text. The spaces Stein left her reader are more sculpted, and with this shaping comes more direction from Stein about what to be thinking in regard to the issues of marriage, equality, and power. The reader is invited to imagine her own struggle for the right to create her own life as she wants, to cast the deciding vote in her own destiny (be it political or theatrical), and to remember the people who both stood in her way and who supported her in her own revolutionary campaign for self-determination.

THE MOTHER OF US ALL AT THE SANTA FE OPERA—1976

In his biography of Virgil Thomson, Anthony Tommasini notes that "the year of Thomson's eightieth birthday, 1976, also the American bicentennial, saw a flurry of productions of that most American of operas, *The Mother of Us All*."[13] Beyond simply feting Thomson, the 1976 productions, and the Santa Fe staging in particular, which Tommasini designated "the most prominent,"[14] were considered part of the celebration of the nation's two-hundredth birthday. This choice of operas is not surprising if one focuses on Thomson's music, but if one concentrates on the words of Gertrude Stein's libretto, these enterprises begin to look riddled with contradictions. One might hope that the Santa Fe Opera was in fact attempting to stage the complexities that imbued bicentennial celebrations—that a nation still reeling from the disasters of Watergate and Vietnam was at the very least skeptical about what it could and ought to be celebrating in 1976—and discovered an opera that metaphorically embodied cynical contradiction in the dissonance between its hyper-patriotic score and its feminist libretto. The visual portions of the performance text, however, force one to rethink this proposition. The Santa Fe Opera production, due in large measure to the visual elements of set and costume design created by Pop artist Robert Indiana working in tandem with Thomson's music, concealed the subversive potential of Stein's words and ideas.

Before looking at the aural and visual details constructing the performance text on the Santa Fe Opera stage, I would first like to explore the tensions that colored bicentennial celebrations in general. Bicentennial celebrations were an occasion for constructing cultural memory. Marita Sturken explains that cultural memory is "a means through which definitions of the nation and Americanness are simultaneously established, questioned, and refigured"[15] and that "Forgetting is a necessary component in the construction of memory. Yet the forgetting of the past in a culture is often highly organized and strategic."[16]

According to cultural historian John Bodnar, the key issue that organizers of bicentennial celebrations were trying to help the nation forget was the very possibility of revolutionary activity:

> Basically and implicitly the ARBA [the American Revolution Bicentennial Administration] treated the American Revolution as the end of history. That is to say that it was not celebrated because it demonstrated that people could engage in radical social and political change whenever they so desired, but it was commemorated because it had produced a nation and a political system that deserved citizen support in the past, present, and future. John Warner [the president of the ARBA] said as much in a letter to the *New York Times* in 1976 when he asserted that America would "honor the great men who forged and then steered a nation so strong and so flexible that one revolution has proved enough."[17]

Bodnar goes on to suggest that John Warner's ARBA had a precise strategy for facilitating this large-scale process of forgetting: it sought to deflate the revolutionary zeal buoying ethnic, racial, and gender-based factions by actively seeking out the participation of these groups in controlled forms.

Lyn Spillman reads the actions of the ARBA in a similar light, finding that the ARBA encouraged diverse participation and that ultimately "many groups were active in the celebrations: they created rituals and reflections on national identity which responded to or were attached to the framework created by central groups."[18] The Santa Fe Opera's effort to celebrate the bicentennial with *The Mother of Us All* fit this model. The Santa Fe Opera joined in the national celebration by staging the "most American of operas." The company jubilantly proclaimed in a press release, "Happy Birthday, America! The Santa Fe Opera's Bicentennial salute will be the production of *The Mother of Us All*." The press release went on to promise a "star-spangled production" and boasted the production's "all American cast." At the time of the production, British conductor Raymond Leppard had recently immigrated to the United States. He was quoted in another press release as saying, "I like America enough to come and live here . . . . My decision to emigrate was a contributory reason for doing *The Mother of Us All*," suggesting that the opera has the power to reinforce feelings of natural(ized) Americanness. The only major contributor to the construction of the performance text who did not join in the flag waving was British director Peter Wood. In his *Autochronology*, Robert Indiana quoted Wood as saying, "Were it not for us, you wouldn't be celebrating anything."[19] Not surprisingly, Wood's quip was left out of the Santa Fe promotional materials.

The themes and ideas in Stein's libretto both were and were not ideologically congruent with the ideals of the bicentennial celebration. The nineteenth-century setting was one of the aspects of the production that blended easily with the parameters of the event. In his program notes for the Santa Fe Opera production, Thomson explained why he was taken with the period and why, when he was approached by Douglas Moore of Columbia University to write an opera, he was drawn to the nineteenth century and why he felt compelled to persuade Stein of the value of the undertaking. He said the nineteenth century was

> A time rare in history, when great issues were debated in great language. . . . Historical changes of the utmost gravity were argued in noble prose by Webster, Clay, and Calhoun in the Senate, by Beecher and Emerson in the pulpit, by Douglas and Lincoln on the political platform. These issues, burning issues after the Missouri Compromise of 1820, dealt with political, economic, racial, and sexual equality. And the changes advocated were embodied in the Constitution, all except woman suffrage, by 1870. In fifty years the United States ceased to be an eighteenth-century country and became a twentieth-century one.[20]

Thomson's comments suggest that the nineteenth century was the period in which ideas of civic enfranchisement were expanded significantly in the United States—that the freedoms that century offered were something to celebrate in conjunction with the colonists' freedom from Great Britain.

As an advocate of voting freedom for both women and African Americans, Susan B. Anthony, the opera's central character, might seem the perfect figure on whose shoulders to place the burden of representing American patriotism since she was a defender of individual liberty. In fact, Anthony seems to bear a great resemblance to the notion of the effigy as described by Joseph Roach. In *Cities of the Dead*, he writes that effigy, when used as a verb, "means to evoke an absence, to body something forth, especially something from a distant past . . . . It fills by means of surrogation a vacancy created by the absence of an original."[21] Though there is no single "authentic" patriot on whom to pin the psychological needs of a country damaged by war and scandal in 1976, Anthony, as depicted in the opera, was nevertheless drafted for the task. But as Roach notes of such surrogations, "The fit cannot be exact. The intended substitute either cannot fulfill expectations, creating a deficit, or actually exceeds them, created a surplus."[22] An interesting historical fact not mentioned in the libretto, and a way that Anthony exceeded the ideological needs of the kind of patriotism promoted by celebration organizers in 1976, was the fact that she and four other women disrupted the centennial celebration in Philadelphia. After *The Declaration of Independence* was read, the women delivered a copy of *The Declaration of Rights for Women* to the vice president, scattered copies of the *Declaration* in the aisles, and then read it aloud to the crowd.[23] Ironically this was the very sort of citizen participation the ARBA was hoping to avoid in 1976. This obscure bit of history may well have been something remembered by audience members as Karen De Crow, president of NOW, reread this same speech only a month earlier at a protest/celebration in Philadelphia.

Another way that the Anthony of Stein's text exceeded the nation's (as defined by the conservative ARBA) needs for patriotism in 1976 was in her position on marriage. In her analysis of *The Mother of Us All*, Jane Bowers notes that Stein's Anthony was much more radically opposed to men and marriage than the historical Anthony. This historical Anthony believed that the answer to women's freedom could be found in the vote; Stein believed that the vote was not a sufficient guarantee of women's civic and social liberties and put this sentiment into the mouth of her character.[24]

Virgil Thomson's music, written after Stein's libretto and ostensibly for the purpose of supporting the libretto, actually served to widen the breach between what Stein's words seem to mean on the page and what they come to represent in the context of performance. Thomson said of his score:

> The music of *The Mother of Us All* is an evocation of nineteenth-century America, its gospel hymns and cocky marches, its sentimental ballads, waltzes, darnfool ditties, and intoned sermons . . . . It is a memory book, a

souvenir of all those sounds and kinds of tunes that were once the music of rural America and that are still the basic idiom of our country, the oldest vernacular that is still remembered and used.[25]

Though the found quality of popular songs and hymns aligned nicely with Stein's borrowing of actual historical speeches of Anthony and Webster, Thomson's invocation of the vernacular and his claim that the nostalgic tunes he used in composing the score are "the basic idiom of our country" and therefore are the basic idiom of the people, calls to mind Homi Bhabha's comments in *Nation and Narration*. He finds that the people and their stories exist in the complicated time of a static moment shored up by past historical events and an ever-unfolding present being reinvented through the constant gathering of stories. In this formulation the people both come into being through the nation and its stories and predate the nation and its stories.[26] The daily artifacts of life, including the aural artifacts of song, rhythm, and sound that were appropriated by Thomson, are implicated in this temporal duplicity. Thomson attempted to use vernacular sound that he deemed emblematic of the nation to mark out the space of the already existing ideal nation and then create, through the performance of these sounds, the nation in the shape of the bucolic, patriotic fantasy. The sounds and their cumbersome symbolic baggage both preexist the people, luring them into the promises of the nation, and are a product of the people, created by them to forge the promise of the nation.

The coerciveness of folk music and patriotic tunes in drawing people into a circle of identification of national unity was, I think, running contrary to what seems to be the agenda of the libretto as discernible on the page. When Bowers explicated the libretto's central theme, she suggested that Stein "dramatizes the conflict between a female's desire for power and authority and her sexual and emotional need to merge with a male other."[27] Thomson's music on the other hand, resolved any conflict the individual might feel about merging with the needs of the nation by suggesting she was always already part of that nation through her identification with and production of vernacular sound.

Robert Indiana and his Pop-inspired designs converted the strategy described by Bhabha (and translated into a musical idiom by Thomson) into a visual idiom (see photo 4.1). The gaps created by the tensions between Stein's text and Thomson's were largely filled by Indiana's painting style, with which Thomson's music is more ideologically aligned. Indiana said, "I've known Virgil's work most of my life . . . but it was in 1964 that I realized that every one of my paintings dealt with a theme that was related to Virgil's music."[28]

Photo 4.1   The Santa Fe Opera's *The Mother of Us All* (photograph © Ken Howard)

The theme that Indiana and Thomson shared was a kind of folk-inspired American-ness. Like Thomson, and Pop artists in general, Indiana appropriated the "scraps, patches, and rags" of everyday American consumer life. His early "herms," reminiscent of the ancient Greek burial totems called "hermes," were made from discarded rafters and painted with the Gothic and Roman lettering stencils he found left behind outside his loft on Coenties Slip. The signs that he saw in the neighborhood as well as those seen during a childhood spent traveling the highways of the Midwest were also a major influence. Indiana, in fact, refers to himself as "an American painter of signs." His flat, bright colors, sharp geometric forms, and reliance on numbers and words of no more than five letters attest to the appropriateness of his self-proclamation.

A key argument in the criticism of Pop is whether, in borrowing images from consumer culture and techniques from billboard and sign painting as well as other forms of advertising, Pop is critiquing American consumer values or applauding them. When he was interviewed by Donald Goodall in 1973, Indiana charted a progression in his work and attitude in his famous *American Dream* Series as follows:

> The first two or three dreams I would say were cynical. I was really being very critical of certain aspects of the American experience. "Dream" was used in an ironic sense. Then, as they progressed, they lost that irony.... And the dreams continue via the autobiographical series, negative aspects have pretty well disappeared. They really are all celebrations.[29]

Later in the course of this same interview, Indiana seemed to grow even less ambivalent about the American represented in his work. He said that his "mature output" could be predicted from a childhood crayon sketch of 1936 because it embodied the "Three C's": it was "commemorative, celebratory, and colorful."[30]

The same "Three C's" also characterize Indiana's vibrant set and costume designs for the Santa Fe Opera. The designs were highly commemorative, but not of revolutionary zeal. Instead the flat cartoon-like set pieces relied heavily on ultra-American symbolic vocabulary such as eagles, stars, and stripes, and architecture reminiscent of the nation's capitol or on images of rural bliss like horse-drawn wagons and honeysuckle-covered gazebos. Indiana seemed set on helping the nation remember both its pageantry and simplicity, but not its revolutionary beginnings.

One aspect of American culture that, like Pop art in general, Indiana seemed to be celebrating was consumerism. An element of Indiana's design that made this clear was the highlighting of the automobile. As fireworks burst open the New Mexico night sky at the top of the show, a vintage Model T pulled onto the stage, driven by the G. S. character. The mode of Gertrude's grand entrance was added by Indiana to the scenario and references a major motif in Pop art and American consumer culture.

Indiana's designs were also extremely colorful. Red, white, and blue drenched the set and costumes, punctuated by searing oranges, screaming yellows, and saccharine pinks. Stars, stripes, and plaids broke up the fields of matte color. These bright, highly saturated, colors are typical of Pop art—a movement that borrowed its hues from street signs and cartoon strips. The flatness and lack of gradation in the colors helped to remove the designs, and with them the characters, from the realm of the realistic. Rather than being imaged as verisimilar historical portraits, the figures gained the iconic quality of comic book heroes. This quality both raised the figures to the status of the mythic, a great aid in creating a national narrative, and made the more mundane sociological issues like marriage, gender equality, and civil rights that Stein was foregrounding seem out of place in the stage picture.

In the end, it was the concept of director Peter Wood that unified Thomson's music with Indiana's visual images in a way that thoroughly overwhelmed what seemed to be the concerns of the libretto on the page. A press release issued by the Santa Fe Opera said of Wood, "His staging concept of the opera which he feels is a 'stream of consciousness process' is a dramatized parade."[31] The concept was not lost on *New York Times* reviewer Peter G. Davis who referred to Indiana's set pieces as pageant "floats" and also noted that "Peter Wood's direction kept the stage pictures in constant motion"[32] a comment suggestive of a parade as Joseph Roach describes it.

He writes that in a parade, "Participants literally succeed themselves before the eyes of the spectators. As the sound of one band dies, another arrives to lift the spirits of the auditors. Generations of marchers seem to arise and pass away."[33] The concept of the parade, characterized by Roach as a form suggesting the perpetual regeneration of its participants, recalls Bhabha's comments about the performative, repetitive component of the people and the nation as constituted by narration. I would also suggest that the parade's marriage of Indiana's Pop imagery with Thomson's patriotic music also embodies the other half of Bhabha's equation. This particular version of the parade was also "continuist" and "accumulative" in its invocation and perpetuation of highly nostalgic (yet carefully selected) cultural forms to celebrate the birth of the nation.

Stein's loosely structured libretto left room for her reader to fill the gaps in the text with the stuff of her own choosing—she offered her reader the opportunity to construct a plan of resistance to the social domination of women in tandem with Susan B. Anthony's battle. In the case of the 1976 Santa Fe Opera production however, Stein's plan was thoroughly subverted by the relentless parade of the patriotic score and scenography that celebrated instead the fiction of a unified nation.

THE GLIMMERGLASS OPERA RE-CREATES
THE MOTHER OF US ALL—1998

Like the producers of the Santa Fe Opera performance text, the Glimmerglass Opera producers were interested in celebrating the Americanness of Thomson's score, but this impulse was coupled with artistic choices that put Stein's work into conversation with contemporary developments in the struggle for women's rights stirred in part by the sesquicentennial of the Seneca Falls Convention, which was celebrated the same weekend the opera opened (see photo 4.2). Unlike the Santa Fe production, which seemed to attempt to defuse any revolutionary potential in Stein's text, the Glimmerglass production seemed to try, through the references to issues connected to the Seneca Falls sesquicentennial, to reveal and extend the subversive qualities in Stein's libretto, thereby exacerbating the dissonance created by the meeting of Stein's work and Thomson's.

In her grant proposal to the National Endowment for the Arts, Associate Director of Development Joan Dessens noted the Glimmerglass's continuing commitment to the staging of a "series of revivals of works which vividly imagine American culture."[34] Dessens also suggested that the Glimmerglass project "gives new life to a true American masterpiece."[35]

Photo 4.2 Left to right: Tracy Saliefendic (Gertrude S.), Joanna Johnston (Susan B. Anthony), Ruthann Manley (Anne). © 1998 George Mott/Glimmerglass Opera

The goals of examining and animating American culture were supported by the geographical and cultural context of Cooperstown, New York. Nestled in the scenic Catskill Mountains, Cooperstown and its mere 2,200 residents seem to exist in blissful, bucolic time warp. Home to the National Baseball Hall of Fame, the James Fenimore Cooper House, and the Farmers' Museum as well as the Glimmerglass Opera, Cooperstown is a veritable repository for Americana in its most picturesque and idealized form. This rustic fantasy world and the opera company centered in it exert a powerful force: according to the company's public relations research, 51 percent of audiences travel more than two-and-a-half hours to attend a performance.

Though the elements of Americana in the opera may have dominated the producing agency's attention (at least while they sought financial support for the production) and the sociocultural context of Cooperstown formed a multidimensional para-aesthetic backdrop to the performance, several of the choices made regarding the aesthetic elements with the performance text seemed more specifically oriented to problematizing the idealized images of Americana conveyed by Thomson's music. Through an exploration of the continuing struggle for women's rights, producers of the performance text reminded the audience that only certain segments of the population have had, and still have, full access to the American dreams of freedom and self-determination. Such a reading of the performance text becomes particularly appealing because the Glimmerglass production coincided with the sesquicentennial of the Seneca Falls Convention, opening the same weekend that this milestone was being observed. The Seneca Falls Convention of 1848 began the public and organized struggle for women's voting and other human rights in the United States. Though Susan B. Anthony was not actually in attendance at this meeting (she was in Canajoharie, New York teaching at the time and not yet involved in the women's movement), the issues discussed there formed the backbone of her life's work. And while the promotional materials from the Glimmerglass Opera note an awareness of the sesquicentennial and not a focus on it, its chronological and geographical proximity make it available for intertextual consideration with the performance text.

Though the Seneca Falls sesquicentennial was hardly marked by the scale of celebration that an event like the American Bicentennial enjoyed, it was an event that occupied the attention of many people in the upstate New York region and one that drew many national luminaries including First Lady Hillary Rodham Clinton, Secretary of State Madeleine Albright, poet Maya Angelou, astronaut Shannon Lucid, and *now* President Patricia Ireland. Though reviews of the production carried in extra-regional newspapers such as *USA Today*, *The Village Voice*, and *The Kansas City Star* declined to mention the sesquicentennial as an influential factor in the creation of the performance text, local newspapers such as *The Ithaca Journal, The Rochester City Newspaper,* and *The Gloversville, New York Leader-Herald* saw the intersection of the two events as significant.

Before examining particular elements of the Glimmerglass Opera performance text that seemed to be engaged in a dialogue with the significant issues at the sesquicentennial celebration of the Seneca Falls Convention, I highlight some of the major moments in the struggle for women's rights that marked the 150 years leading up to this event. I suggest that while it was women's suffrage that concerned the delegates to the original Seneca Falls Convention and Anthony herself once she became involved in the movement, it was the battle over the Equal Rights Amendment (ERA) that haunted the last quarter century preceding the Glimmerglass production of *The Mother of Us All.* It is that issue that has become the contemporary analogue to the suffrage campaign and gives added resonance to many of the artistic choices in the Glimmerglass production.

In 1923, shortly after women received the right to vote with the passage of the nineteenth amendment to the Constitution in 1920, the first ERA was introduced in Congress. Though this attempt at an ERA did not make it to the Senate floor for a vote, its successor, introduced in 1946 (the year Stein finished her libretto on Anthony) won a simple majority, but did not gain the required two-thirds support to move the issue on to the states. When an ERA was again introduced in 1972, it did win the two-thirds vote and was sent to the states for ratification. Though six states voiced their support for the ERA within one week, by 1982, the year by which the ERA had to gain acceptance, only thirty-five of the thirty-eight states required for ratification of the new amendment had agreed. Though significant moves toward reinstating legislative debate of the ERA were nonexistent in the next sixteen years, according to *American Bar Association Journal* writer Debra Baker, 1998 marked a significant turning point:

> For the first time since the defeat of the federal ERA in 1982, two states—Iowa and Florida—passed amendments to include women in their state constitutions. In Missouri the general assembly debated passage of the federal ERA. And legislation calling for the ratification of the federal ERA was introduced in Illinois and Virginia, though no action was taken in either state.[36]

Once again, Baker goes on to suggest, the ERA was becoming a hot political issue. This resurgence of interest in an ERA is not unlike the changing tides of opinion and energy in regard to women's suffrage. Since the battle for female suffrage lasted multiple generations before it was ultimately won, perhaps the ERA can be viewed, particularly in light of the legislative events of 1998, as a contemporary analogue to the struggle for female suffrage.

Two kinds of virtual ERAs were in fact part of the Seneca Falls sesquicentennial festivities. *The Buffalo News* reported that one aspect of Forum 98, the part of the celebration held at Hobart and William Smith Colleges that united various politicians, academics, business leaders, and others to draft a document called a "declaration of principles and a call for action" that was then presented to a larger group of women at a public meeting, called for Congress to pass a National Women's Equality Act "that wants legislative guarantees of equity in education, employment, family responsibilities, taxation, health care, the justice system, and access to the media"[37] and "the Senate to ratify the United Nations 1979 Convention to Eliminate All Forms of Discrimination Against Women." Though these documents are not the same as the ERA, they certainly have similar goals.

If one views the Seneca Fall Convention celebration and the renewed interest in the ERA at both state and national levels as related and influential factors in the creation of the Glimmerglass performance text, then one also has to acknowledge that this production participated in the creation of cultural memory, which as Marita Sturken writes, "is a field of cultural negotiation through which different stories vie for a place in history."[38] The struggle for female suffrage is re-remembered as one that is vital, potent, and far from over as it is being restaged in the fight for an ERA; its story looks like one that deserves a significant place in history and in contemporary consciousness. Anthony also emerges as a cultural surrogate. She is figured as an anachronistic and passionate protector of contemporary women's rights in a variety of arenas.

Several elements of the Glimmerglass performance text, the surreal set and lighting design, the characterization of Susan B. Anthony, and the overt inclusion of homosexuality as a motivating factor in several of the principal characters' physical behavior, all can be read as creating a kind of dissonance with the patriotic score and the idyllic locale in which the performance was staged. At the same time, these choices reflected issues involved in the renewed struggle for the ERA, thereby recharging the subversive qualities in Stein's text. A fourth and final notable aesthetic choice in the Glimmerglass staging, a modernization of the pageant form, worked toward co-opting the celebration and animation of Americana for service in the campaign to update the written text, transforming it into a meditation on the continuing struggle for the ERA.

The setting, designed by Allen Moyer, had two distinct areas. The one first visible to the audience was Susan B. Anthony's study. Stage right was a cluttered writing desk topped with two towering stacks of books that stretched to the height of the proscenium arch under which Anthony sat. Stage left was a wood-burning stove with an almost equally tall chimney beside which sat Anne, Anthony's companion, in a parlor chair knitting a red scarf. Enveloping these set pieces were disproportionately tall walls that seemed to extend beyond the proscenium arch. Near the top of the upstage wall were two shutters that opened so that the actors playing G. S. and V. T. could watch Susan and Anne in the study from a dizzying height. The study walls, clad in horrifying red, white, and blue tapestry wallpaper, called to mind the yellow wallpaper of Charlotte Perkins Gillman's novella chronicling the spiral into insanity of a Victorian woman imprisoned in such a room. Maddening passions of Anthony's both for the speeches she wrote here and the love she had for Anne, also flared dangerously in this room, but for Anthony and for the audience, this private sphere merged with the public sphere when the walls of the study lifted to reveal the second area of the setting, a classroom or lecture hall.

Bedecked in red, white, and blue bunting and adorned with multitudinous tiny flags, framed black-and-white portraits of American presidents, six-foot-tall chalkboards on which character names were initially written and later on which G. S. wrote important words conveying themes from the opera such as "men afraid," and an enormous wooden lectern, the schoolroom would seem a relic from Robert Indiana's Pop-inspired designs for the Santa Fe Opera production of *The Mother of Us All* were it not for the skewed proportions provided by the too-small flags and too-large lectern and chalkboards. The distortion of the set elements (coupled with a logic-defying scene in the schoolroom involving giant snowmen not hinted at in the written text beyond mention that it is cold) gave the opera a very surreal physical environment.

Meanwhile the actors were clothed rather realistically, in costumes appropriate to the play's historical setting. In her review of the production for *The Independent Press of New Jersey*, Liz Keill reported, "Gabriel Berry, who designed the costumes, says she looked at the fashions of the time as versatile and risk-taking for women, while men kept to their same staid styles."[39] Thus it seems that the conventional dress of the period was imbued with a symbolic tone automatically. The palette for the period-inspired costumes was limited—to black, gray, red, white, and blue—but the general impression of the human figures when seen in close-up production stills is quite conventional. The actors simply look like participants in a well-funded and quite patriotic period drama. When the actors are seen in broader shots however, standing behind the enormous lectern or sitting at a desk topped with a twenty-foot stack of books, they seem to shrink down beyond the scale of realism.

Though the costumes rendered the characters in strokes of ordinary period detail, when they were placed within the distorted environment of the setting, they began to look shockingly unfamiliar as the logic and the reality of the stage images seemed to dissolve. Spectators were invited to abandon the confines of ordinary perception and the so-called reality it filters. Such a perceptual position would, at least theoretically, motivate spectators to want more than just imaginative freedom, but concrete social freedom, like equal rights for women as well. In this sense, creating a surreal atmosphere for the opera is a way of linking the aesthetic with the political.

The lighting of the figures within these settings also contributed to the surreal atmosphere. The stage was alternately awash in deeply saturated hues of fuchsia and violet, and rather starkly lit in a drab, gray-white light thanks to the design of Mark L. McCullough. More remarkable than the alternation of intense color with a near absence of color were the enormous shadows projected onto the walls of the set. The shadows worked in tandem with the skewed proportions of the set pieces to toy with the audience's perceptions of the figures on the stage. The shadows produced the sense that there were layers of action taking place, the one directly in front of the viewer, and a less immediately tangible layer behind it. The shadows urged the spectator to read the stage images allegorically and to seek deeper connection within those images.

Larry McGinn, the *Syracuse Post-Standard* reviewer, suggested that Moyer's classroom setting might be "a metaphor for educating all of the population."[40] I would suggest that McGinn's point might be refined. The classroom was a metaphor for educating the population, but more specifically it was a forum for educating the population about the struggle for women's rights. Further, the classroom setting was particularly appropriate for such a project because among the issues being debated at the original Seneca Falls Conventions and its sesquicentennial celebration were those pertaining to women's educational rights and several of the skirmishes that occurred between the ERA's defeat in 1982 and the staging of the opera had to do with education.

In 1848 in addition to women's suffrage, one of the prime issues on the minds of delegates to the Seneca Falls Convention was the right of women to "expanded educational opportunities . . . including higher education and professional training"[41] and this goal was prominent in the *Declaration of Rights and Sentiments* drafted at the convention. Though women's desire for equal educational opportunity was considered less radical than their demand for voting rights in 1848, the latter was granted in 1920 while the former was not gained until 1972 with the passage of *Title IX*, which outlawed gender discrimination in school programs and activities that receive federal funding.

Though *Title IX* was made law in 1972, the scope of the law was challenged in the succeeding decades. In 1984, after the ERA had been defeated, for example, the Supreme Court ruled in *Grove City College v. Bell* that *Title IX* "applied only to discrimination in admission and federally funded programs"[42] (not all educational situations, thereby keeping the focus of the law quite narrow. According to Baker it was Congress that corrected the court's ruling, forcing *Title IX* "to apply to all programs within a school that receives federal funding."[43]

A major ruling related to *Title IX*, which also dealt with women's right to equal educational opportunity, came in 1996 with *Virginia v. U.S.*, which forced the Virginia Military Institute to admit women. This ruling made it significantly more difficult for institutions to discriminate on the basis of gender. In *Reed v. Reed* (1971) and *Frontiero v. Richardson* (1973), the court had established that there had to be "a rational basis for laws that contained sex-based classifications."[44] This standard was raised by *Craig v. Borne* (1976) to what is known as the "intermediate scrutiny standard" when the court ruled that gender-based discrimination had to be "substantially related to the achievement of an important governmental interest."[45] The culmination of these related ruling then came with *Virginia v. U.S.* when, according to Baker, Justice Ruth Bader Ginsburg, author of the court's opinion, "heightened the immediate scrutiny standard, holding that sex-based classification requires an 'exceedingly persuasive justification.' "[46] When Ginsburg addressed the University of Virginia Law School graduates shortly after this ruling, she told them, "There in no practical difference between what has evolved and the ERA."[47] Though the official ERA failed, these various court cases deciding the limits of women's educational freedom have established a virtual ERA to protect women's rights in scholastic endeavors until another serious movement for a federal ERA is born. Thus, the Glimmerglass Opera's classroom setting is the perfect place to explore both the historical and contemporary struggles for women's rights.

A second notable feature of the Glimmerglass performance text and one that reflects an interest in the renewed struggle for the ERA is the characterization of Susan B. Anthony. Joanna Johnston, who played Anthony, and director Christopher Alden created a character who seemed not to belong in the world of an opera. Peter G. Davis reported in *New York Magazine* that:

> In most of the productions I've seen, Anthony is presented as a marbleized monument even before her singing statue is unveiled in the finale. Alden however, easily persuades us that she is a very complete, complex, and responsive woman, one who fearlessly tackles male adversaries, comforts the down-trodden, sees two side to everything, shows a delicious sense of humor,

is subject to bouts of self-doubt, and clearly enjoys the physical presence of her companion Anne. Looking startlingly like photographs of the real Susan B. Anthony, Joanna Johnston turned in a virtuoso acting performance, rightly dominating every scene in which she appeared.[48]

As Anthony, Johnston pounded her fists on the walls of the set and on the lectern, threw herself on the floor, as she was unable to sit primly at her desk while writing her speeches, and kissed Anne passionately on the lips. Rather than suggesting that Anthony is merely an iconic figure who belongs on the face of a coin as her work is done and her battle belong in the annals of history, this characterization made her struggles seem alive and immediate. Johnston's physically aggressive portrayal reinforced the idea that a battle is currently being waged and that it cannot be fought with delicacy and decorum. Johnston's characterization reveals that this struggle demands corporeal as well as intellectual commitment.

Johnston and Alden's approach to Anthony ran contrary to Thomson's. Musically, Thomson treats Anthony sympathetically as he does the rest of the characters. Thomson's biographer Anthony Tommasini explains,

> Moment after whimsical moment turns tender, taking listeners by surprise. When Susan B. complains, "Men are so conservative, so selfish, so boresome, and they are so ugly, and they are so gullible, anybody can convince them," she does this to pointed music in a minor mode. Suddenly her outburst seems all too justified and terribly sad.[49]

While Thomson does take Stein's Anthony seriously, he expected his music to be the shaping force in characterizations of her, and that directors and actors not interfere with the aural image he created of her. Evidence in support of this argument may be found in Thomson's approach to the actors and director who staged the first production of *The Mother of Us All* at Columbia University's Brander Matthews Theater in 1947. The man first tapped to direct the production, Milton Smith, withdrew from the production team after hearing the score and libretto, feeling overwhelmed by the unconventional opera and unsure how to stage it without major alterations. As Tommasini reports, Thomson was thrilled by Smith's absence because this meant he got to handpick a replacement—someone who shared his artistic views. His choice was John Tara, a director who worked with Lincoln Kirstein, a close associate of Thomson's. As Tommasini states, "As in *Four Saints*, his singers would be moved and placed, not directed, which was Thomson's preference."[50]

The Anthony created by Johnston and Alden did not conform to Thomson's ideal. Physically, Johnston took complete possession of the acting space, using all its resources—the floor, the walls, the air—as media from which she could craft her strong-willed character. As David Raymond of *The Rochester City Newspaper* commented, "Some of Susan B.'s movements seem a little *too* forceful for a Victorian lady."[51] Johnston's Anthony was so forceful in fact, that she even seemed to control the music and other actors at key moments. At the top of the opera, the music did not begin for several minutes. Anthony sat her desk, apparently stuck for an idea as she was trying to write a speech. When she seized upon it, and threw her whole body into the act of writing, only then did the music begin to unfurl. Later in the first act, as the suffragettes were frozen in a tableau at a rally, placards aloft and limbs sculpturally arranged, Anthony swept her arms over her head and the action recommenced.

Vocally Johnston's performance was perceived as being less than perfect. Peter Davis noted that, "the role lies too high for her voice, which spread, splintered and ran out of breath more often than not."[52] Larry McGinn observed that, "Johnston plays the suffragette with total commitment. Sometimes this passion pulls her enormous mezzo-soprano off pitch or causes the tone to spread unpleasantly at the top."[53] Though these vocal shortcomings were surely unintentional, as evidenced by the fact that Lauren Flanigan replaced Johnston when the production was transposed to the New York City Opera in March 2000, paradoxically they worked to make Johnston's performance all the more compelling from a theatrical and thematic standpoint. The emotions with which Johnston endowed Anthony were so potent that they interfered with her singing, at the same time shattering the image of Thomson's perfect musical Americana. As the music failed, perhaps so too did its ideology. The Glimmerglass Anthony was not "moved and placed" within the carefully contained environment of Thomson's musical creation, but was powerfully and richly acted to such an extent that it interfered with the music as it was written.

Anthony's passionate physical involvement with Anne as well as the suffrage movement was a clearly discernible element of the Glimmerglass performance text, and one that points to the third characteristic that relates to the 1990s struggle for ratification of the ERA. An issue that continues to fuel the fires of ERA opponents is the issue of same-sex marriage. Phyllis Schlafly, president of the conservative Eagle Forum and longtime opponent of the ERA is quoted by Baker as saying, "Abortion rights and gay marriage continue to be real concerns"[54] about the passage of an ERA. Baker also notes that the NOW Executive Vice President Kim Gandy said that her organization agreed to leave out issues of abortion rights and same-sex marriage in 1972, but that they would not be so reticent again: "People who oppose equal rights for women are going to believe those things are covered anyway . . . . We may as well have the issues in there and gain the support of a broader coalition."[55]

The issue of same-sex marriage in the renewed struggle for the ERA was paralleled in the Glimmerglass performance text's foregrounding of the difficulty of maintaining homosexual relationships in the public eye and the difficulties imposed on homosexual couples when heterosexual marriage is the enforced norm. In Act 2, Anthony and Anne sing:

> Susan B.: What is marriage, is marriage protection, or religion, is marriage renunciation or abundance, is marriage a stepping stone or an end. What is marriage.
> Anne: I will never marry . . . .
> Susan B.: I am not married and the reason why is that I have had to do what I have had to do, I have had to be what I have to be, I could never be two in one as married couples do and can, I am but one all one, one and all one, and so I have never been married to anyone.
> Anne: But I have been, I have been married to what you have been to that one.
> Susan B.: No no, no, you may be married to the past one, the one that is not the present one, the one, the one, the present one.

Because there are several other characters on stage at this moment, the other characters even have lines interrupting the passage as noted by the ellipses above, and because Stein's meaning in the passage is not entirely clear, the lines can be played in a variety of ways depending on the director's interpretation of Anthony and Anne's relationship. Alden had Anthony sing directly to Anne who looked crestfallen at Anthony's renunciation of marriage.

Despite the impossibility of marriage, Anne and Anthony touched, embraced, and kissed frequently. Anne also mirrored some of Anthony's gestures and blocking, as an emblem of the spiritual union between the two characters. After they kissed in Act 2, Anne wrapped the long red scarf she had been knitting around Anthony's shoulders, a coded sign of their affection that Anthony could carry with her into the public realm. When Anthony left the parlor to go out and deliver more speeches, Anne beat her fists against the parlor wall, splayed her arms across it, and slid down to the floor exactly as Anthony had done earlier. Anne was overwhelmed and frustrated by the fact that she had to sacrifice her own happiness for that of the suffrage cause.

The obstacles in the way of same-sex unions also appeared in the relationship between Jo the Loiterer and Chris the Citizen, who are, in Alden's interpretation of the libretto, male lovers split up by Jo's impending marriage to Indiana Elliot. In the libretto it is Elliot who struggles with the idea of marriage and particularly the business of taking a new surname, but as David Raymond observed, Alden

> Interprets the characters of Jo the Loiterer and Chris the Citizen as male lovers torn apart when Jo marries. The decision turns the characters from amusing minor figures to very dramatic ones, giving an extra emotional charge to Anthony's assertion that marriage is "rather horrible." There's nothing in the words or music to indicate this, and it may sound tacky and polemical on paper, but it works very well in this production.[56]

Alden made his interpretation clear, despite the lack of textual support for the reading, through his blocking choices. As two bare-chested men engaged in a snowball fight while the chorus sang that, "Naughty men, naughty men, they are always quarreling," Chris and Jo stood in a barely lit downstage corner locked in an embrace until they most reluctantly forced themselves apart.

A fourth characteristic of the Glimmerglass performance text is one that molds the producing agency's initial interest in the "Americanness" of the opera to fit the renewed interest in an ERA and the celebration of the Seneca Falls Convention. The directorial concept that linked the somewhat contradictory concerns surfacing in the Glimmerglass production was the historical pageant. In her requests for funding to both the NEA and the Virgil Thomson Foundation, Joan Dessens wrote, "We seek your help to enable us to do justice to this extraordinary pageant."[57] The idea of the pageant was also emphasized in the Glimmerglass's impressive audience education program called the Summer Seminar Weekend. Dr. Jenny Kalick, Chair of the Amherst College Music Department, and Dr. Robert Bezucha, Professor of History at Amherst College, conducted a session on historical pageants as part of the day-long program, "The History Behind the Opera: Susan B. Anthony and the Women of Seneca Falls."

The pageant was a particularly useful production metaphor given the various historical and cultural concerns that enveloped the 1998 performances. First, pageantry is directly linked to the Progressive Era, the period in which women finally did gain the right to vote, and the period in which the final scene of the libretto is set. Women assumed leadership roles in the production of pageants, many of which dealt with the suffrage issue.[58]

Formally and thematically, pageants are also commensurate with the performance of *The Mother of Us All* at the Glimmerglass. First, pageants aimed toward the epic. The production of Stein's libretto was considered epic in scope, at least by the producing agency faced with the task of orchestrating its staging. In her requests for funding, Dessens wrote,

"Thomson's work is a mammoth and expensive undertaking. It brings with it extraordinarily high royalties, . . . requires a huge cast, and any production of it must convey the sweep of American history and the forces involved on both sides in the struggle for women's suffrage."[59] In addition, pageants were not confined to proscenium arch theatres; instead their presentations were usually mounted in the open air. This tradition was mirrored in the Alice Busch Theatre of the Glimmerglass Opera: a 900-seat, open-air house. Furthermore, the figures in a pageant were usually tied to the community in which the work was being presented and/or significant figures in American history. Anthony was of particular interest to the New York State community at the time the opera was being staged. Though Anthony, as noted earlier, did not attend the original Seneca Falls Convention, she was nevertheless celebrated at the sesquicentennial with special tours going to Rochester to the Susan B. Anthony House and the world premiere of Ken Burns's documentary on Anthony and Elizabeth Cady Stanton, *Not for Ourselves Alone*, was screened as one of the main events on the sesquicentennial program. Dessens said the Glimmerglass production "would honor a great American" in both her grant proposals and noted in her proposal to the Thomson foundation that their production would come at a time "when national attention will be focused on the historical foundations of the Thomson/Stein opera."[60] Clearly the subject of the libretto, like the subjects of the pageants, comes from the pages of American history and was of interest to the community of people at least in the region, and perhaps in the nation.[61]

Perhaps most significantly, the ideological aims of the pageant, as described by David Glassberg in *American Historical Pageantry: The Uses of Tradition in the Early Twentieth Century*, align nicely with the artistic choices in the Glimmerglass performance text that seemed directed toward making connections between the nineteenth-century struggle for voting rights and the late-twentieth-century quest for an ERA. Glassberg writes:

> Another legacy of the era of pageantry is the conception, evidenced by the pageant-masters and their clients, of the role of public historical imagery in fostering a sense of connection between past and present, between locale and nation, as a springboard to a particular, if severely circumscribed vision of an ideal future.[62]

The pageant's drive to make connections between periods as well as connections between the local and the national was mirrored in the Glimmerglass staging choices that worked intertextually with the Seneca Falls Convention and renewed interest in the ERA. This similarity suggests that perhaps a goal of *The Mother of Us All* at the Glimmerglass, in a manner akin to the Progressive Era pageant, was to inspire audience members to take action in the current battles over women's rights. Instead of only allowing Anthony to function as a surrogate for modern-day political warriors on the stage, the audience member was also encouraged, through the pageant metaphor, to act as Anthony's surrogate in the world outside the theatre, struggling as aggressively in the political sphere as Joanna Johnston's Anthony did within the confines of the opera. While this process of surrogation is indisputably coercive, it seems related to the key concern manifested in Stein's libretto. Stein left room for the reader to fill the gaps in the text with the stuff of her own choosing. She gave her reader the opportunity to construct a plan of resistance to the social domination of women in tandem with Susan B. Anthony's battle.

CONCLUSION

The Santa Fe Opera and the Glimmerglass Opera created richly imaginative performance texts that both joined in and referenced celebrations that coincided with their productions. The celebrations and their attendant issues were not separate from the productions, but instead seemed to shape what was on the stage, thus filling the spaces in Stein's text. And since the productions became a part of the celebrations officially or unofficially, the productions and their images shaped the nature and message of the celebrations as well. Nevertheless, these celebrations might have been impossible had the producing artists known or acknowledged the multiple dimensions of Stein's persona evident in her World War II writings and the details of her domestic life with Alice B. Toklas.

The Santa Fe Opera and Glimmerglass Opera productions emphasize the fact that celebrations are highly selective ritual reflections. Essential to these rituals is the curbing of time—in an effort to hold the present and the future in check so that participants can make a nostalgic return to the past, repeating it and performing it, in highly discriminating ways. In order to meet a set of ideological needs, the architects of a celebration create an abstraction of the past, often disconnected from current and evolving ideas that might force them to reconceive the historical icons they venerate. Likewise the artists involved in the production of Stein's opera drew their images of Stein in broad strokes so that her memory could be integrated into the theatrical events without creating the kind of critical dissonance that might rewrite the celebration and its values. These performance celebrations prove that a crucial phase of constructing public cultural memory, about Gertrude Stein or otherwise, is strategic, ritualized forgetting.

In chapter 5, I continue to explore the ways that contemporary culture both shapes perceptions of Stein and infiltrates the spaces in her texts. Ideas about the importance of Stein's sexual orientation to her writing in the 1990s "outed" elements of her persona and her texts that she had kept closeted during her lifetime. These shifts in perception had a profound impact on the available range of meanings in two productions of her opera, *Doctor Faustus Lights the Lights,* and on a new work about Stein and adapted from her writings in several genres, *Gertrude and Alice: A Likeness in Loving.*

5. Coded Statements of Desire: Outing Meaning in Robert Wilson's *Doctor Faustus Lights the Lights*, the Wooster Group's *House/Lights*, and Anne Bogart's *Gertrude and Alice* ᴄ⌒

Before the subtext of lesbian desire in Gertrude Stein's plays and literary texts was decoded—and in some cases recoded—on American stages in the 1990s by Robert Wilson in *Doctor Faustus Lights the Lights*, Elizabeth LeCompte and the Wooster Group in *House/Lights*, and Anne Bogart in *Gertrude and Alice: A Likeness in Loving*, Stein staged her relationship with Alice B. Toklas in some carefully coded ways during their American tour in 1934–5. Like the stage performances in the 1990s, some people seemed able to read Stein's relationship with Toklas as they journeyed across the American landscape as erotic, lesbian, and for the time period, subversive, while others did not. Further, the code breaker's choice to embrace or shun the staged image or its sexually charged double was perceived as having significant consequences. Stein's tour performance of her sexuality is a crucial piece of the history of the highly selective ways she staged herself and the ways that others interpreted and remounted that performance as they brought her writings to life in the theatre. In this case, however, 1990s artists and critics chose to stage a side of Gertrude Stein counter to the one that she herself most publicly promoted.

DRESSING THE PART: GERTRUDE STEIN, MARY PICKFORD, AND CLOAKED LESBIANISM

A prime part of Stein's performance in America was her dress and hairstyle. The theatricality of her personal presentation was not lost on Toklas who wrote in *What is Remembered,* "I now prepared the costumes for Gertrude's voyage."[1] Stein reveals in *Everybody's Autobiography* that Alice's and her attire for the trip was all new and made for them in Belley.[2] That the two women decided against packing the clothing they usually wore in Paris is not surprising given the fact that it was Stein's first trip to the United States in thirty years and that she was returning as a conquering celebrity. Certainly many people buy new clothing to take on special trips. But the decision may suggest something more: that both women were planning to cast themselves and their relationship to each other in a way that they were not accustomed to doing in Paris.

Throughout her adult life in Paris, Stein had exhibited two tendencies in her personal style. Bravig Iambs, one the visitors to her Paris salon, described them as follows:

> There was never anything equivocal about Gertrude's hats; they were either excessively mannish, Napoleonic and severe, or of a dowdy, blousy, flower-bedecked femininity which was disconcerting to behold. The same tendency was marked in her dress. She could be very handsome, indeed, in austere brown monastic gowns—there was one made out of some Egyptian cloth that I liked very much, falling straight from the shoulder to foot and giving her the height she needed, for she was rather small in stature. But Gertrude also had a penchant for brightly colored cloths, bearing patterns of tiny flowers, and for blouses, both of which should have been forbidden, because they made her look dumpy and old.[3]

Joseph Allen Boone describes Stein (and Oscar Wilde) as "geniuses at commodifying larger-than-life images of themselves for general public consumption; in both cases, Wilde's and Stein's personae as celebrity artists with odd mannerisms and odder wardrobes encode the sexual difference they disguise as eccentricity."[4] But when he was analyzing eccentricity and encoded sexual difference, he was describing the monastic gowns that Stein did not wear in public on her tour of America. Photographs from the tour consistently show Stein dressed instead in the second style Iambs described: she looked quite matronly wearing longish tweed skirts and jackets, brocade vests, demure blouses topped with a brooch, and flat Mary Jane–style shoes. Her hats, like "the leopard skin cap from which she refused to be parted"[5] might have been slightly eccentric, but overall she cut a fairly subdued figure not demonstrating clear signs of her lifestyle or sexual preference.

The shape of her body within these clothes, as Catherine Stimpson has argued, further removed Stein from the image of the lesbian most popular in the 1930s. Stimpson writes, "A popular icon of the lesbian, which *The Well of Loneliness* codified—that of a slim, breastless creature who cropped her hair and wore sleek mannish clothes—did little to reinforce an association between the ample Stein and deviancy."[6] Stein's physical form served as a kind of sexual masking.

More revealing than Stein's tastes in dress was the way she chose to wear her hair—in the same style she had adopted since 1927, which was much like the cut Stimpson described earlier. While the bob had offered adventurously stylish women freedom from the hassles of long hair since 1910,[7] Stein took her hairstyle a step further. Impressed with the cut the Duchesse de Clermont-Tonnerre was sporting at the time, Stein asked Alice to give her the same haircut. Alice tells the story of the haircut as follows:

> That night Gertrude said to me, Cut off my braids. Which I agreed to do. The following day I spent gradually cutting it off because I did not know how you did it, and I got it shorter and shorter. The more I cut off, the better Gertrude liked it. Finally toward the end of the afternoon, it was done and the doorbell rang . . . . It was Sherwood Anderson and he said, giving Gertrude one look, You look like a monk. Later Gertrude forgot that she had ever had two long braids.[8]

As interesting as the anecdote of the haircut is in and of itself, what is perhaps more revealing is the place Toklas positioned the incident in constructing what was remembered of her life with Stein. The haircut incident immediately precedes Toklas's story of the preparations for the tour despite the fact that the event had taken place some seven years before. While Toklas had been able to design Gertrude's costumes very carefully, the monkish haircut was far more masculine than popular female coifs of the day. This may have been causing Toklas anxiety as their departure date drew nigh. While Stein's dress was carefully coded to reveal little about her sexuality and lifestyle, her haircut was much more susceptible to decoding information that the two women were not planning to reveal.

In addition to Stein's dress, a particular role was designed for Toklas on tour: rather than playing wife to Stein's husband as she did in Paris, Toklas was recast for the trip as Stein's secretary. Biographer Linda Wagner-Martin writes,

> Toklas's craft in playing secretary was superb; few people thought of her as other than Gertrude's secretary and maid. For the seven months of the tour,

Alice said nothing that would have given away the real situation—that she and Gertrude were a couple and that much of her own considerable ability had gone into making Stein successful. . . . For all the news coverage of Gertrude, very little mentioned Toklas. The media's failure to connect the women, even after the publication of the best-selling *Autobiography*, suggests that it, too, was sensitive to lesbian issues.[9]

While Wagner-Martin does a fine job of identifying Toklas's tour persona, I believe she misreads the reaction of the press. As Mark Goble noted in "Cameo Appearances: Or, When Gertrude Stein Checks into *Grand Hotel*," several headlines in newspapers and periodicals during the visit seemed to be trying to crack the coded signals about her relationship with Toklas, even in stories purporting to be about some other subject. B. F. Skinner's title for his article about Stein's connection to automatic writing in *The Atlantic*, "Has Gertrude Stein a Secret," provides a prime example.[10]

The consequences of cracking Stein's coded message about her sexuality were, according to Goble, significant for Mary Pickford. At the beginning of *Everybody's Autobiography*, Stein tells the story of meeting the actress in New York. Initially, Pickford, according to Stein, suggests that the two women be photographed together, but then reconsiders:

Mary Pickford said it would be easy to get the Journal photographer to come over, yes I will telephone said someone rushing off, yes I said it would be wonderful we might be taken shaking hands. You are not going to do it, said Belle Greene excitedly behind me, of course I am going to I said, nothing would please me better of course we are said I turning to Mary Pickford, Mary Pickford said perhaps I will not be able to stay and she began to back away, Oh yes you must I said I will not be long now, no no she said I think I had better not and she melted away. I knew you would not do it said Belle Greene behind me. And then I asked everyone because I was interested just what it was that went on inside Mary Pickford . . . . They all said that what she thought was if I were enthusiastic it meant that I thought it would do me more good than it would do her and so she melted away or others said perhaps after all it would not be good for her audience that we should be photographed together.[11]

While no one now knows for sure what made Pickford back away from Stein, Goble wonders "whether something about the sexuality of Stein's modernity contributes to Pickford's concerns that the association 'would not be good for her audience.' "[12] Goble's reading of the Pickford incident suggests that Pickford was able to decode Stein's performance and that she feared that her fans might prove equally skillful. Pickford's own carefully constructed persona as America's Sweetheart might begin to appear false when juxtaposed with Stein's persona, leading to serious professional and material consequences for Pickford.

The 1930s were not an easy time to be, or be perceived as, a lesbian in the United States. Despite an expanding lesbian subculture, as Lillian Faderman succinctly puts it in *Odd Girls and Twilight Lovers: A History of Lesbian Life in Twentieth-Century America*, "to live as a lesbian in the 1930s was not a choice for the fainthearted."[13] Faderman notes that the struggle a single woman would have supporting herself, the mounting hostility from the general public during the Depression toward women outside the traditional family structure (as they competed with men for jobs and further undermined shaky gender roles already threatened by economic instability as men had difficulty playing the part of the masculine "bread winner") and the dissemination of medical and psychological theories stressing the abnormality of physical love between women all made life difficult, if not outright dangerous, for lesbians.

Though these might not have been Pickford's concerns specifically, she was no doubt aware of Hollywood's effort to censor gay images on screen. As George Chauncey explains in *Gay New York: Gender, Urban Culture, and the Making of the Gay Male World, 1890–1940*,

> In response to the chaos created by the existence of a host of local censorship authorities, each with a somewhat different perspective on the boundaries of acceptable content, the Hollywood studios adopted a production code in 1930 designed to establish a single national standard for the production of morally unobjectionable films. The code allowed for the depiction of adultery, murder, and a host of other immoral practices, so long as they were shown to be wrong, but it prohibited any reference whatsoever to homosexuality, or "sex perversion," along with a handful of other immoral practices. The code initially had little affect on the studios, but in 1934, in response to the threat of a national boycott organized by the Catholic-led Legion for Decency, the studios established an independent Production Code Administration, which enforced the ban for another thirty years. After a generation in which films had depicted homosexuals and homosexually tinged situations, such images were prohibited altogether.[14]

Thus, by the time Pickford and Stein met, lesbian and homosexual celluloid images were being strictly policed.

A star of Pickford's stature would have been cognizant of the ways her offscreen activities might impact the interpretation and appreciation of her onscreen persona. The studios were adamant that stars stay completely closeted,[15] and while a photograph with Stein was not erotically compromising, the gossip it might generate could nevertheless be damaging to Pickford's image. As Edith Becker has noted, "Gossip feeds into audience expectation and interpretation. Long denigrated in our culture, gossip nevertheless serves a crucial purpose in the survival of subcultural identity within an oppressive society."[16] While Becker points out the positive power of gossip for cultivating a lesbian identity, the flip side of gossip's power for Pickford would have been that had a photograph with Stein led to innuendo about Pickford's sexual preferences, her currency as a mainstream screen icon might have been seriously devalued.

Pickford seemed to assume that despite Stein and Toklas's best efforts while traveling in America, the code of their lifestyle together could be cracked by some segments of the public, could alter the reading of her own carefully preserved image, and then could be passed on to the movie-going public through gossip.

THE CRITICAL CONTEXT SURROUNDING
1990s STAGE PERFORMANCES

Though Stein and Toklas quite clearly (though at times unsuccessfully) sought to conceal the subtext of their private life from a broad American audience while on tour in the mid-1930s, literary and dramatic critics in the 1990s often focused on Stein's lesbianism as a key to unlocking the subtext of her published work. This critical tendency suggested that lesbian desire is present in Stein's writing and is or can be made visible to the most competent of readers while the confusion of Stein's style created an elaborate ruse to mask the lesbian desire from unsympathetic eyes. If the artists who produced Stein in this era were at all interested in current academic critical opinion on Stein, they would have been hard-pressed to avoid encountering such ideas.

Elizabeth Fifer, in her 1992 study of Stein, *Rescued Readings: A Reconstruction of Stein's Difficult Texts*, attempts to decode this desire, making the logic of the text readily apparent to the reader.

> For the most part, Stein's difficult texts pursue simultaneously two contradictory goals—to conceal the author's deepest [sexual] feelings by drawing excessive attention to the surface of her text and to extend her experimental narrative technique to include as much personal information as possible. . . . Her manipulation forces knowledgeable readers into a special relationship, one of "rescuing" her meaning, based on their willingness to persevere in the face of verbal anomalies and accumulating "errors" meant to distract unsympathetic readers and evade Stein's own internal censors.[17]

Fifer outlines a relationship between surface and interior regarding both Stein and her writing. She suggests that both Stein's textual and psychological interiors are readable by a particular class of reader willing and able to negotiate her elaborate surface ruses.

Sue-Ellen Case provided another notable critical reading emphasizing the importance of Stein's sexual identity in the formulation of her writing style. In her 1996 work, *The Domain-Matrix*, Case compares Stein's compositional strategies to the messages on Sappho, an electronic bulletin board devoted to lesbian issues, finding that both Stein and the Sappho posters "encrypt" forms of address so that voyeuristic heterosexual readers will fail to access their meanings. Case writes:

> Although Stein was not strictly cyber, the Cubist element in her experiments made spatial organization central to her writing. These spatial subversions were not mere formal folly to Stein, but a component of her lesbian security system. In Stein's script, the spatial traditions of meaning inscribe not so much the problem of late capitalism as high heterosexism, which is laid, like land mines, within the linear prescriptions of grammatical conventions. . . . Spatial reorganizations divert this drive to heterosexist coupling, helping to create an encrypted lesbian address.[18]

Case reads the manner in which Stein organizes her words on the page as well as her rejection of traditional grammatical and dramatic structures as a secret code that scrambles her messages of lesbian desire, making this layer of the text "available only to the reader who 'knows' Stein as a lesbian and can read the intimations."[19]

Case goes on to suggest that the cyberlesbian can borrow Stein's techniques in order to address other lesbians either on Sappho or in other media. Though Case does acknowledge that Internet users in the mid- to late-1990s were generally of a particular advantaged class, she does seem to assert that all members of this class should be equally able to encode and decode fractured messages of desire. While Fifer is less specific as to whom her designated "knowledgeable" and "unsympathetic" readers might be, both she and Case seem to suggest that the most competent members of Stein's interpretive community are lesbians.

If lesbian readers are truly the most competent interpreters of Stein's written texts, then it would follow that lesbian spectators would be the most agile and insightful viewers of her works in performance. The contexts in which these particular works of Stein were produced, however, trouble this neat alignment. While reading is a private act, theatre spectatorship is a public one, very much influenced by the nature of the community for which the play is performed. In *Theatre Audiences*, Susan Bennett argues that "the mainstream theatre addresses an audience which is white, male, middle class, and heterosexual."[20] Two of the productions of Stein's works I discuss took place in venues that comply with Bennett's assessment: Lincoln Center and the Washington University campus theatre.[21] The avant-garde exception, the Wooster Group's Performing Garage, does not have a reputation of catering to particularly lesbian audiences.[22]

Issues of competency in reception thus become stickier when homosexual artists—like Wilson and Bogart—create texts for audiences not primarily composed of homosexuals, or when heterosexual artists—like LeCompte— produce performance texts founded on homosexual scripts for audiences that are at best mixed. In " 'Lesbian' Subjectivity in Realism: Dragging at the Margins of Structure and Ideology," Jill Dolan posed these questions for her readers:

> As lesbian work is brought out of its marginalized context and traded as cultural currency in heterosexual academic and theatre venues, the question of the performance's "readability" becomes complicated. What does it mean for lesbian texts to circulate on the heterosexual marketplace? Is a lesbian performance transported to a heterosexual context readable, or is it illegible because it is inflected with subcultural meanings that require a lesbian viewer to negotiate? . . . If lesbian performance is now being created for mixed audiences, will the new context prompt a return to more conventional forms and their meanings?[23]

The works based on Stein's texts produced by Wilson, LeCompte, and Bogart begin to probe the issues Dolan's questions identify. While the most knowledgeable and informed viewers of Stein's written texts may be lesbians, they were likely to be a minority population in the theatres in which these three artists transformed Stein's work into performance texts. Attempts to stimulate the "most competent" viewers in the audience—intellectually, emotionally, and erotically—often seemed clandestine. Layers of meaning that literary critics sought to reveal, at least to lesbian readers, were once again concealed behind a facade of ambiguity, and those willing or able to peer behind it likely found themselves isolated from the rest of the audience.

As Richard Dyer reminds us, "Audiences cannot make media images mean anything they want to, but they can select from the complexity of the image the meanings and feelings, the variations, inflections and contradictions, that work for them."[24] Lesbian viewers surely had this opportunity with all three performance texts. Wilson, LeCompte, and Bogart built multifaceted images, at once filling the spaces in Stein's texts with material charged with lesbian or homosexual desire visible to the most competent interpreters of the performance text, and leaving the theatrical signs quite ambiguous, resulting in the appearance of open or unfillable space for many viewers who were unable or unwilling to crack coded messages of desire.

THE CULTURAL CONTEXT SURROUNDING
THE 1990s STAGE PERFORMANCES

The issues raised by Stein's performance in America and by literary critics interpreting her work had parallels in mainstream 1990s culture. These forces converged in Wilson's, LeCompte's, and Bogart's performance texts, influencing the ways Stein's textual spaces were filled or seemed to be unfilled. In "Commodity Lesbianism," Danae Clark discussed the "dual marketing strategy of gay window advertising."[25] This practice, Clark explains, is one in which advertisers attempt to target homosexual consumers, appealing to what they perceive to be this market group's taste, without alienating the heterosexual consumer. Clark cites examples from advertising and mainstream fashion magazines that offer a gay or lesbian viewer the potential to construct an eroticized narrative—based on posture, gesture, attitude, and clothing style—that would be largely unavailable to heterosexual readers. Clark goes on to caution that the gay window advertising strategy is not evidence of the acceptance of either lesbian politics or identities by the marketplace: "capitalists welcome lesbians as consuming subjects but not as social subjects."[26] In fact, she suggests, gay window advertising is a way of "ining" rather than "outing" gays and lesbians:

> This type of advertising invites us to look *into* the ad to identify with elements of style, invites us *in* as consumers, invites us to be part of a fashionable "*in* crowd," but negates an identity politics based on the act of coming out. Indeed, within the world of gay window advertising, there is no lesbian community to come out to, no lesbian community to identify with, no indication that lesbianism or lesbian style is a political issue.[27]

Here, Clark shows that while lesbianism may not be repressed into absolute silence, its visibility and intelligibility are strictly policed within public discourse.

The problems that Clark reveals have particular applications to the staging of Stein's work. When artists reencode signals of desire so that only some members of the audience can read them, the very productions that seek, on some level, to celebrate Stein's lesbianism by outing the supposedly long closeted meaning in these texts might be inadvertently driving other viewers into the closet and cultural isolation. New strategies would need to be developed for making the images presented on the stage accessible as positive choices for viewers.

Ann M. Ciasullo's arguments in "Making Her (In)Visible: Cultural Representations of Lesbianism and the Lesbian Body in the 1990s" resonate with Clark's position. Ciasullo looks at the mainstream media's fascination with images of lesbians in the 1990s (she quotes Ann Northrop's quip, "lesbians are the Hula-Hoop of the nineties")—from *People* magazine and *Newsweek*, to popular television shows like *Friends*, and movies like *Chasing Amy* and *Set it Off*—finding that:

> The mainstream lesbian body is at once sexualized and desexualized: on the one hand, she is made into an object of desire for straight audiences through her heterosexualization, a process achieved by representing the lesbian as embodying a hegemonic femininity and thus, for mainstream audiences, as looking "just like" conventionally attractive straight women; on the other hand, because the representation of desire between two women is usually suppressed in these images, she is de-homosexualized.[28]

Ciasullo argues that the specifically femme lesbian body is allowed to appear on mainstream 1990s cultural stages, but while she is "out" in culture in this way, the containment of any images of overtly lesbian sexual desire drives her back into a kind of representational closet. Her specific kind of sexuality—just like the images Clark described above—becomes unreadable to heterosexual viewers who replace her choices with their own desires. Likewise in the theatres that produced Stein, lesbian and gay male bodies (or their simulations when straight actors brought Stein's words to life and her subtext to the fore) were simultaneously visible and invisible to different segments of the audience, particularly in those moments devoid of physically explicit sexual content.

Judith Butler provides another angle from which to view the cultural intelligibility of homosexuality and its role in and as discourse, both theatrical and general. Throughout *Excitable Speech: A Politics of the Performative*, Butler aims to examine the performative power of hate speech and its relationship to the body and body politic. Particularly salient to the discussion of some stagings of Stein's work in the 1990s are her points on the policy formulated by the U.S. military toward homosexuality during the 1990s. If an individual violates "the don't ask, don't tell" rule, announcing that "I am a homosexual," Butler suggests that in the eyes of the military the implication of this declaration "is not simply that the utterance performs the sexuality of which it speaks, but that it transmits sexuality through speech: the utterance is figured as a site of contagion,"[29] and that in the world of the military the utterance is perceived to threaten a kind of bodily injury.

Butler also compares the declaration of sexual orientation in the military to coming out in other contexts, noting its importance and positive power within queer activism. Ultimately, however, she contends, contrary to the military appraisal of sexual declaration, "a discursive production of homosexuality, a talking about, a writing about, and institutional recognition of, homosexuality, is not exactly the same as the desire of which it speaks" and "when we think we are acting homosexually when we speak about homosexuality we are, I think, making a bit of a mistake."[30]

Butler's suggestion that speaking about homosexuality is not the same thing as physically engaging in a homosexual act intersects in interesting ways with some of Stein's theories about the relationship between sound, an analogue of speaking, and sight, a visual perception of physical being or action. In her lecture, *Plays*, Stein said:

> Nothing is more interesting to know about the theatre than the relation of sight and sound. It is always the most interesting thing about anything to know whether you hear or you see. And how one has to do with the other. It is one of the important things in finding out how you know what you know.[31]

On some level, the concerns of Stein and Butler are similar. Speaking and sound, according to Butler and Stein respectively, are not identical to physical acts or seeing: they elicit different responses and have different consequences. These ideas become even more interesting when they are considered in regard to the ways Stein's works were sometimes staged in the 1990s. Though directors may have been seeking to give voice to the passion encoded in Stein's texts by coaching actors to speak lines in ways that left double entendres in Stein's texts audible to the most competent listeners, the fact that some of these vocalizations emanated from bodies engaged in virtually or entirely platonic acts, rendered the disclosure of desire less complete than if the physical text had been constructed otherwise. I suggest that the most complete and also the most culturally subversive cues were those that were both aural and visual. Cues occupying both dimensions simultaneously were at risk of decoding from two angles instead of one, but the assumption of the risk on the part of the artist creating the image and on the part of the audience member in engaging with and embracing the image, opened culturally and psychically transformational possibilities.

ROBERT WILSON AND THE WOOSTER GROUP
STAGE DESIRE: *DOCTOR FAUSTUS LIGHTS
THE LIGHTS* AND *HOUSE/LIGHTS*

The competing cultural demands for expression of homosexual desire and
its erasure were felt in the productions of Stein's work directed by Robert
Wilson and Elizabeth LeCompte. Though neither of these directors are particularly noted for an interest in queer political and/or theatrical activism,
the performance texts created by both artists contained cues that led me to
conclude that they were, at the very least, willing to open Stein's text to
readings cognizant of lesbian desire. Because these cues were ambiguous,
the most competent readers of the performance texts were probably able to
access these meanings while the same signals were likely to go unnoticed by
many spectators, as evidenced by the lack of attention these issues were paid
in the many reviews of these productions. These performance texts also suggest that if speaking homosexuality is not the same as engaging in it, then
perhaps the most complete expressions of homosexual desire on these stages
were the ones constructed of physical/visual elements as well as verbal/aural
elements.

Robert Wilson's first foray into Stein's work, *Doctor Faustus Lights the
Lights*,[32] performed at Lincoln Center (as well as Frankfurt's Theater am
Turm, and the Hebbel Theatre in Berlin in 1992 and in the Royal Lyceum
Theatre as part of the Edinburgh International Festival in 1993), demon-
strated an inclination to decode the latent desire in Stein's writing through
casting decisions and blocking. These elements were, however, cloaked in
aspects of Wilson's trademark highly aesthetic and abstract style that
rendered them less than obvious at first glance (see photo 5.1).

Wilson makes clear how well suited Stein's work is to his signature style
in an interview with *Guardian* reviewer John O'Mahony:

> With Gertrude Stein you have to almost invent a theatrical situation . . . . There
> is a lot of freedom for the director. The text is just a block of words and
> you can divide it up between two people or twenty people . . . Stein was a
> composer. Her pieces always remind me of a musical composition. They
> always sound like music for dance so it lends itself to my work which is all
> dance.[33]

Even *Doctor Faustus Lights the Lights*, one of Stein's most conventional
texts containing identifiable characters and some semblance of a plot, does
not clearly differentiate side and spoken text, leaving the director plenty

Photo 5.1   Mr. Viper and the three Marguerite Ida and Helena Annabels from Robert Wilson's *Doctor Faustus Lights the Lights* (photograph © Johan Elbers 2004)

of freedom to create his own, in this case quite abstract, score for the performers.

Wilson explains further, in an interview printed in the program for the Edinburgh production of *Doctor Faustus Lights the Lights*, "[Stein] is something special. The architecture, the structure, the rhythm, the humour. . . . They invite mental pictures. Even if she's describing something, the text has so much space for pictures—for each person's own picture."[34] The space in *Doctor Faustus Lights the Lights* left plenty of room for Wilson's picture since the libretto's most overt theme, the glory and price of technological innovation, seems tailor-made for Wilson and his particular brand of theatrical creation. The fit was so precise that one reviewer wrote, "One might infer that Faustus is a stand-in for none other Robert Wilson, the ultimate control-freak of a theatrical form that enslaves the actor to the almighty light bulb."[35] In Stein's libretto, Faustus sells his soul to the devil in exchange for the invention of electric light. While light is a prominent feature in many Wilson productions, the beauty of Andreas Fuchs's design in this one made Mephistopheles's bargain seem not altogether unreasonable. Light was, in fact, central to all aspects of the production. In addition to its narrative importance, it was also of absolute scenographic importance. Wilson stated:

> The light is the set. . . . I wanted to have one element that could change the space. It could be high or low, brighter or darker. And it was a bar of light. It could be anything, a table, a ceiling, anything. It is the only scenic element. Without light there is no space.[36]

Wilson's perception did not go unnoticed in the production's reviews. As one reviewer put it, "Although 15 fetching young actors appear in *Doctor Faustus*, the real star is a long fluorescent light strip."[37]

The performances began with a stunning image of light and as that one began to fade, a flood of new images was generated in its place. Faustus, dressed in black, stood before a field of stark white light, compass in hand slowly making arcs in the air. Throughout the production this and other planes of light danced among and with the actors taking turns with the aforementioned strip of light that rose and fell, filling a myriad of scenographic functions. Finally, toward the end of the play, bulbs descended from the heavens on sinewy cords to taunt Faustus and tantalize the spectator.

While the lighting accentuated the most prominent theme in Stein's text, Wilson's casting decisions and blocking could be read as filling the spaces in the text with references to homosexual desire for those audience members not blinded by the lighting's beauty. Wilson cast the libretto with theatre students from Berlin instead of professional actors. More interesting than their level of experience was the fact that none of the young Germans spoke English. Wilson said of this decision, "I had the feeling that it would be more interesting in English [than translated into German] even if they didn't understand what they were saying, or if they had German accents. There was something interesting about the fact they didn't necessarily know what they were saying."[38] The interesting effect of his decision came in the actors' line delivery. The rhythms and intonations of the performers were slightly off kilter throughout the show. As Robert Gore-Langton of *The Daily Telegraph* put it, "the slight German accents merely add to the alien tone of the proceedings."[39] Jamie James of *The Times* saw this choice as "a deliberate ploy on the director's part to further abstract Stein's Cubist language."[40] Combined with very mechanical movements and sharp angular gestures, the delivery of the lines gave the actors a very artificial quality. On one level the performance style might be read as a comment on the soul-deadening influence of technology and endless mechanical reproduction, but on another level, the artificiality of the performances might open up a space in theatrical landscape for something more optimistic. If the mechanical bodies and alien voices representing conventional heterosexual relationships—an interaction between Marguerite Ida and Helena Annabel and Faustus or the Man from Over the Sea—make them seem strange and unnatural, the performance text begins to grant the viewer permission to imagine an alternative emotional and sexual configuration. As Colin Donald of the *The Scotsman* suggested, "Resonant wads of meaning are squashed into the slightest exchanges between characters, their flickering expression and clean-lined acrobatic movements kaleidoscoping words into many potential meanings."[41] While Donald does not identify these meanings as having to do with sexual orientation specifically, the fact that he perceived an opening spectrum of nameless possibility is significant.

Cross-gender casting further emphasized this denaturalization of conventional givens. Reviewers rarely singled out the work of individual performers with the exception of Martin Vogel, who played The Country Woman, and Karla Trippel, who played the Dog (a genderless figure in the libretto) wearing a man's suit and tie. While these characters occupy relatively peripheral spots in the libretto compared to Marguerite Ida and Helena Annabel, Faustus, and Mephisto, they loomed large, in one case quite literally, in production. Vogel, eight-feet tall in his stark white, high-necked and full-skirted Victorian dress that concealed stilts, was visually stunning, but the diminutive Trippel was equally attention grabbing in her dapper menswear. Cross-gender casting and costuming worked together to mark these roles as prominent and enticing for at least the specialized segment of the audience called reviewers.

Perhaps this critical interest was generated because no attempt was made to make either performer pass completely in his or her cross-gendered role: Vogel was clearly male playing a female character while Trippel was clearly female in male dress. In short, this was an example of deliberately unconvincing drag, which as Kirk Ormand and Marjorie Garber have pointed out, has the goal not of passing but of destabilizing "gender and normative sexuality by blurring the lines between them."[42] Likewise, Vogel and Trippel's casting, costuming, and performances were not important for their unconvincing playing of roles, but for their transgressing norms of behavior and dress that contemporary culture insists on reading as having sexual implications. Their stage images drew attention to the coding and decoding of desire.

Another striking aspect of the casting that sheds light on subtextual decoding was Wilson's strategy to cast three women as the multiply named yet singular heroine Marguerite Ida and Helena Annabel and three men as Doctor Faustus and two men as Mephisto. *Times* critic John Peter described this choice: "Characters are played by several actors for no discernable reason, theatrical or any other."[43] While for some viewers such as Peter, the multiple castings may have seemed an unnecessary abstraction of an already quite abstract text, David Savran saw Wilson's choice in a very different light:

> As if in *hommage* to his queer predecessor, he seems to allow that the proliferation of heroes and heroines will unleash an uncanny and narcissistic homoeroticism, as one Faustus or one Marguerite Ida and Helena Annabel appears almost to cruise his or her fantasmatic double. By so allowing sexual desire to circulate in unexpected directions, Wilson underscores Stein's achievement in this text of presenting heterosexuality not as a "natural" state, but as an artificial one, as patently—and banally—constructed as Doctor Faustus's electric lights.[44]

The distinctions between these critical readings are significant. A mainstream newspaper reviewer either didn't see, or chose not to report, any homosexual subtext to his readers. Savran, on the other hand, a critic who frequently addresses issues of homosexuality and who was writing for an academic audience, emphasized this point. Savran invites his reader into the community of most astute and skillful viewers. It is also worth noting that because academic journal reviews are published months after a production closes for a readership not based in the city of performance, Savran's readers are very likely not to have seen the performance he describes. His reading goes uncontested with reader experience, rewriting the production in an assertive way and making the desire in the performance very prominent.

Savran's assertions about the character's interactions with their doubles can be taken even further. Heterosexual interaction was parodied in moments such as the one when one of the Doctor Faustuses, in an unusual interaction with one of the Marguerite Ida and Helena Annabels rather than one of his doubles, squeezed one of the Marguerite Ida and Helena Annabel's breasts. He touched her mechanically, never looking directly at her instead keeping his gaze fixed straight ahead, his fingers spread and tense as he quickly grabbed and released her breast, eliciting chuckles from the audience. There was no show of sexual pleasure here for either party, only comic pleasure from the audience aroused by the incongruity of this coupling. In contrast to the humor of this moment was the eroticism of the slow tango of the male Mephistos, with their bodies pressed tightly together shortly after Mr. Viper, the symbol of phallic power, appeared wielding an oversized lance and his plastic serpent coiled about his arm. While the penetrating bite of the serpent rends the heroine's psyche in Stein's script, represented in performance by the three scantily clad actresses frozen in poses of terror, the possibility of this thrill drew the two male Mephistos into a tight embrace, zinging with erotic electricity.

These moments that contained collisions between the verbal intimations of Stein's text and the visual suggestions of Wilson's performance text were the ones that offered the richest array of possibilities for spectators interested in processing cues of homosexual desire. These cues were, however, so enmeshed in the highly abstract world of the performance text that they were not readily apparent to all viewers. Thus, while the spaces in Stein's text might have appeared to be filled by suggestions of homosexual desire for some viewers, they might have appeared wide open to others.

I found that a subtext of Stein's lesbian desire was more readily available in the Wooster Group's production of *House/Lights*, which paired the 1960s cult film by Joseph Mawra, *Olga's House of Shame*, with *Doctor Faustus Lights the Lights* (see photo 5.2). Like Wilson's production, this performance text seemed filled swith queer performance strategies for those viewers already attuned to them. At the same time, *House/Lights* presented a highly abstract and aestheticized facade to other audience members.

As soon as the audience entered the Performing Garage and viewed the set, they had to expect that they had a challenging evening of theatre before them. Assembled on stage was what reviewers of the Columbus, Chicago, and Minneapolis performances had variously dubbed "a way too busy industrial set," "an electronic media jungle," "the laboratory of a mad scientist," and "an industrial torture chamber."[45] Before the show even began, it was clear that a barrage of sensory stimuli would ensue: six video monitors dotted the set otherwise crowded with dual metal seesaws, a stool trapped in a sliding track, a ballet bar, a video camera, a computer workstation, wheeled artificial trees blooming with red plastic flowers and lights, and up- and downstage battens heavy with overgrown clear light bulbs.

As the first moments of the performance unfolded the multiple foci of attention suggested by the still and unpeopled set came to life. Kate Valk, who played Faustus and Marguerite Ida and Helena Annabel from the Stein piece and Elaine from *Olga's House of Shame*, was seated downstage on the stool, breathing heavily into the microphone stationed in front of her, as though she had been chased. She then swiveled around to face one of the upstage video monitors where the movie was playing. On the screen, a car was pulling up a mountain road, as if to suggest her pursuers were drawing ever nearer. The lights lowered on the batten and then began to angle out from their previous position of straight down. Valk raised her arms to grab hold of the downstage batten while the video continued to play on the monitors. From the downstage right corner where the computer station was located, Tanya Selvaratnam, who was identified in the program as portraying Nadja, a character from the *Olga* film, and Powerbook, typed on the computer, inducing it to emit intermittent duck quacks.

Photo 5.2 *House/Lights* directed by Elizabeth LeCompte; pictured: Suzzy Roche and Kate Valk (upside down) (photograph © Mary Gearhart)

These multiple points of attraction simultaneously present on the stage recall Case's comments on Stein's organization of words on the printed page. I found that I could not simply read the happenings on the stage as a singular, grammatical image revealing itself neatly in a linear sequence. Instead I had to scan the multiple sites of activity, reorganizing the scenic and aural icons until they cohered into some form of personal meaning. And while this particular moment in the performance did not seem to me to be revelatory of coded signals of lesbian desire as much as a statement of female creative power and authority, the general technique of multiple points of interest that require reassembly by the individual viewer, would be revelatory of lesbian desire later in the performance.

Another step made by the Wooster Group that allowed me to glimpse a subtext of lesbian desire in the performance was the choice of an intertext. Directors frequently seek out an additional structure to augment a Stein text in order to make it more stage-ready. Writing of her experience directing *For the Country Entirely, A Play in Letters*, Ellen Donkin quotes a letter she received from Virgil Thomson noting the wisdom she found in his remarks as she worked intimately with the text:

> I have always found it embarrassing when directors attempt to illustrate any meaning they may find in the words. These plays need a structure added. There must be invented for each one a scenario, which the actors can mime while reciting the text. This does not need to have any connection with the text; often this method works best when there is no obvious connection.[46]

The Wooster Group both did and did not follow Thomson's advice that suggests that Stein's texts resist mimetic illustration. *Olga's House of Shame* did provide the main physical scenario for the performance.[47] The actors frequently copied the action sequences and even the moves of the camera illustrated in the video rather than the fragments of plot suggested by the libretto. As Bevya Rosten's interview with Kate Valk revealed,[48] the Wooster Group accentuated the hybrid Stein-Olga text by borrowing from Cantonese Opera for Valk's distinctive high-pitched mode of speaking and from Marx Brothers' films for the frenetically goofy style of movement employed by all the performers.

But despite Thomson's admonition and surface appearances to the contrary, there are some connections between *Doctor Faustus Lights the Lights* and *Olga's House of Shame* that the performance came to reveal. Once I suspended my disbelief that there is something worthwhile in a low-budget flick depicting a crisis in an s/m girl gang with an original intent of titillating a male viewer, and simultaneously agreed to enjoy the rollicking play of

Stein's language rather than trying to make concrete and specific sense of every phrase, I found myself moving beyond the surfaces of both texts, discovering that both can be read as dealing with power, its connection to sexuality, and what the cost can be of taking the power one desires, sexual or otherwise. As such, when the Wooster Group mimed the excesses of *Olga's House of Shame* punctuated by further frivolities of style, certain aspects of *Doctor Faustus Lights the Lights* began to loom large if the viewer was willing to peek behind the Wooster Group's facade of manic activity. If the viewer wished, she could find hints of lesbian desire flashing elusively across the crowded screen of the performance.

Such a moment came midway through the performance. Peyton Smith,[49] who played both Olga and Mephistopheles, sat downstage, lit a cigarette and proceeded to break away from the texts of both *Olga's House of Shame* and *Doctor Faustus Lights the Lights* in order to sing an extremely campy rendition of Johnny Cash's "Burning Ring of Fire." As she sang, Valk was sprawled on the couch upstage of her, her willowy limbs cascading over its edges, face ecstatically flushed, and echoing along the "burning ring of fire" line in a breathy version of the voice she used for her Stein characters. One reviewer commented on the levity of this moment,[50] but none read the moment as a staging of lesbian desire. The connection is, however, not hard to make. As Smith puffed on a cigarette, blowing rings of smoke at the microphone, Valk's body convulsed in time behind her, responding directly to the stimuli Smith's performance provided. Earlier, when in the Stein text Marguerite Ida and Helena Annabel was supposed to have been bitten by a viper, Smith took a slow, delicious bite of Valk's inner thigh as Valk was hanging upside down. The burning ring of fire seemed to refer back to the mark of the viper (an episode of sexual overtones in the Stein text that causes the doubly named heroine an identity crisis), the blown smoke, and the aroused genitals of one or both women.

Throughout the performance, the use of video had both problematized and expanded the notion of actorly presence, and thus was the third device that allowed some viewers to access signals of lesbian desire. Valk frequently appeared both in real time and space and as a distanced image on the video monitors. During the course of the production, the audience members learned to accept this convention, reading the moments when Valk appeared both immediately in front of them and as a disembodied image in the various more remote monitors, as dramatically significant. And though this refraction of Valk's image in some ways distanced the audience from her physically, it also helped catapult them into another dimension with her, a reconfiguration of space and perception, or a further manifestation of the hybrid cyber-Cubism described by Case as descriptive of Stein. The splintered images, usually of Valk's face, gave me the impression that I was seeing Valk from several perspectives, figuratively as well as literally, creating a kind of digitized, visual aside,[51] that revealed more about her than the singular purely present image of her material body.

The performance closed with what was perhaps the most fascinating image of the entire evening, and one that required that I use all the viewing strategies I had accumulated during the course of the performance. Valk returned to the camera downstage. She sat on the stool, seductively massaging her nipple (visible through the lace bra exposed by an unzipped vent traveling the front of her dress) while the video monitor displayed the image of her hand superimposed on the still photograph of a torso of a smooth, sinewy, rather androgynous, but apparently very young male body. As she erotically touched her own body in real time and space, her hand simultaneously caressed this simulated body on the video.

In this final image, the video frustrated any desire on the part of the spectator to respond to the immediate physical image alone. The video demanded to be read simultaneously. When I acquiesced, I found a tantalizing array of possibilities opening before me, and a great deal of satisfaction in pursuing them as intellectual and erotic stimuli became thoroughly intertwined in this interaction with Valk's fractured image. The reading that most appealed to me was seeing the video image as a description of Valk's internal desires—the autoeroticism fueling a fantasy scenario of escape from the singularly gendered body to one between or even among genders. This closing image also provided a physical analogue to the lines in the vicinity of the conclusion of Stein's text spoken by Marguerite Ida and Helena Annabel: "I am Marguerite Ida and Helena Annabel and I know no man or devil no viper and no light I can be anything and everything and its always always alright."[52]

As the performance closed the three main strategies used by the Wooster Group in staging *House/Lights*, multiple foci of attention, provocative intertextual weavings, and video distancing, all cohered to provide a stunningly complex moment that could potentially be unraveled by each viewer differently. Lesbian desire was staged in such a way that it seemed clearly present in the spaces of Stein's text and the spaces between Stein's text and the intertext, *Olga's House of Shame*, but only to the specific portions of the audience with the will to see it and the desire to participate in the pleasures it offered.

ON STAGE AGAIN: *GERTRUDE AND ALICE*

An interesting juxtaposition to the stagings of Stein's work by Robert Wilson and the Wooster Group and Stein's own staging of her relationship with Alice is Anne Bogart's 1999 staging of a work about Stein called *Gertrude and Alice: A Likeness in Loving.* The piece, written and performed by Lola Pashalinski and Linda Chapman, was a compilation of Stein's writings from various genres used to illustrate the evolving relationship Stein had with Alice B. Toklas (see photo 5.3). Beyond most literally dramatizing the critical trend of reading Stein's works as coded statements of lesbian desire, *Gertrude and Alice: A Likeness in Loving* provides an interesting example of the problem of the cultural intelligibility of staged representations of Stein's lesbianism. Though this sexual relationship and its impact on Stein's writing was the main concern of the performance, it utilized very little overt eroticism, suggesting once again that there is considerable space between utterance and act when it comes to representing homosexual desire on stage.

As the audience entered the Edison Theatre on the Washington University campus in St. Louis, Missouri,[53] the set was immediately visible. On the stage in front of a white drop were placed a podium with an open book, a chintz-covered chair with a figure seated in it, her head covered by a linen handkerchief, a table beside that chair with cigarettes, an ashtray and matches on top of it and a leopard-print hat on the shelf below it, a settee, another chair, and an upholstered footstool.

Photo 5.3 Lola Pashalinski as Gertrude Stein and Linda Chapman as Alice Toklas in *Gertrude and Alice* (photograph © Carol Rosegg)

The most interesting thing about this pared-down domestic scene was the partially covered figure. Given the shape of the body that was visible, I guessed that this was Alice, a hypothesis confirmed once the play began. Below the white handkerchief was a slim female body clothed in a raspberry silk tunic, black mid-calf straight skirt, dark hose and raspberry Mary Jane pumps. Whether this was the intention of the director and writers or not, the association I immediately made with this image was Picasso's "Portrait of Gertrude Stein" and Robert Lubar's analysis of the portrait in "Unmasking Gertrude: Queer Desire and the Subject of Portraiture."

In this article, Lubar recounts some of the well-known history of Picasso's painting as well as a new analysis of his problems in painting it. As I mentioned in chapter 2, when Gertrude sat for her portrait, Picasso had little trouble capturing her hands and the form of her body swathed in voluminous folds of brown fabric, but her face, according to legend, eluded him. When Picasso's frustration became overwhelming, he simply wiped out the head. The portrait supposedly remained decapitated by the smear until Picasso found a solution to the problems posed by Gertrude's head in the mask-like visages of fifth- and sixth-century Iberian stone carving. Of primary interest to both Lubar and this study are not the historical influences on the portrait or even the portrait's step in the development of Picasso's Cubism, but what it suggests are the problems with representing the lesbian subject. Lubar writes:

> I submit that Picasso's effacement of Gertrude's head and his delayed substitution of a mask are the outward signs of that something that eludes representation yet remains ever present within the structure of the visual field: the complex trajectory of desire. Picasso's inability to recognize Gertrude Stein as intelligible subject of portraiture may, in this light, be approached as a problem in representation that exceeds the traditional limits of subject-object relations.[54]

I would suggest that the handkerchief over Alice's head in *Gertrude and Alice: A Likeness in Loving* serves a similar function, erasing it (and Alice) from the view of the audience. At various moments in the performance, the artists staging the piece seemed to experience a failure of representation, finding themselves unable to fill the space inside the dramatic frame they created with the intimate details of a desire-rich lesbian relationship.

In the first moments of the show, when Alice sat in the chair with the hanky over her head, Gertrude stood behind the upstage podium writing in a book. At the same time a voice-over spoken by the actor playing Gertrude repeated several times, "Put something down someday in my own handwriting." Alice then removed the handkerchief and lit a cigarette. Gertrude came over, blew it out, and repeated only, "Put something down," as if to refer to her desire for Alice to extinguish the cigarette. These actions immediately connect Gertrude's words with the domestic scene, suggesting that her words have double meanings that relate to life with Alice.

Alice, however, was more difficult to depict. Her most famous autobiography was, after all, written for her, by Stein. Her letters, *What is Remembered*, and *The Alice B. Toklas Cookbook* offer some literary evidence of her own composition on which to base her depiction or from which to extrapolate her desire, but Toklas remains elusive. A telling line of Alice's spoken early in the production was "I reflect what you reflect about me." With this line, Chapman and Pashalinski seemed to be trying to convince the audience that we can find in Gertrude's writing a reflection of Alice and that her image is created by Stein's reflections about her. I would suggest, however, that we need to be wary of being quickly satisfied by this statement and assuming that Alice is as easy to see as the line suggests because it eliminates all agency on the part of the sitter of the portrait in constructing her own image. Lubar, for example, believed that Stein was very active in her desire to create a self-image in the portrait she was sitting for for Picasso, and that this was in fact, part of the struggle that led to her effacement by Picasso. Lubar suggests that Stein met Picasso's gaze with a lesbian gaze that he was both unable to seduce into heterosexuality and unable to represent pictorially:

> Gertrude's mask serves a proscriptive function at the site of a symbolic trespass. It marks the artist's anxious apprehension of Gertrude's appropriation and redeployment of the terms of signification . . . . In effect, Gertrude's refusal to occupy the position of lack mobilized a complex fantasy of castration for Picasso; the mask signifies at once his conflicted desire for the lost maternal object through specular identification with a queer woman and his anxious apprehension that the very terms governing sexual identity and normative heterosexuality are unstable and subject to revision. The mask, then, is an elaborate charade, a site of dissimulation that can never make good on what it promises. In his attempt to shield himself from Gertrude's penetrating gaze, Picasso in effect acknowledges the complex trajectory of his own desire and the fantasy of a unitary subject of gender and sexuality.

Bogart, Chapman, and Pashalinski, despite Chapman and Pashalinski's long-term lesbian relationship and Bogart's own sexuality,[55] also seemed unable to return Alice's lesbian gaze and thus found themselves in a representational quagmire not unlike Picasso's.

While there was a certain kind of intellectual pleasure in recognizing the snippets of texts they wove together, in knowing the source works where these snippets were originally located, and in appreciating the clever ways they made lines from Stein's work resonate with periods in her relationship with Alice, these pleasures hardly qualify as erotic. The fact that Alice's head was frequently effaced during the course of the production, both by several returns to the opening image and a recurrent pose of her frozen in a position with her face turned upstage, might suggest that as an erotic subject with her own desire and as an erotic object of Stein's desire, Alice was still not completely representable—her picture could not be painted in the dramatic medium without considerable masking—and she could not, thus, be available as an object of visual desire for the audience member.

The recurring poses seem to be an example of Bogart's use of the Japanese theatre term, "kata." In *A Director Prepares*, Bogart explains her attraction to set forms in performance:

> If you allow the emotions free rein to respond to the heat of the moment, then what you set is the form, the container, the kata. You work this way, not because you are ultimately most interested in form, but paradoxically, because you are most interested in the human experience. You move away from something in order to come closer to it. To allow for emotional freedom, you pay attention to form. If you embrace the notion of containers or katas, then your task is to set a fire, a human fire, inside these containers and start to burn.[56]

While the kata of Alice's turned head and body provided a set form to structure the performance, no emotional fire—and more particularly no erotic fire—ever seemed to burn within it.

In this production, the most sexual scene featured Gertrude putting her head on Alice's lap while reciting, "when she came late, I did not wait," emphasizing the double entendre in the word "came." Other intimations of sexuality between two women also had to be inferred from the delivery of lines—emphasis and tone of voice conveyed the sexual subtext of "I can make good sentences," the two women occupying a shared domestic space, an occasional tango, and a little dance the two women did while sitting on the couch—sitting close together, feet moving in unison, tracing circles on the floor while Gertrude said "we are careful to move together for pleasure." While a viewer would have to be either very naive or very closed-minded to miss these cues, they were hardly graphic and their comic execution rendered them generally unerotic.

CONCLUSION: STRIKING A DISRUPTIVE POSE

In her 1992 essay, "Practicing Cultural Disruptions: Gay and Lesbian Representation and Sexuality," Jill Dolan wrote:

> Perhaps the regressive outlawing of gay and lesbian images as prurient and obscene will prompt the reradicalization of their meaning in the 1990s. Perhaps representations of gay and lesbian sexuality will regain their potential to disrupt hegemonic meanings by invoking the excess of sexual practice, after a brief period of neutralizing assimilation into the dominant discourse on sexuality as alternative lifestyles and identities.[57]

From the vantage point provided by the productions of Stein's work staged by Wilson, LeCompte, and Bogart, Dolan's prediction looks premature. Rather than disrupting hegemonic systems in and of themselves, images of lesbian desire used to fill the spaces in Stein's work were coded and concealed, as spoken and visual imagery were often segregated, instead of "invoking the excess of sexual practice" as Dolan had hoped such images might. But the fact that these images were constructed on a variety of stages by some of the most well-known directors of the period is, nonetheless, a significant beginning. Images of lesbian desire were available for identification by the most competent viewers, and with this potential for unhegemonically sanctioned identification comes the opportunity for a countermobilization of social power. If a spectator chooses to read an image—aural or visual—as an embodiment of culturally unsanctioned desire, and then embraces that image psychically, identifying with it and incorporating it into an evolving perception of the self, that identification may also be insurrectionary.

The stage was set for the individual spectator to find psychically, and from that socially, revolutionary possibility. Though Mary Pickford feared the consequences of having her image linked with Stein's in the 1930s, the most competent reader of the 1990s stagings of Robert Wilson's *Doctor Faustus Lights the Lights*, the Wooster Group's *House/Lights*, and Anne Bogart's *Gertrude and Alice* had the opportunity to assume a pose next to Stein, full of powerful and disruptive possibility.

Epilogue: Dreams of a New Frontier—Mapping Gertrude Stein's Twenty-First-Century Identity on a Global Stage ➹

In *Everybody's Autobiography*, Stein wrote, "In this epoch the only real literary thinking has been done by a woman."[1] Lest her reader have any confusion about which woman was doing this important work, she followed up a few pages later with, "so then the important literary thinking is being done. Who does it. I do it."[2] In her own characteristically brazen opinion, Stein was the quintessential twentieth-century literary visionary.

As the preceding chapters have suggested, several generations of American theatre artists concurred with Stein's self-assessment. During the twentieth century, artists from Judith Malina to Al Carmines to Robert Wilson sought to find some part of their image reflected in, or derived some part of their image from, Gertrude Stein's. Since Stein figured herself as the embodiment of twentieth-century innovation, it stands to reason that the custodians of her image—both artistic and critical—might now need to borrow from someone else—someone quintessentially twenty-first century—in order to maintain her force in a new epoch's theatrical landscape. As Stein is being refigured and repositioned for the new century, a person whose artistic strategies might be appropriated for the task is Heiner Goebbels. Goebbels already shares many points of contact with Stein, but the differences between them chart a new course for productions of Stein (and the stagings of her persona that always seem to ensue) in the twenty-first century.

OPENING THE TEXTUAL LANDSCAPE: SEEING
STEIN THROUGH GOEBBELS

As I've surveyed major performances of Stein's work from the 1930s until the end of the twentieth century, I've been exclusively concerned with the work of American directors. But as I conclude the study by imagining where Stein production might go in the twenty-first century, I'd like to broaden my scope by investigating the work of a non-American who has been drawn to her work and who has presented her work to an American audience. Heiner Goebbels adapted Stein's *Making of Americans* for his musiktheater piece, *Hashirigaki*, which played at the Brooklyn Academy of Music in March of 2003 after previous tour stops in Los Angeles, Paris, Berlin, London, Rome, Hamburg, Moscow, Singapore, and Istanbul. The works of Robert Wilson and the Wooster Group that I discussed in chapter 5 also played internationally as well as nationally, and both Wilson and LeCompte are known for non-Western performance techniques, some of which appeared in their productions of Stein,[3] but Goebbels's *Hashirigaki* significantly extends and intensifies the trends represented by both *Doctor Faustus Lights the Lights* and *House/Lights* in this regard. *Hashirigaki* was a prime example of intercultural performance, which is, as Patrice Pavis has argued, the kind of theatre that "creates hybrid forms drawing upon more or less conscious and voluntary mixing of performance traditions traceable to distinct cultural areas."[4] And while Stein may have staged herself as quintessentially American, even one of her most American of texts, *The Making of Americans*, seemed ideal for the tradition-mixing global project by the end of the seventy-five-minute performance. *Hashirigaki* suggests a model for shuffling Stein and her American texts with various international components in the new century, thereby opening all the constituent elements to a broader and richer array of intercultural theatrical possibilities.

Robert Wilson is responsible for forging the link between Stein and Goebbels. The first time Goebbels heard Stein's *Making of Americans* was when Wilson read from the novel at Heiner Müller's funeral in 1996.[5] Without such a powerful introduction, the two artists might never have come together since their personal histories seem almost irreconcilably different. Stein, an American writer, born in 1874, studied medicine, was influenced by William James, moved to Paris, and sat in the center of the revolutions in twentieth-century modernist art and literature. Goebbels, a German composer, musician with the So-Called Radical Left Wing Brass Band and Cassiber, and director, born in 1952 in Germany (where he maintains his home base), studied sociology and music, was influenced by Hans Eisler, sits at the center of the postmodern revolution in concert hall music, a position that rather than keeping him locked in one spot, has taken him on tours to more than thirty countries in the last fifteen years.[6] Despite occupying such different points in the historical and cultural landscape, Goebbels's aesthetic theory and practice is remarkably well suited to Stein. Just as disparate international elements collide in his work creating unforeseen combinations, so too does the encounter of a Stein text with Goebbels's style of stage composition.

Perhaps the most startling point of intersection is in the notion of landscape itself. Goebbels, like Stein, explores what it might mean to conceive of the text as landscape. In his article "Text as Landscape," he wrote, "To treat the text as a landscape means not to pass through it superficially in the manner of a tourist or, to remain in the picture, to grab hold of it from inside a moving car, but to travel through it like an expedition."[7] His vision of textual landscape, more emphatically than Stein's, explicitly animates the process of the reader, suggesting the need for a close and rigorous physical intimacy.

The exertion that he expects of his audience on their expedition through the textual landscape shares Stein's desire to separate the processes of perception. While she wondered if she could hear and see in the theatre at the same time, Goebbels makes a point of prying these perceptions apart in his productions. In regard to hearing in the theatre and the actor's relationship to the text, he writes:

> On stage I try to blur or even break the identity between speech and speaker in order to make the "speaker" disappear. There are two reasons for this: first, to rescue the language, to develop the hearing of language independently, and second, to acquire an actor who can not only physically elaborate what he or she has already said but who can present himself or herself as an independent body—to arrive finally at having two bodies: the text as a body and the body of the actor.[8]

The attention that Goebbels gives to the embodied nature of the text through the work of the actor is a significant addition to Stein's theory. While Stein was very much interested in rescuing language, she lacked the practical theatre experience to understand how the performer might be enlisted for the task. Goebbels, a master of this form of knowledge, traverses the boundary between the theoretical and the practical, taking these ideas farther than Stein was able. As I explain in more detail later, in *Hashirigaki*, he made the body of the actor extremely visible by casting an array of physical types and he revealed the relationship between body and text by making the process of verbal production plain—by having a Swedish actor sing a Japanese song or by having a Japanese actor recite a passage from a circuitous American novel. The actors' collision with the text made seeing and hearing independently prominent.

But like Stein, Goebbels is also much concerned with the play's scenery—its visual aspects—not just the auditory landscape. In an interview in *The Wire*, he said, "I try not to match words and people, words and pictures, music and words in an illustrative way. Distance on stage keeps our senses awake and curious, and actualizes our longings and desires for the matches."[9] Instead of creating a gesamtkunstwerk, Goebbels allows the elements to remain distinct, and sometimes dissonant in his work. That he succeeds in this project should not be too surprising given the fact that he blends Prince and the Revolution with Alain Robbe-Grillet, griots accompanied by a kora with Joseph Conrad and Heiner Müller, and the Beach Boys with Japanese folk music with Gertrude Stein. The space between the visual, verbal, and musical elements in a Goebbels text is a variation on the kinds of space that I have shown that is so characteristic of Stein's texts.

This particular kind of textual space is fundamental to Goebbels's practice of intercultural performance because it is through carefully cultivated distance that he works to maintain the juxtaposed elements' cultural identity. He says,

> It is often true that I only manipulate the structure of outside material . . . and that I don't want to touch their identity at all. For me, it is vital to preserve clarity in the contradictions between different styles. I don't want to blend them. I would rather let them conflict with one another than have something new arise out of them that lacks the strength of the independent parts. That being said, I do of course hope that something new will come out of it all, whereby the separate musical identities, so to speak, don't lose anything in the process.[10]

It is the space in the text that allows new possibilities to flourish both for the constituent elements and the audience perceiving them. Difference, like absence, makes substantial demands on the audience as they try to sort through the medley of stimuli. This method of activating audience sensory and mental perception, in both Stein and Goebbels, gives the audience considerable responsibility and freedom.

But while Stein and Goebbels share many points of contact, they differ significantly on the character of the artist. Stein, as this chapter's opening quotations from *Everybody's Autobiography* make clear, sought to characterize herself as a genius, standing alone at the vanguard of twentieth-century art.

Goebbels has a very different understanding of the artist's relationship to his community:

> I believe it to be a key characteristic of my work that the individual genius of authorship is not essential to me and that vital elements in the composition of my musical theatre pieces do not even stem from my own pen. Essentially, my pieces are different because I work with various ensembles, hands, musicians, and singers and give them their own space. I consider it old-fashioned to believe one has to create everything oneself—that's a 19th century concept—or that one has something inside that has to come out. It doesn't work that way with me. There's nothing inside me that's crying to come out.[11]

Whereas Stein always suggested there was something very special in her crying to come out—something that made her work unique and herself a genius—Goebbels shares artistic power and at least claims to be as interested in what his collaborators bring to the table as what he himself has to offer.[12] This spirit of openness and respect, which is I think, the same source of inspiration that motivates his care with the diverse cultural strands he weaves together, is an essential tool for reanimating Stein's image for the twenty-first century. Though Stein also granted her audience freedom, it was less explicit than Goebbels's invitation, and while she also mixed various kinds of found material into her plays and librettos, she did so without the extreme care for preserving the integrity of the source material.

As Sarah Bay-Cheng has noted, people continually write off Stein's contribution to a production as non sensical.[13] Despite Goebbels's equally whimsical concatenations, critics grant him considerably more respect than they do Stein's drama. They take his experiments seriously, and gladly follow where he leads, I would argue due in large measure to the very democratic and appealing spirit in which he does so. As John Rockwell wrote in his piece on *Hashirigaki* in *The New York Times*, "The amazing thing about Mr. Goebbels's wildly heterogeneous musico-poetical-theatrical collages is that they almost always work. They cohere, they compel, they beguile."[14] Tom Service of *The Guardian* conveyed a similar sentiment about the London staging: "Goebbels creates an inexplicable but coherent theatrical grammar."[15] Goebbels's manner and method work to restage an element of Stein's personality that is not always widely appealing, and one that seems to goad reviewers, and in their wake audience members, into belittling or dismissing her contribution to the performance text, no matter how much directors seem to revere her work. But more importantly, Goebbels's treatment of textual space teaches future directors how wide a range of materials can be brought into conversation with a Stein text and how creating a distance between textual filling and text is liberating. Increasing the space in the performance text rather than attempting to fill it up gives viewers a greater responsibility to make connections and to see possibilities than when text and filling seem to match. Splicing Eastern and Western, high culture and low speaks to the general condition of transnational twenty-first-century life without shutting down viewer freedom or textual possibility.

HASHIRIGAKI: A MODEL FOR
TWENTY-FIRST-CENTURY PRODUCTION

The performances of *Hashirigaki*, staged March 19–23, 2003 at the Brooklyn Academy of Music, were sponsored by the swisspeaksFESTIVAL, an eight-week celebration designed to acquaint New Yorkers with Swiss culture. At first glance, the luminous *Hashirigaki* might seem the ideal ambassador of experimental Swiss theatre as it was created at the adventurous Le Théâtre Vidy-Lausanne in 2000. But beneath its veneer of candied Technicolor delight, the production—created by an international team from an eclectic array of source material—proffered a meditation on the pleasures of living in a world unfettered by boundaries, national or otherwise and a model for adventurous productions of Gertrude Stein's texts in the new century (see photo 6.1).

In *Hashirigaki*, Goebbels controlled the collision of three textual forces: traditional Japanese music, Gertrude Stein's epic novel *Making of Americans* finished in 1911 but not published until 1925, and the music of the Beach Boys from their 1966 album, "Pet Sounds." Though these elements hail from far-flung locales, periods, media, and cultural strata, a complex network of alliances emerged from them by the end of the ninety-minute show, suggesting that the lines demarcating East and West, high art and kitsch, the exotic and the banal, are quickly eroding.

After the dimming of the houselights and the chiming of four bells, the audience was greeted by a mysterious rustling sound—like the wings of a flock of birds—in the dark. Slowly the lights came up on three crouching figures and it became evident that they were generating this sound by wiggling the papery collars on their black jumpsuits. This playfulness with sound and its slippery metamorphosis in the presence of sight was a trademark characteristic of the production. The performers' bodies eventually unfurled, revealing the scale of statures of the tiny Japanese performer, Yumiko Tanaka, the middle-sized Canadian, Marie Goyette, and the willowy Swede, Charlotte Engelkes. Projected on the wall behind them and on their black-clad bodies was a painted landscape on which a flickering gobo

Photo 6.1   *Hashirigaki* directed by Heiner Goebbels; set design, light, and photograph by Klaus Grünberg

of a bird appeared as if to tease the audience about its initial misperception of the show's opening sounds. The figures became native elements of the landscape until travel commenced with Tanaka exiting right, Goyette left, and Engelkes departing head first through a torso-high trap in the wall. Opening a performance based on the text of Gertrude Stein with a land-scape was highly appropriate, as she wanted theatre to be like a landscape: free from the syncopated nervousness of narrative, embracing instead a pure and immediate interaction of sight and sound. This goal was one realized by Goebbels (with the help of his immensely talented light and set designer Klaus Grünberg) in this moment and throughout the show.

In next tableau—the show was structured, in a manner Stein would have applauded, around chunks of reverberating image and sound—the land-scape disappeared. The title track from "Pet Sounds" underscored the deliv-ery of lines excised from Stein's novel as the performers brought on an assortment of objects—from a framed version of the first scene's pro-jected landscape to a surfboard to a chainsaw to perambulators both toy and life-sized—taking them through the openings in the wall. The sundry items provided a visual analogue for Stein's words. Freed from the search for nar-rative sense, one could take pleasure in the shape, size, and color of the props and appreciate Stein's language for the musicality of its repetitions and its rhythms that were further enhanced by the French, Swedish, and Japanese accents flavoring the performers' pronunciation. The pop sound-scape resonated with the Stein text, rescuing each element from its usual station in the cultural hierarchy. The scene also began to explain the production's title. *Hashirigaki* means talking while walking or a flowing, cursive script. The first half of the definition was very literally what the performers were doing, but augmenting this rather mundane sense, the production's amalgamation of alien cultures and artistic styles might be imagined as a style of writing characterized by rolling links and multiple connections.

In the thematic center of the production, the performers built a Western city from cardboard cutouts. Bathed in the shifting hues of Grünberg's glowing cyc, the three sang in Japanese while lugging on stage a silhouetted church, house, skyscraper, factory, and car. The pieces partially masked the theramin and Japanese percussive instruments left on the floor from a previous scene, while bells hanging languidly from the flies were transformed into hot air balloons by means of cardboard baskets. Shifting the means of production of aural stimulation into visual images responded to Stein's theoretical queries about whether one could see and hear in the theatre at the same time. In these moments Eastern culture became embedded in, rather than antithetical to, Western progress. Later an instrumental version of "God Only Knows" played beneath the show's most sustained story fragments and behind less narrative cuttings from Stein's novel that circled around and back through the ideas of saying, feeling, thinking, and repeating. The marriage of music and word in this section linked the worlds of popular and high culture, making both feel familiar even to those for whom one half of the pairing might have been alien. Midway through the scene, the cast traded the tan fedoras and trench coats they had been wearing for neon-bright wigs and more feminine raincoats and pumps. Simultaneously embodying bubblegum 1960s back-up singers and witty, international avant-garde performance artists, the trio did something akin to the twist while they sang "Don't Talk." Tanaka's performance persona was inept with the step, denaturalizing the bizarre gyrations of mid-twentieth-century Western youth further. Frustrated, she stalked offstage to the strains of gleeful laughter from the audience. She returned with a shamisen and began elegantly accompanying the song, creating a seamless union of Eastern and Western sound. Finally a hanger flew into view ordering the performers to demolish the city. A perceptible wave of melancholy washed over the audience as the ruins of the utopian cosmopolis flew out. The possibility of such international and cultural accord seemed once again a fragile, paper dream.

In the show's coda, the performers, costumed in various elegant white suits, knelt downstage, each behind an instrument. A bare bulb nested in a rotating, mesh box aloft in the upstage left corner. The shadows it cast spilled out into the orchestra, uniting performers and audience, and enacting the quotation from *Making of Americans* in the program about many people uniting to "see some see something, to see some hear something, to see some do something . . . to feel something, to feel some feel something." Goyette and Engelkes sang "I Just Wasn't Made for These Times." Tanaka offered the audience a last taste of Stein—a bit of text spooling around the issue of sadness—as Engelkes responded on the theramin and Goyette chimed the bells. As the final light cue faded, and I braced myself to emerge into a tense New York City night at the beginning of Gulf War II, I found myself wishing that the lines of culture and status could be so deftly navigated outside the theatre.

CONCLUSION

In Chicago and Santa Fe, Cooperstown and Saint Louis, Hartford and New York, American audiences saw their collective fixations and aspects of Gertrude Stein's persona reproduced in the spaces of her texts during the twentieth century. As the twenty-first century unfolds, American cultural concerns and Stein herself will surely be bodied forth anew, through the kind of imaginative intercultural collisions modeled by Goebbels's *Hashirigaki* on an increasingly global stage. Could Stein reclaim the bird's eye view she had from her airplane ride over the Midwest and gaze down upon these exquisite new theatrical landscapes, she would, no doubt, be thrilled and amazed by her texts' new topography and the evolving landscape of American alternative theatre that owes so much to her work.

Notes

INTRODUCTION

1. Gertrude Stein, *What are Masterpieces* (Los Angeles: The Conference Press, 1940), 62.
2. Edward M. Burns and Ulla E. Dydo, eds, *The Letters of Gertrude Stein and Thorton Wilder* (New Haven: Yale University Press, 1996), 3.
3. Stein was traveling with her partner, Alice B. Toklas.
4. Edward Burns, ed., *The Letters of Gertrude Stein and Carl Van Vechten, 1913–1946* (New York: Columbia University Press, 1986), 359.
5. Shari Benstock makes a related argument in *Women of the Left Bank, Paris 1900–1940* (Austin: University of Texas Press, 1986), 157.
6. Stein refused to speak to audiences of greater than 500. Marvin Ross lost his job at Columbia University for selling more than 1,700 tickets to one of the Columbia University lectures, according to Linda Wagner-Martin in *Favored Strangers: Gertrude Stein and Her Family* (New Brunswick: Rutgers University Press, 1995), 212.
7. Gertrude Stein, *Lectures in America* (Boston: Beacon Press, 1985), 94.
8. Ibid., 122.
9. Ibid., 125.
10. Ibid., 122.
11. Gertrude Stein, *The Geographical History of America* (Baltimore: Johns Hopkins University Press, 1995), 55.
12. Ibid., 230.
13. I discuss this issue in chapter 3 in regard to *Doctor Faustus Lights the Lights* and in chapter 4 in regard to *The Mother of Us All*.
14. The term is Jane Palatini Bowers's from her seminal study, *They Watch Me As They Watch This: Gertrude Stein's Metadrama* (Philadelphia: University of Pennsylvania Press, 1991), 25–71.

1 GERTRUDE STEIN: LIVING AND WRITING THE AMERICAN LANDSCAPE

1. Gertrude Stein, *Everybody's Autobiography* (Cambridge, Mass.: Exact Change, 1993), 208.

2. In *ThirdSpace: Journeys to Los Angeles and Other Real-and-Imagined Places* (Cambridge, Mass.: Blackwell, 1996), Soja outlines the biography of Henri Lefebvre before he begins exploring his theories.

3. S. J. Kleinberg, *The Shadow of the Mills: Working Class Families in Pittsburgh, 1870–1907* (Pittsburgh: University of Pittsburgh Press, 1989), 41.

4. See http://digital.library.pitt.edu/maps.

5. Kleinberg, 51.

6. Janet Hobhouse, *Everybody Who Was Anybody: A Biography of Gertrude Stein* (New York: G. P. Putnam and Sons, 1975), 2.

7. Michael North, *Reading 1922: A Return to the Scene of the Modern* (Oxford: Oxford University Press, 1999), 203.

8. Gertrude Stein, *The Autobiography of Alice B. Toklas* (New York: Vintage, 1961), 71.

9. Ibid., 71.

10. Ibid., 71–2.

11. Stein wrote of this experience in "Plays," *Lectures in America* (New York: Vintage, 1965), 112–3: "I think the play really was Pinafore in London but the theatre there was so huge that I do not remember at all seeing a stage I only remember that it felt like a that is the theatre did. I doubt if I did see the stage."

12. Hobhouse, 73.

13. Hobhouse (5) reports that Stein's "early essays at Harvard in the 1890s show that as late as age twenty-one (her detractors would claim even later), Gertrude Stein was writing simple English sentences with great difficulty, failing in her command of basic grammatical constructions and simple spelling. On this and on the later stylistic practices of the accomplished writer—if only in terms of the fascination with simple words which that writing conveys—Gertrude's early years without English must have had some bearing."

14. See Jane Palatini Bowers's reading of the Daniel Webster figure in *Mother of Us All*, Stein's 1946 libretto in *They Watch Me As They Watch This: Gertrude Stein's Metadrama* (Philadelphia: University of Pennsylvania Press, 1991).

15. Gertrude Stein, *The Autobiography of Alice B. Toklas*, 73.

16. Alice B. Toklas, *The Alice B. Toklas Cookbook* (Garden City, N.Y.: Anchor Books, 1960), 131.

17. Ibid., 131.

18. See *Hometown Chinatown: The History of Oakland's Chinese Community* (New York: Garland, 2000), 7.

19. Ibid., 6.

20. See Lisa Ruddick's chapter on *Making of Americans* in *Reading Gertrude Stein: Body, Text, Gnosis* (Ithaca: Cornell University Press, 1990) for an insightful analysis of Martha Hersland as Stein's literary double and David Hersland as her father's.

21. Gertrude Stein, *Wars I Have Seen* (New York: Random House, 1945), 4.

22. Gertrude Stein, "Plays," 119.

23. Ibid., 119.

24. Ibid., 75.

25. Ibid., 112–4.

26. Ibid., 115.

27. Ibid., 116–7.

28. Michael Stein would share these same interests as an adult.

29. Linda Wagner-Martin, *Favored Strangers: Gertrude Stein and Her Family* (New Brunswick: Rutgers University Press, 1995), 21.

30. See Michel de Certeau's "Walking in the City" in *The Practice of Everyday Life* trans. Steven Rendall (Berkeley: University of California Press, 1988). See also Joseph Boone's reading of the DeCerteau and the mobility of the modern urban space as a tool for creating homosexual male identity in "Queer Sites of Modernism," in *The Geography of Identity*, ed. Patricia Yaeger (Ann Arbor: University of Michigan Press, 1996).

31. See Linda Simon's *Genuine Reality: A Life of William James* (New York: Harcourt Brace and Company, 1998), 129–36 for a description of James's teaching style at Harvard and the effect of teaching on his mental health and James R. Mellow's *Charmed Circle: Gertrude Stein and Company* (New York: Avon, 1974), 46–7.

32. Qtd. in James R. Mellow, *Charmed Circle: Gertrude Stein and Company*, 46.

33. Lisa Ruddick, *Reading Gertrude Stein*, 4.

34. Qtd. John Malcolm Brinnin, *The Third Rose: Gertrude Stein and Her World* (Reading, Mass.: Addison-Wesley, 1987), 30–1.

35. Gertrude Stein, *Everybody's Autobiography*, 275.

36. Qtd. Hobhouse, 15.

37. Stein was given the option of taking one more course during the summer session to make up for her failing grade in obstetrics. She elected not to do so.

38. Wagner-Martin, 48–51.

39. Shari Benstock, *Women of the Left Bank: Paris, 1900–1940* (Austin: University of Texas Press, 1986), 57.

40. As noted earlier, Stein's first publication was in *The Harvard Psychological Review*. During her American tour, Stein also wrote a series of pieces on American life and manners for *Harper's*.

41. See Hobhouse, 35 and Wagner-Martin, 63.

42. Stein tells of Stieglitz's impressions of her in *Everybody's Autobiography*, 74–5.

43. See the work of Janet Hobhouse, Linda Wagner-Martin, John Malcolm Brinnin, James Mellow, and Diana Souhami.

44. Gertrude Stein, *The Autobiography of Alice B. Toklas*, 5.

45. Emily Hahn tells the story in *Mabel, A Biography of Mabel Dodge Luhan* (Boston: Houghton-Mifflin, 1977): Stein was staying next door to Dodge in the villa when she was visited by her son's tutor. Dodge claims to have been aware of Stein's listening to the encounter and the next day at a meal, Stein's "strong look" was interpreted as a sexual advance by Dodge and Alice, who abruptly left the dining room.

46. *Vanity Fair* June 10, 1918: 31.

47. See Michael North's fascinating reading of the sexual undertones of this account in *Reading 1922*.

48. Wilson, Edmund. "Mr. Hemingway's Dry Points," *Dial 77* October 1924: 340–1.

49. Joseph Boone, "Queer Sites of Modernism," 261.

50. In Wagner-Martin's biography of Stein, she offers a different reading: "The heterosexual dominance of the salon had been one reason Alice sat with the 'wives.' She did not want to talk with a segregated audience anymore than Gertrude did; what they like best was to entertain as a pair, which they did in smaller, more intimate groups" (188).

51. Ulla Dydo, *A Stein Reader* (Evanston: Northwestern University Press, 1993), 326.

52. Virgil Thomson, *Virgil Thomson* (New York: Knopf, 1966), 89.

53. Ibid., 89.

54. Ibid., 90.

55. Stein also saw the adaptation of *They Must. Be Wedded. To Their Wife* as the ballet *A Wedding Bouquet* at the Sadler Wells Theatre in London in April of 1937.

56. Many critics read Stein's difficult works of the 1920s as making coded allusions to domestic life with Alice.

57. A detailed chronology of Stein's tour is published in *The Letters of Gertrude Stein and Thornton Wilder*, 339–51. A narrative account is available in *Everybody's Autobiography*.

58. Gertrude Stein, *Everybody's Autobiography*, 226.

59. Ibid., 237.

60. Ibid., 298.

61. Ibid., 180.

62. A recent popular treatment of this issue is found in *The New Yorker*, June 2, 2003: 58–81.

63. Gertrude Stein, "The Winner Loses," in *Wars I Have Seen*, 176.

64. Ibid., 181.

65. Ibid., 181.

66. Denise's lines read as follows: "Oh dear I am so tired of working I wish I could be rich again, oh dear. I want to rich, anyway I never want to shell a pea or dig a potato or wash a dress. I want all vegetables to grow in cans not in the ground. I want all clothes washed in a laundry and I want all stockings bought new and thrown away. That is what I want, oh dear."

67. Hobhouse, 222.

68. Gertrude Stein, *Wars I Have Seen*, 162.

69. Ibid., 163.

2   BEHIND THE MASK OF PRIMITIVISM: UNTANGLING THE IMAGES OF GERTRUDE STEIN AND AFRICAN AMERICANS IN *FOUR SAINTS IN THREE ACTS* AND FRANK GALATI'S *EACH ONE AS SHE MAY*

1. For a fascinating analysis of the portrait, see Robert S. Lubar's article, "Unmasking Pablo's Gertrude: Queer Desire and the Subject of Portraiture," *Art Bulletin* 1.79 (March 1997).

2. Gertrude Stein, *The Autobiography of Alice B. Toklas* (New York: Vintage, 1961), 57.

3. See Colin Rhodes's *Primitivism and Modern Art* (London: Thames and Hudson, 1994) for an extended discussion of these issues.

4. Richard Dyer, *White* (London: Routledge, 1995), 2.

5. Paul Gilroy, "Modern Tones," in *Rhapsodies in Black: Art of the Harlem Renaissance* (Berkeley: University of California Press, 1997), 104.

6. Carl Van Vechten, "Foreword to *Four Saints in Three Acts*."

7. Qtd. Steven Watson, *Prepare for Saints: Gertrude Stein, Virgil Thomson, and the Mainstreaming of American Modernism* (New York: Random House, 1998), 199.

8. See Barbara Webb, "The Centrality of Race to the Modernist Aesthetics of Gertrude Stein's *Four Saints in Three Acts*," *Modernism/modernity* 3 (2000), 447–69. Barbara Webb's work (from an earlier conference paper version of this article and from her unpublished Master's thesis) was a tremendous influence on this study. I am most grateful for the generous ways she shared her excellent work with me.

9. See Steven Watson's *Prepare for Saints* for a fine reading of the production as developing from this set of assumptions.

10. Virgil Thomson, *Virgil Thomson* (New York: Alfred A. Knopf, 1966), 239.

11. Qtd. Watson, 252.

12. Ibid., 258.

13. Qtd. in Anthony Tommasini, *Virgil Thomson: Composer on the Aisle* (New York: W.W. Norton, 1997), 250.

14. John Houseman, *Run-Through: A Memoir* (New York: Simon and Schuster, 1972).

15. Qtd. Tommasini, 231.

16. Ibid., 232.

17. Stein, *The Autobiography of Alice B. Toklas*, 64.

18. Ibid., 238.

19. Rhodes, 18–9.

20. Gertrude Stein, *Everybody's Autobiography* (Cambridge: Exact Change, 1993), 112.

21. Ibid., 287–8.

22. Houseman, 101.

23. Gertrude Stein, *Four Saints in Three Acts*, in *Last Operas and Plays* (Baltimore: Johns Hopkins University Press, 1993), 478.

24. Stein, *Everybody's Autobiography*, 124.

25. *Vogue*, Virgil Thomson Collection, clippings, Beinecke Library.

26. Olin Downes, "The Stein-Thomson Concoction," *New York Times*, February 25, 1934.

27. Tommasini, 169.

28. "Stein Opera: First-Nighters Hear Four Acts of 4 Saints in 3 Acts," *Newsweek*, February 17, 1934.

29. Stark Young, "One Moment Alit," *New Republic*, March 7, 1934: 103.

30. "Dressmakers for Art." *The Saturday Review*, March 3, 1934.

31. Qtd. David Harris, "The Original *Four Saints in Three Acts*," *The Drama Review* 26.1 (1982): 123.

32. *Hartford Courant*, March 1934, Virgil Thomson Collection, clippings.

33. Harris, 127.

34. John Martin, "The Dance: Four Saints," *New York Times*, February 25, 1934.

35. Barbara Bloemink, *The Life and Art of Florine Stettheimer* (New Haven: Yale University Press, 1995), xii.

36. *Women's Wear Daily*, Virgil Thomson Collection, clippings.

37. Qtd. Houseman, 117.

38. Joseph Wood Krutch, "A Prepare for Saints," *The Nation*, April 4, 1934.

39. Tommasini, 420.

40. "Amos 'n' Andy's Transition," *Newsweek*, July 9, 1951: 56.

41. Ibid., 56.

42. John Martin, "NAACP Objects," *Newsweek*, July 23, 1951: 59.

43. Richard Watts, "Revival of an Enchanting Opera," *New York Post*, April 17, 1952.

44. William H. Beyer, "The State of the Theatre: Modern Dance and Opera," *School and Society*, June 21, 1952.

45. Brooks Atkinson, "Four Saints in Three Acts Restaged by ANTA at the Broadway Theatre," *New York Times*, April 17, 1952.

46. See Robert Coleman, "Four Saints in Three Acts is for Limited Audience," *Daily Mirror*, April 17, 1952; Miles Kastendieck, "A Unique Experience; A Handsome Show," *New York Journal American*, April 17, 1952; Walter F. Kerr, "Four Saints in Three Acts," *New York Herald Tribune*, April 17, 1952; "Not Four-Thirty Six," *Newsweek*, April 28, 1952: 52; Robert Sylvester, "Four Saints in Three Acts Again Musical, Mystical, and Very Funny." *Daily News*, April 17, 1952; and "Old Pigeons," *Time*, April 28, 1952.

47. See Clarence Thomas, "Concurrence to Majority Opinion," in *Adarand Construction Company v. Peña* (1995), http://www.caselaw.findlaw.com.

48. David Krasner, *Resistance, Parody, and Double Consciousness in African American Theatre* (New York: St. Martin's Press, 1997), 26.

49. Tom Valeo, "Director's Adaptation of Melanctha Seeks Out the Coherent and Dramatic," Arlington, *Illinois Daily Herald*, February 17, 1995: sec. 6, 16–7.

50. Connie Lauerman, "Thinking of Her: Galati Revives Gertrude Stein at Goodman," *Chicago Tribune*, February 12, 1995.

51. Stein, *The Autobiography of Alice B. Toklas*, 54.

52. Michael North, *The Dialect of Modernism: Race, Language and Twentieth-Century Literature* (New York: Oxford University Press, 1994), 24.

53. While critics do, as I mentioned, agree on the source material for "Melanctha," they don't all agree about which character represents Stein. Major Stein critics such as Jane Palatini Bowers and Harriet Chessman see Melanctha, rather than Jefferson, as Stein's representative in the text. See Jane Palatini Bowers, *Gertrude Stein* (New York: St. Martin's Press, 1993) and Harriet Chessman, *The Public is Invited to Dance: Representation, the Body, and Dialogue in Gertrude Stein* (Stanford: Stanford University Press, 1989).

54. North, 61.

55. Program, Goodman Theatre Archives.

56. North, 73.

57. Adam Langer, "Beautiful Bore," *Chicago Reader*, February 24, 1995.

58. Lauerman, February 12, 1995.

59. Richard Christensen, "Winning Way with Words. 'Each One' Captures Melody of Gertrude Stein's Language," *Chicago Tribune*, February 14, 1995: 25.

60. Edward A. Berlin, *Ragtime: A Musical and Cultural History* (Berkeley: California University Press, 1980), 71–2.

61. Ibid., 104.

62. David A. Jasen and Trebor Jay Tichenor, *Rags and Ragtime: A Musical History* (New York: The Seabury Press, 1978), 14.

63. Krasner, 26–7.

64. Ibid., 82.

65. Langer, February 24, 1995.

66. Frank Galati, *Gertrude Stein: Each One As She May*, Unpublished script, 69 or Gertrude Stein, "Melanctha," in *Selected Writings of Gertrude Stein*, ed. Carl Van Vechten (New York: Vintage, 1990), 394.

67. Galati, 42; Stein, "Melanctha," *Selected Writings of Gertrude Stein*, 379.

68. Galati, 1–3; Stein, 349–50.

69. Galati, 8; Stein, 364.

70. Cornell West, *Race Matters* (New York: Vintage, 1994), 119–20.

71. Krasner, 26.

3   EXILE FROM MASS CULTURE: CHARTING THE OPEN SPACES OF PERCEPTUAL FREEDOM IN THE LIVING THEATRE'S *DOCTOR FAUSTUS LIGHTS THE LIGHTS* AND THE JUDSON POETS THEATRE'S *IN CIRCLES*

1. Picasso's portrait of her hung on her studio wall in Paris. When she was forced to flee Paris during World War II, the Picasso was one of only two paintings she took with her into the countryside.

2. Stein had hoped to secure a movie deal during her American tour of 1934–5. She was not successful in this pursuit.

3. Gertrude Stein, *Everybody's Autobiography* (Cambridge, Mass.: Exact Change, 1993), 1.

4. Ibid., 2.

5. Hellman was a success in her own right by this time, as *Children's Hour* had played on Broadway in 1934. Nowhere, however, does Stein record an anxiousness to meet her or anything about what exchanges they might have had during the dinner party. Hellman retaliated for this snub in a 1965 interview in *The Paris Review* (33 Winter-Spring 1965: 64–95). Hellman said, "There was this magnificent china and lace tablecloth. Chaplin turned over his coffee cup, nowhere near Stein, just all over this beautiful cloth, and the first thing Miss Stein said was, 'Don't worry, it didn't get on me.' She was miles away from him. She said it perfectly seriously. Then she told Dash he was the only American writer who wrote well about women. He was very pleased." The

interviewer then asks, "Did he give you any credit for that?" Hellman responds, "He pointed to me, but she didn't pay any attention. She wasn't having any part of me. I was just a girl around the table. I talked to Miss Toklas. We talked about food. It was very pleasant."

6. Alice B. Toklas, *What is Remembered* (San Francisco: North Point, 1985), 152.
7. Sinda Gregory, *Private Investigations: The Novels of Dashiell Hammett* (Carbondale and Edwardsville, Ill.: Southern Illinois University Press, 1985), 18.
8. Cynthia Hamilton, *Western and Hard-Boiled Detective Fiction in America: From High Noon to Midnight* (Iowa City: University of Iowa Press, 1987), 145.
9. Gertrude Stein, *The Geographical History of America* (Baltimore: Johns Hopkins University Press), 112.
10. Toklas, 152.
11. Stein, *Everybody's Autobiography*, 292.
12. Ibid., 292.
13. Michael North, *Reading 1922: A Return to the Scene of the Modern* (Oxford: Oxford University Press), 171.
14. While Chaplin's politics would eventually imbue his persona and his films, they had not yet done so at the time he met Stein. This shift would begin to occur with *Modern Times*.
15. See Charles J. Maland's *Chaplin and American Culture: The Evolution of a Star Image* (Princeton: Princeton University Press, 1989), 73.
16. North, 165.
17. In "Antigone's Example: A View of The Living Theatre's Production, Process, and Praxis," *Theatre Survey* 41.1 (May 2000), Cindy Rosenthal writes, "The Living Theatre is a metaphor for the sixties, its very name conjuring up the undulating movement, the pulsing flow, the argumentative spirit that characterized that time" (69).
18. Judith Malina, *The Diaries of Judith Malina, 1947–1957* (New York: Grove Press, 1984), 169.
19. Even before Julian Beck and Judith Malina began producing theatre under the banner of the Living Theatre, they were producing Gertrude Stein. On August 16, 1951 they opened their project, Theater in the Room, as a rebellion against the constraints of the commercial theatre. In the front room of their apartment, they seated ten people on a bench against one wall; in front of them sat ten more on cushions on the floor. These twenty audience members, who had received hand-drawn invitations, were treated to several short theatrical pieces: "Crying Backstage," a comic curtain-raiser by Paul Goodman, "He Who Says Yes and He Who Says No" by Bertolt Brecht, The Young Man and the Mannequin scene from Gabriel Garcia Lorca's *Once Five Years Pass*, and Gertrude Stein's short play, "Ladies' Voices." That I choose to emphasize Stein here is in part a result of my own interest in Stein's work. But beyond my own distinct prejudice in favor of Stein, Beck and Malina seemed to have a prejudice for her work as well. Of the Theatre in the Room pieces, only "Ladies' Voices" was revived for their Evening of Bohemian Theatre in January of 1952. Their

audience was also especially taken with "Ladies' Voices." In her diary, Malina records that, "The Stein drew calls for encores."

20. Marty Jezer, *The Dark Ages: Life in the United States, 1945–1960* (Boston: South End Press, 1982).

21. "Peace but with our Guard Up," *Newsweek*, July 9, 1951: 17.

22. Elaine Tyler May, "Explosive Issues: Sex, Women, and the Bomb," in *Recasting America: Culture and Politics in the Age of the Cold War*, ed. Larry May (Chicago: Chicago University Press, 1989).

23. Bevya Rosten, *The Fractured Stage: Gertrude Stein's Influence on American Avant-Garde Directing as Seen in Four Productions of Dr. Faustus Lights the Lights* (UMI Dissertation Service, 1998), 41.

24. Clifford Geertz, "Thick Description: Towards an Interpretive Theory of Culture," in *The Interpretation of Cultures: Selected Essays* (New York: Basic Books, Inc., 1973), 23.

25. Stephen J. Whitfield, *The Culture of the Cold War*, 2nd ed. (Baltimore: Johns Hopkins University Press, 1996), 10.

26. Daniel Belgrad, *The Culture of Spontaneity: Improvisation and the Arts in Postwar America* (Chicago: University of Chicago Press, 1998), 15–6.

27. Belgrad observed:

> At the San Remo bar in Greenwich Village in the early 1950s, a visitor would sooner or later run into scores of people engaged in some aspect of the postwar aesthetic of spontaneity—Paul Goodman, Julian Beck and Judith Malina, John Cage and Merce Cunningham, Miles Davis, Jackson Pollock, Allen Ginsberg, Gregory Corso, and Jack Kerouac—among others (5).

Though Belgrad notes Beck and Malina's participation in the aesthetic of spontaneity and proximity to other artists of the movement, he does not analyze their work (or other theatrical work) in any significant depth.

28. Rosten, 31.

29. See chapters 1 and 4 for further discussion.

30. *Doctor Faustus Lights the Lights* Program, Billie Rose Theatre Collection.

31. Living Theatre Papers, Billie Rose Theatre Collection, Series XIII, Box 63.

32. Malina, 182.

33. John Tytell, *The Living Theatre: Art, Exile, and Outrage* (New York: Grove Press, 1995), 76.

34. The list of opening night viewers is in Series 3, Box 7, Folder 1 of the Living Theatre Papers in the Billie Rose Theatre Collection.

35. Jack Wright, "The Living Theatre: Alive and Committed," diss., University of Kansas, 1969, 51.

36. For analysis of suburban life see such texts as Lynn Spiegel's *Welcome to the Dream House*, Roger Silverstone's *Visions of Suburbia*, Linda McDowell's *Undoing Place? A Geographical Reader*, and Margaret Marsh's *Suburban Lives*.

37. Publicity letter, dated 1951. Contained in Series IX, Box 54, Folder 2 in Living Theatre Papers, Billie Rose Theatre Collection.

38. Publicity letter, dated 1951. Contained in Series VII, Sub 1, Box 17, Folder 10 in Living Theatre Papers, Billie Rose Theatre Collection.

39. Publicity letter, dated 1951. Contained in Series IX, Box 54, Folder 2 in Living Theatre Papers, Billie Rose Theatre Collection.

40. *New York Times*, December 3, 1951.

41. Malina, 180. Malina's uncertainty about Banks before the production is also evident in her letter to Van Vechten dated August 2, 1951 in The Living Theatre's Papers. She writes, "We saw Dick Banks the other night and I had long discussion concerning *Doctor Faustus*. I want to thank you for suggesting him for the music as I think it may lead to a successful collaboration."

42. Gertrude Stein, "A Circular Play, A Play in Circles," *The Gertrude Stein Reader*, ed. Ulla Dydo (Evanston, Ill.: Northwestern University Press, 1993), 341.

43. Harold Clurman, "Theatre," *Nation*, November 27, 1967: 572–3.

44. Michael Smith, "Theatre Journal," *Village Voice*, Billie Rose Newspaper Clipping of Dramatic Criticism, Clippings File "I" 1967–8.

45. *In Circles* program, Billie Rose Collection.

46. Jon C. Teaford, *The Twentieth-Century American City*, 2nd ed. (Baltimore: Johns Hopkins University Press, 1993), 130.

47. Ibid., 133.

48. Unfortunately, the publisher and the executor of production photographer Peter Moore's estate could not reach a mutually satisfactory agreement about publishing images of this production. All the photographs I describe are, however, available for public review in the New York Public Library.

49. Marilyn Stassio, "Al Carmines: Religion's Answer to Busby Berkeley," *Cue*, February 24, 1968: 10.

50. "Perfect Circles," *New Yorker*, November 18, 1967: 131–3.

51. Robert Pasolli, "Theatre: *In Circles*," Village Voice, July 11, 1968: 35–6.

52. See Dan Sullivan, "Another Delightful Look at *In Circles*, A Drama of Obfuscation," *New York Times*, June 28, 1968: 36; Jerry Talmer, "Gertrude in a Garden," *New York Post*, October 16, 1967, and Diesel, Leota. "The Theatre," *Greenwich, Connecticut Villager*, July 4, 1968. Billie Rose Newspaper Clippings of Dramatic Criticism, Clippings File "I" 1967–8.

53. Sullivan, 36.

54. Allan Wallach, "He is Gertrude Stein's Soul Mate," *Newsday*, July 24, 1968: 56A.

55. Dominick Cavallo, *A Fiction of the Past: The Sixties in American History* (New York: St. Martin's Press, 1999), 3.

56. Jack Kroll, "Stein Songs," *Newsweek*, November 27, 1967: 105.

57. *New Yorker*, November 18, 1967: 131–3.

58. Clive Barnes, "Theater: Gertrude Stein Words at the Judson Church," *New York Times*, October 14, 1967: 12.

59. Sullivan, 36.

60. Jerry Talmer, "Gertrude in a Garden," *New York Post*, October 16, 1967. Billie Rose Newspaper Clipping of Dramatic Criticism, Clippings File "I" 1967–8.

61. Sherwood Anderson, xv.
62. Michael Quinn, "Celebrity and the Semiotics of Acting," *New Theatre Quarterly* 6.22 (1990): 154–61.

4 POP PARADES AND SURREAL PAGEANTS: STAGING
NATIONAL IDENTITY AND THE STRUGGLE FOR
WOMEN'S RIGHTS IN *THE MOTHER OF US ALL*

1. Gertrude Stein, *The Mother of Us All, Last Operas and Plays* (Baltimore: Johns Hopkins University Press, 1995), 59.
2. Gertrude Stein, *Wars I Have Seen* (New York: Random House, 1945), 171.
3. Qtd. in Phoebe Stein Davis, "Even Cake Gets to Have Another Meaning: History, Narrative, and Daily Living in Gertrude Stein's World War II Writings," *Modern Fiction Studies* 44.3 (1998): 571. Davis reports that the advertisement ran on February 3, 1945.
4. Wanda Van Dusen, "Portrait of a National Fetish: Gertrude Stein's 'Introduction to the Speeches of Marechal Petain' (1942)," *Modernism/Modernity* 3.3 (1996): 70.
5. Notable examples include Lisa Ruddick in *Reading Gertrude Stein: Body, Text, Gnosis* (Ithaca: Cornell University Press, 1990), and Marianne DeKoven in *A Different Language: Gertrude Stein's Experimental Writing* (Madison: University of Wisconsin Press, 1983).
6. See Catherine Stimpson, "Gertrice/Altrude: Stein, Toklas, and the Paradox of the Happy Marriage," in *Mothering the Mind: Twelve Studies of Writers and Their Silent Partners*, ed. Ruth Perry and Martine Watson Brownley (New York: Holmes and Meier, 1984), 135.
7. Gertrude Stein, *Everybody's Autobiography* (Cambridge, Mass.: Exact Change, 1993), 225.
8. Lisa Walker makes this argument in *Looking Like What You Are: Sexual Style, Race, and Lesbian Identity* (New York: New York University Press, 2001).
9. Ibid., 27.
10. Jane Palatini Bowers, *They Watch Me as They Watch This: Gertrude Stein's Metadrama* (Philadelphia: University of Pennsylvania Press, 1991), 108, 110.
11. Ibid., 114.
12. Stein, *The Mother of Us All in Last Operas and Plays*, 70.
13. Anthony Tomassini, *Virgil Thomson: Composer on the Aisle* (New York: W.W. Norton and Company, 1997), 517.
14. Ibid., 518.
15. Marita Sturken, *Tangled Memories: The Vietnam War, the AIDS Epidemic, and the Politics of Remembering* (Berkeley: California University Press, 1997), 13.
16. Ibid., 7.
17. John Bodnar, *Remaking America: Public Memory, Commemoration, and Patriotism in the Twentieth Century* (Princeton: Princeton University Press, 1991), 234.
18. Lynn Spillman, *Nation and Commemoration: Creating National Identities in the United States and Australia* (Cambridge: Cambridge University Press, 1997), 95–6.

19. Robert Indiana, "Autochronology," in *Robert Indiana* (Austin: University of Texas Press, 1977), 54.
20. Santa Fe Opera program, 47.
21. Joseph Roach, *Cities of the Dead: Circum-Atlantic Performance* (New York: Columbia University Press, 1996), 36.
22. Ibid., 2.
23. Spillman, 46; Bodnar, 237.
24. Bowers.
25. Santa Fe Opera program, 47.
26. Homi K. Bhabha, "DissemiNation: Time, Narrative, and the Margins of the Modern Nation," in *Nation and Narration*, ed. Homi Bhabha (London: Routledge, 1990), 297.
27. Bowers, 109.
28. Santa Fe Opera Press Release, August 3, 1976: 4.
29. Donald Goodall, *Robert Indiana* (Austin: University of Texas Press, 1977), 27.
30. Ibid., 33.
31. Santa Fe Opera Press Release, Santa Fe Opera Archives.
32. Peter G. Davis, "Opera: Mother of the Mesas," *New York Times*, August 13, 1976.
33. Roach, 285.
34. Joan Dessens, Project Proposal to the National Endowment for the Arts and Project Proposal to the Virgil Thomson Foundation, 1.
35. Ibid., 3.
36. Debra Baker, "The Fight Ain't Over," *American Bar Association Journal* 85 (August 1999): 53.
37. Pat Swift, "Thinking about the Next Set of Issues to Tackle," *Buffalo News*, July 25, 1998, Glimmerglass Opera Archives, clippings file.
38. Sturken, 1.
39. Liz Keill, "Character from City History Featured in Glimmerglass Opera," *Independent Press of New Jersey*, August 1998: B3. Glimmerglass Opera Archives, clippings file.
40. Larry McGinn, "Masterful Mother," Syracuse, *New York Post Standard*, July 25, 1998, Glimmerglass Opera Archives, clippings file.
41. Judith E. Harper, *Susan B. Anthony: A Biographical Companion* (Santa Barbara: ABC-CLIO, Inc., 1998), 259.
42. Baker, 55.
43. Ibid., 55.
44. Ibid., 54.
45. Ibid., 55.
46. Ibid., 54.
47. Ibid., 55.
48. Peter G. Davis, "Farce-Fed," *New York Magazine*, August 31, 1998: 161.
49. Tomassini, 392.
50. Ibid., 393.
51. David Raymond, "From Glimmerglass, a Masterful Mother," *Rochester City Newspaper*, July 30, 1998, Glimmerglass Opera Archives, clippings file.

52. Davis, 161.

53. McGinn.

54. Baker, 55.

55. Ibid., 56.

56. Raymond.

57. Dessens, 1 and 3.

58. Naima Prevots, *American Pageantry: A Movement for Art and Democracy* (Ann Arbor: Michigan University Press, 1990), 49. One famous pageant even had Susan B. Anthony as its subject. In 1915, Hazel MacKaye directed and produced *The Pageant of Susan B. Anthony* for the National Women's Party. MacKaye explained why the pageant form was the appropriate vehicle for disseminating the suffragists' message: "Women are becoming more and more alive to the act that the working world is man-made, and that women will have to put up a good fight to get a fair share as bread-winners . . . . Through pageantry, we women can set forth our ideals and aspirations more graphically than in any other way."

59. Dessens, 3.

60. Ibid., 5.

61. Prevots, 4.

62. David Glassberg, *American Historical Pageantry: The Uses of Tradition in the Early Twentieth Century* (Chapel Hill: University of North Carolina Press, 1990), 290.

5   CODED STATEMENTS OF DESIRE: OUTING MEANING IN ROBERT WILSON'S *DOCTOR FAUSTUS LIGHTS THE LIGHTS*, THE WOOSTER GROUP'S *HOUSE/LIGHTS*, AND ANNE BOGART'S *GERTRUDE AND ALICE*

1. Alice B. Toklas, *What is Remembered* (New York: Holt, Rinehart, and Winston, 1963), 139.

2. Gertrude Stein, *Everybody's Autobiography* (Cambridge, Mass.: Exact Change, 1993), 168–9.

3. Bravig Iambs, *Confessions of Another Young Man* (New York: Henkle-Yewdale, 1936), 166.

4. Joseph Allen Boone, *Libidinal Currents: Sexuality and the Shaping of Modernism* (Chicago: University of Chicago Press), 262.

5. Toklas, 139.

6. Catherine Stimpson, "Somagrams of Gertrude Stein," in *The Female Body in Western Culture: Contemporary Perspectives*, ed. Susan Rubin Suleiman (Cambridge: Harvard University Press, 1986), 32.

7. In *Daring Do's: A History of Extraordinary Hair* (Paris: Flammarion, 1994), Mary Trasko reports, "Antoine had cut his first 'bob' in 1910 to make the actress Eve Lavalliere look younger for a role she play at the Comedie Francaise. Though he was deluged with requests for the cut, he did not feel that the time was right for it. Nevertheless two years later he succumbed" (109).

8. Ibid., 138.

9. Linda Wagner-Martin, *Favored Strangers: Gertrude Stein and Her Family* (New Brunswick: Rutgers University Press, 1995), 209.

10. Mark Goble, "Cameo Appearances; or, When Gertrude Stein Check into *Grand Hotel*," *Modern Language Quarterly* 62.2 (2001), see page 141 and endnotes 23 and 24.

11. Stein, *Everybody's Autobiography*, 6.

12. Goble, 141.

13. Lillian Faderman, *Odd Girls and Twilight Lovers: A History of Lesbian Life in Twentieth-Century America* (New York: Columbia University Press, 1991), 93.

14. George Chauncey: *Gay New York: Gender, Urban Culture, and the Making of the Gay Male World, 1890–1940* (New York: Basic Books, 1994), 353.

15. Andrea Weiss, "A Queer Feeling When I Look at You: Hollywood Stars and Lesbian Spectatorship in the 1930s," in *Multiple Voices in Feminist Film Criticism*, ed. Diana Carson, Linda Dittmar, and Janice R. Welsh (Minneapolis: Minnesota University Press, 1994), 331.

16. Edith Becker, Michelle Citron, Julia Lesage, and B. Ruby Rich, "Lesbians and Film," in *Out in Culture: Gay, Lesbian, and Queer Essays on Popular Culture* (Durham: Duke University Press, 1995), 31.

17. Elizabeth Fifer, *Rescued Readings: A Reconstruction of Gertrude Stein's Difficult Texts* (Detroit: Wayne State University Press, 1992), 90.

18. Sue-Ellen Case, *The Domain-Matrix: Performing Lesbian at the End of Print Culture* (Bloomington: Indiana University Press, 1996), 84–5.

19. Ibid., 87.

20. Susan Benett, *Theatre Audiences: A Theory of Production and Reception* (London: Routledge, 1998), 85.

21. *Gertrude and Alice* later moved to New York City where it played at the Foundry Theatre.

22. I draw a distinction here between the Performing Garage and a venue like the WOW Café.

23. Jill Dolan, " 'Lesbian' Subjectivity in Realism: Dragging at the Margins of Structure and Ideology," in *Presence and Desire: Essays on Gender, Sexuality, and Performance* (Ann Arbor: University of Michigan Press, 1993), 159.

24. Richard Dyer, *Heavenly Bodies: Film Stars and Society* (New York: St. Martin's Press, 1986), 5.

25. Danae Clark, "Commodity Lesbianism," in *Out in Culture: Gay, Lesbian, and Queer Essays on Popular Culture*, ed. Corey K. Creekmur and Alexander Doty (Durham: Duke University Press, 1995), 486.

26. Ibid., 492.

27. Ibid., 494.

28. Ann M. Ciasullo, "Making Her (In) Visible: Cultural Representations of Lesbianism and the Lesbian Body in the 1990s," *Feminist Studies* 27.3 (Fall 2001), 578.

29. Judith Butler, *Excitable Speech: A Politics of the Performative* (New York: Routledge, 1997), 108.

30. Ibid., 108–9.

31. Gertrude Stein, "Plays," in *Lectures in America* (New York: Vintage, 1965), 113–4.

32. He subsequently directed *Four Saints in Three Acts* and *Saints and Singing*.

33. October 25, 1993.

34. Program, 6

35. Jan Stuart, "Robert Wilson Tackles Doctor Faustus," *Los Angeles Times*, July 11, 1992: 8.

36. John O'Mahony, "Unnatural Acts," *The Guardian*, August 25, 1993: 6.

37. Jan Stuart, "Faustus: Squaring Circles or Vice Versa," *Newsday*, July 9, 1992: II: 63.

38. Program, 6.

39. Robert Gore-Langton, "Doing the Lights Fantastic," *Daily Telegraph*, August 27, 1993: 15.

40. Jamie James, "Meeting of Minds Over a 50-Year Gap," *Times*, July 18, 1992.

41. Colin Donald, "Risk pays dividends," *The Scotsman*, August 26, 1993: Sec. III.

42. Kirk Ormand, "Oedipus the Queen: Cross-Gendering without Drag," *Theatre Journal* (March 2003): 5.

43. John Peter, "Heaven and Earthy," *Times*, August 29, 1993: Features.

44. David Savran "Whistling in the Dark," *Performing Arts Journal* XV.1 (January 1993): 26.

45. See reviews in *Chicago Tribune*, November 14, 1997, *Chicago Sun-Tribune*, November 13, 1997, and *Columbus Dispatch*, October 9, 1997.

46. Ellen Donkin, "Directing Stein," in *Upstaging Big Daddy*, ed. Ellen Donkin and Susan Clement (Ann Arbor: Michigan University Press, 1992), 212.

47. Other intertextual weavings were made with *I Love Lucy, Young Frankenstein*, and *Footlight Parade*.

48. Bevya Rosten, "The Gesture of Illogic," *American Theatre* February 1998: 16–9.

49. When I saw the performances live in 1998, Smith played this role. Suzzy Roche later took over the part.

50. See review in *Minneapolis Star-Tribune*, November 22, 1997.

51. This idea is both supported and rejected by Valk's comments in interviews. In the *Chicago Sun-Times*, November 7, 1997, Valk was quoted as saying, "It's more like an internal conflict manifested on stage. Like everything you see is happening inside one person's head." While in *American Theatre* (February 1998) she noted the ways the group's work in general freed her from having to produce psychological motivation: "I channel the text. It's liberating. I don't have to search for a psychological thrust." While the aside is generally thought of as being psychologically motivated, the use of video in this performance suggests it doesn't have to be.

52. Gertrude Stein, *Doctor Faustus Lights the Lights. A Gertrude Stein Reader*, ed. Ulla E. Dydo (Evanston: Northwestern University Press, 1993), 624.

53. I saw the two public performance of this production in St. Louis, Missouri during February 1999. The production later moved to New York City in June 1999, produced by the Foundry Theater.

54. Robert S. Lubar, "Unmasking Pablo's Gertrude: Queer Desire and the Subject of Portraiture," *Art Bulletin* 1.79 (March 1997): 57.

55. In "A Fresh Look at a Syntax Skewer: A New Play Depicts the Life and Love of Gertrude Stein," June 9, 1999: E4, Dinita Smith of the *New York Times* reports that Pashalinski and Chapman had been lovers for nineteen years at the time of the performances.

56. Anne Bogart, *A Director Prepares: Seven Essays on Art and Theatre* (London: Routledge, 1992), 102.

57. Jill Dolan, *Presence and Desire: Essays on Gender, Sexuality, and Performance* (Ann Arbor: Michigan University Press, 1993), 191.

EPILOGUE: DREAMS OF A NEW FRONTIER—MAPPING GERTRUDE STEIN'S TWENTY-FIRST-CENTURY IDENTITY ON A GLOBAL STAGE

1. Gertrude Stein, *Everybody's Autobiography* (Cambridge, Mass: Small Change, 1993), 210.

2. Ibid., 214.

3. Arguably the presence of a puppet in Wilson's production called to mind Bunraku; performer Kate Valk of the Wooster Group noted that her voice had a distinct Cantonese influence.

4. Patrice Pavis, *The Intercultural Performance Reader* (London: Routledge, 1996), 8.

5. John Rockwell, "Call Him What You Will, He's Too Busy to be Bothered," *New York Times*, March 16, 2003 and "Wie Heiner Goebels 'Hashirigaki versteht: Ein Stuck, offen fur Interpretation,' " *Liberation*, March 8, 2001. In the *Liberation* interview, Goebbels also says that the only one of Wilson's three stagings of Stein that he saw was the last one, *Saints and Singing*.

6. Biography of Goebbels on heinergoebbels.com.

7. Heiner Goebbels "Text as Landscape: With the Qualities of Libretto, Even if Unsung," 2, http://www.heinergoebbels.com/english/writings/landscape.htm.

8. Ibid., 3.

9. Nicholas Till, "Street Fighting Mensch," *Wire*, March 2003: 50.

10. More like an architect, interview with Stephan Buchberger, March 15, 1995, www.heinergoebbels.com/English/interv/inter02e.htm, 1.

11. Ibid., 3.

12. As John Tusa noted in his BBC Radio 3 interview with Goebbels on March 3, 2003, though Goebbels claims collaboration, *Hashirigaki* is still listed as being "conceived" as well as directed by Goebbels in programs for the show. He doesn't completely forego the notion of "auteur."

13. Sarah Bay-Cheng, "Stage Lights: Gertrude Stein's Doctor Faustus Lights the Lights and Wooster Group's House/Lights," Association for Theatre in Higher Education, 2003 Annual Conference.

14. Rockwell, 6.

15. Tom Service, *The Guardian*, November 21, 2002.

Selected Bibliography

Aronson, Arnold. *American Avant-Garde Theatre: A History*. London: Routledge, 2000.

Baker, Deborah. "The Fight Ain't Over." *The American Bar Association Journal* 85 (August 1999).

Barnes, Clive. "Theater: Gertrude Stein Words at the Judson Church." *New York Times*. October 14, 1967.

Beach, Sylvia. *Shakespeare and Company*. New York: Harcourt and Brace, 1956.

Belgrad, Daniel. *The Culture of Spontaneity: Improvisation and the Arts in Postwar America*. Chicago: University of Chicago Press, 1998.

Bennett, Susan. *Theatre Audiences: A Theory of Production and Reception*. 2nd ed. London: Routledge, 1998.

Benstock, Shari. *Women of the Left Bank: Paris, 1900–1940*. Austin: University of Texas Press, 1986.

Berlin, Edward A. *Ragtime: A Musical and Cultural History*. Berkeley: California University Press, 1980.

Bhabha, Homi. *Nation and Narration*. London: Routledge, 1990.

Bloemink, Barbara. *The Life and Art of Florine Stettheimer*. New Haven: Yale University Press, 1995.

Bodnar, John. *Remaking America: Public Memory, Commemoration, and Patriotism in the Twentieth Century*. Princeton: Princeton University Press, 1991.

Bogart, Anne. *A Director Prepares*. London: Routledge, 2001.

Boone, Joseph Allen. *Libidinal Currents: Sexuality and the Shaping of Modernism*. Chicago: University of Chicago Press, 1998.

Bowers, Jane Palatini. *They Watch Me As They Watch This: Gertrude Stein's Metadrama*. Philadelphia: University of Pennsylvania Press, 1991.

Brinnin, John Malcolm. *The Third Rose: Gertrude Stein and Her World*. Reading, Mass.: Addison-Wesley, 1987.

Bryer, Jackson R. *Conversations with Lillian Hellman*. Jackson: University of Mississippi Press, 1986.

Buchberger, Stephan. "More Like an Architect: An Interview with Heiner Goebbels." March 15, 1995, www.heinergoebbels.com/english/interv/inter02e.htm.

Burns, Edward. *The Letters of Gertrude Stein and Carl Van Vechten, 1913–1946*. New York: Columbia University Press, 1986.

Burns, Edward and Ulla E. Dydo. *The Letters of Gertrude Stein and Thorton Wilder.* New Haven: Yale University Press, 1996.

Butler, Judith. *Excitable Speech: A Politics of the Performative.* New York: Routledge, 1997.

Case, Sue-Ellen. *The Domain-Matrix: Performing Lesbian at the End of Print Culture.* Bloomington: Indiana University Press, 1996.

Cavallo, Dominick. *A Fiction of the Past: The Sixties in American History.* New York: St. Martin's Press, 1999.

Chaplin, Charlie. *My Autobiography.* New York: Simon and Schuster, 1964.

Chessman, Harriet. *The Public is Invited to Dance: Representation, the Body, and Dialogue in Gertrude Stein.* Stanford: Stanford University Press, 1989.

Clark, Danae. "Commodity Lesbianism." In *Out in Culture: Gay, Lesbian, and Queer Essays in Popular Culture.* Ed. Corey K. Creekmur and Alexander Doty. Durham, N.C.: Duke University Press, 1995.

Clurman, Harold. "Theatre." *Nation.* November 27, 1967.

Davis, Peter G. "Farce-Fed." *New York Magazine.* August 31, 1998.

———. "Opera: Mother of the Mesas." *New York Times.* August 13, 1976.

Davis, Phoebe Stein. "Even Cake Gets to Have Another Meaning: History, Narrative, and Daily Living in Gertrude Stein's World War II Writings." *Modern Fiction Studies* 44.3 (1998).

De Certeau, Michel. *The Practice of Everyday Life.* Trans. Stephen Randall. Berkeley: University of California Press, 1984.

DeKoven, Marianne. *A Different Language: Gertrude Stein's Experimental Writing.* Madison: University of Wisconsin Press, 1983.

Diesel, Leota. "The Theatre." *Greenwich, Connecticut Villager.* July 4, 1968.

Dolan, Jill. *Presence and Desire: Essays on Gender, Sexuality, and Performance.* Ann Arbor: Michigan University Press, 1993.

Donkin, Ellen. "Directing Stein." In *Upstaging Big Daddy.* Ed. Ellen Donkin and Susan Clement. Ann Arbor: Michigan University Press, 1992.

Downes, Olin. "The Stein-Thomson Concoction." *New York Times.* February 25, 1934.

"Dress Makers for Art." *The Saturday Review.* March 3, 1934.

Dyer, Richard. *White.* London: Routledge, 1995.

Fifer, Elizabeth. *Rescued Readings: A Reconstruction of Gertrude Stein's Difficult Texts.* Detroit: Wayne State University Press, 1992.

Geertz, Clifford. *Interpretation of Cultures: Selected Essays.* New York: Basic Books, 1973.

Gilroy, Paul. "Modern Tones." In *Rhapsodies in Black: Art of the Harlem Renaissance.* Berkeley: University of California Press, 1997.

Glassberg, David. *American Historical Pageantry: The Uses of Tradition in the Early Twentieth Century.* Chapel Hill: University of North Carolina Press, 1990.

Goble, Mark. "Cameo Appearances; or, When Gertrude Stein Check into *Grand Hotel.*" *Modern Language Quarterly* 62.2 (2001).

Goebbels, Heiner. "Text as Landscape: With the Qualities of a Libretto, Even if Unsung." http://www.heinergoebbels.com/english/writings/landscape.htm.

Goodall, Donald. *Robert Indiana*. Austin: University of Texas Press, 1977.

Gregory, Sinda. *Private Investigations: The Novels of Dashiell Hammett*. Carbondale and Edwardsville: Southern Illinois University Press, 1985.

Hahn, Emily. *Mabel: A Biography of Mabel Dodge Luhan*. New York: Houghton-Mifflin, 1977.

Hamilton, Cynthia S. *Western and Hard-Boiled Detective Fiction in America: From High Noon to Midnight*. Iowa City: University of Iowa Press, 1987.

Harper, Judith E. *Susan B. Anthony: A Biographical Companion*. Santa Barbara: ABC-CLIO, Inc., 1998.

Harris, David. "The Original *Four Saints in Three Acts*." *The Drama Review* 26.1 (1982).

Hobhouse, Janet. *Everybody Who Was Anybody: A Biography of Gertrude Stein*. New York: Putnam, 1975.

Houseman, John. *Run-Through: A Memoir*. New York: Simon and Schuster, 1972.

Iambs, Bravig. *Confessions of Another Young Man*. New York: Henkle-Yewdale, 1936.

Jasen, David A. and Trebor Jay Tichenor. *Rags and Ragtime: A Musical History*. New York: The Seabury Press, 1978.

Jezer, Marty. *The Dark Ages: Life in the United States, 1945–1960*. Boston: South End Press, 1982.

Keill, Liz. "Character from City History Featured in Glimmerglass Opera." *Independent Press of New Jersey*. August 1998.

Kleinberg, S. J. *The Shadow of the Mills: Working Class Families in Pittsburgh, 1870–1907*. Pittsburgh: University of Pittsburgh Press, 1989.

Krasner, David. *Resistance, Parody, and Double Consciousness in African American Theatre*. New York: St. Martin's Press, 1997.

Kroll, Jack. "Stein Songs." *Newsweek*. November 27, 1967.

Krutch, Joseph Wood. "A Prepare for Saints." *The Nation*. April 4, 1934.

Lubar, Robert S. "Unmasking Pablo's Gertrude: Queer Desire and the Subject of Portraiture." *Art Bulletin* 1.79 (March 1997).

Ma, L. Eve Armentrout. *Hometown Chinatown: The History of Oakland's Chinese Community*. New York: Garland Publishing, Inc., 2000.

Maland, Charles J. *Chaplin and American Culture: The Evolution of a Star Image*. Princeton: Princeton University Press, 1989.

Malina, Judith. *The Diaries of Judith Malina, 1947–57*. New York: Grove Press, 1984.

Martin, John. "The Dance: *Four Saints in Three Acts*." *New York Times*. February 25, 1934.

May, Elaine Tyler. "Explosive Issues: Sex, Women, and the Bomb." In *Recasting America: Culture and Politics in the Age of the Cold War*. Ed. Larry May. Chicago: Chicago University Press, 1989.

McGinn, Larry. "Masterful Mother." *Syracuse, New York Post Standard*. July 25, 1998.

Mellow, James. *Charmed Circle: Gertrude Stein and Company*. New York: Avon, 1974.

North, Michael. *The Dialect of Modernism: Race, Language, and Twentieth-Century Literature*. New York: Oxford University Press, 1994.

———. *Reading 1922: A Return to the Scene of the Modern*. Oxford: Oxford University Press, 1999.

Ormond, Kirk. "Oedipus the Queen: Cross-Gendering Without Drag." *Theatre Journal* (March 2003).

Pasolli, Robert. "Theatre: *In Circles.*" *Village Voice.* November 11, 1968.

Pavis, Patrice. *The Intercultural Performance Reader.* London: Routledge, 1996.

"Perfect Circles." *New Yorker.* November 18, 1967.

Prevots, Naima. *American Pageantry: A Movement for Art and Democracy.* Ann Arbor: University of Michigan Press, 1998.

Raymond, David. "From Glimmerglass, a Masterful Mother." *Rochester City Newspaper.* July 30, 1998.

Rhodes, Colin. *Primitivism and Modern Art.* London: Thames and Hudson, 1994.

Roach, Joseph. *Cities of the Dead: Circum-Atlantic Performance.* New York: Columbia University Press, 1996.

Rockwell, John. "Call Him What You Will, He's Too Busy to be Bothered." *New York Times.* March 16, 2003.

Rosten, Bevya. *The Fractured Stage: Gertrude Stein's Influence on American Avant-Garde Directing as Seen in Four Productions of Dr. Faustus Lights the Lights* (UMI Dissertation Service, 1998).

———. "The Gesture of Illogic." *American Theatre.* February 1998.

Ruddick, Lisa. *Reading Gertrude Stein: Body, Text, Gnosis.* Ithaca: Cornell University Press, 1990.

Savran, David. "Whistling in the Dark." *Performing Arts Journal* 15.1 (January 1993).

Service, Tom. *The Guardian.* November 21, 2002.

Smith, Dinita. "A Fresh Look at a Syntax Skewer: A New Play Depicts the Life and Love of Gertrude Stein." *New York Times.* June 9, 1999.

Soja, Edward W. *Thirdspace: Journeys to Los Angeles and Other Real-and-Imagined Places.* Cambridge, Mass.: Blackwell Publishers, Inc., 1996.

Spillman, Lyn. *Nation and Commemoration: Creating National Identities in the United States and Australia.* Cambridge: Cambridge University Press, 1997.

Stassio, Marilyn. "Al Carmines: Religion's Answer to Busby Berkeley." *Cue.* February 24, 1968.

Stein, Gertrude. *The Autobiography of Alice B. Toklas.* New York: Vintage, 1961.

———. *Doctor Faustus Lights the Lights. A Gertrude Stein Reader.* Ed. Ulla Dydo. Evanston, Ill.: Northwestern University Press, 1993.

———. *Everybody's Autobiography.* Cambridge, Mass.: Exact Change, 1993.

———. *Four Saints in Three Acts.* In *Last Operas and Plays.* Baltimore: Johns Hopkins University Press, 1993.

———. *The Geographical History of America or the Relationship of Human Nature to the Human Mind.* Baltimore: Johns Hopkins University Press, 1995.

———. *In Circles.* In *A Gertrude Stein Reader.* Ed. Ulla Dydo. Evanston, Ill.: Northwestern University Press, 1993.

———. *Lectures in America.* Boston: Beacon Press, 1985.

———. *Making of Americans.* New York: Something Else Press, Inc., 1966.

———. *The Mother of Us All.* In *Last Operas and Plays.* Baltimore: Johns Hopkins University Press, 1995.

————. *Paris, France*. New York: Liveright, 1970.

————. *Wars I Have Seen*. London: B. T. Batsford, Ltd., 1945.

————. *What are Masterpieces*. Los Angeles: The Conference Press, 1940.

"Stein Opera: First-Nighters Hear Four Saints in Three Acts." *Newsweek*. February 17, 1934.

Sturken, Marita. *Tangled Memories: The Vietnam War, The AIDS Epidemic, and the Politics of Remembering*. Berkeley: University of California Press, 1997.

Sullivan, Dan. "Another Delightful Look at *In Circles*, A Drama of Obfuscation." *New York Times*. June 28, 1968.

Swift, Pat. "Thinking About the Next Set of Issues to Tackle." *Buffalo News*. July 25, 1998.

Talmer, Jerry. "Gertrude in a Garden." *New York Post*. October 16, 1967.

Teaford, Jon C. *The Twentieth-Century American City*. 2nd ed. Baltimore: Johns Hopkins University Press, 1993.

Thomson, Virgil. *Virgil Thomson*. New York: Alfred A. Knopf, 1966.

Till, Nicholas. "Street Fighting Mensch." *Wire*. March 2003.

Toklas, Alice B. *The Alice B. Toklas Cookbook*. Garden City, New York: Anchor Books, 1960.

————. *What is Remembered*. San Francisco: North Point Press, 1985.

Tommasini, Anthony. *Virgil Thomson: Composer on the Aisle*. New York: W.W. Norton and Company, 1997.

Trasko, Mary. *Daring Do's: A History of Extraordinary Hair*. Paris: Flammarion, 1994.

Tusa, John. "Interview with Heiner Goebbels." BBC Radio 3. March 3, 2003.

Tytell, John. *The Living Theatre: Art, Exile, and Outrage*. New York: Grove Press, 1995.

Van Dusen, Wanda. "Portrait of a National Fetish: Gertrude Stein's 'Introduction to the Speeches of Marechal Petain' (1942)." *Modernism/Modernity* 3.3 (1996).

Wagner-Martin, Linda. *Favored Strangers: Gertrude Stein and Her Family*. New Brunswick: Rutgers University Press, 1995.

Wallach, Allan. "He is Gertrude Stein's Soul Mate." *Newsday*. July 24, 1968.

Watson, Steven. *Prepare for Saints: Gertrude Stein, Virgil Thomson, and the Mainstreaming of American Modernism*. New York: Random House, 1998.

Webb, Barbara. "The Centrality of Race to the Modernist Aesthetics of Gertrude Stein's *Four Saints in Three Acts*." *Modernism/Modernity* 3 (2000): 447–69.

Whitfield, Stephen J. *The Culture of the Cold War*. 2nd ed. Baltimore: Johns Hopkins University Press, 1996.

Will, Barbara. *Gertrude Stein, Modernism, and the Problem of "Genius."* Edinburgh: Edinburgh University Press, 2000.

Wilson, Edmund. "Mr. Hemingway's Dry Points." *Dial*. October 7, 1924.

Wright, Jack. *The Living Theatre: Alive and Committed*. Dissertation, University of Kansas, 1969.

Yaeger, Patricia. *The Geography of Identity*. Ann Arbor: University of Michigan Press, 1996.

Young, Stark. "One Moment Alit." *New Republic*. March 7, 1934.

Index